IMAGES
of America

MADEIRA

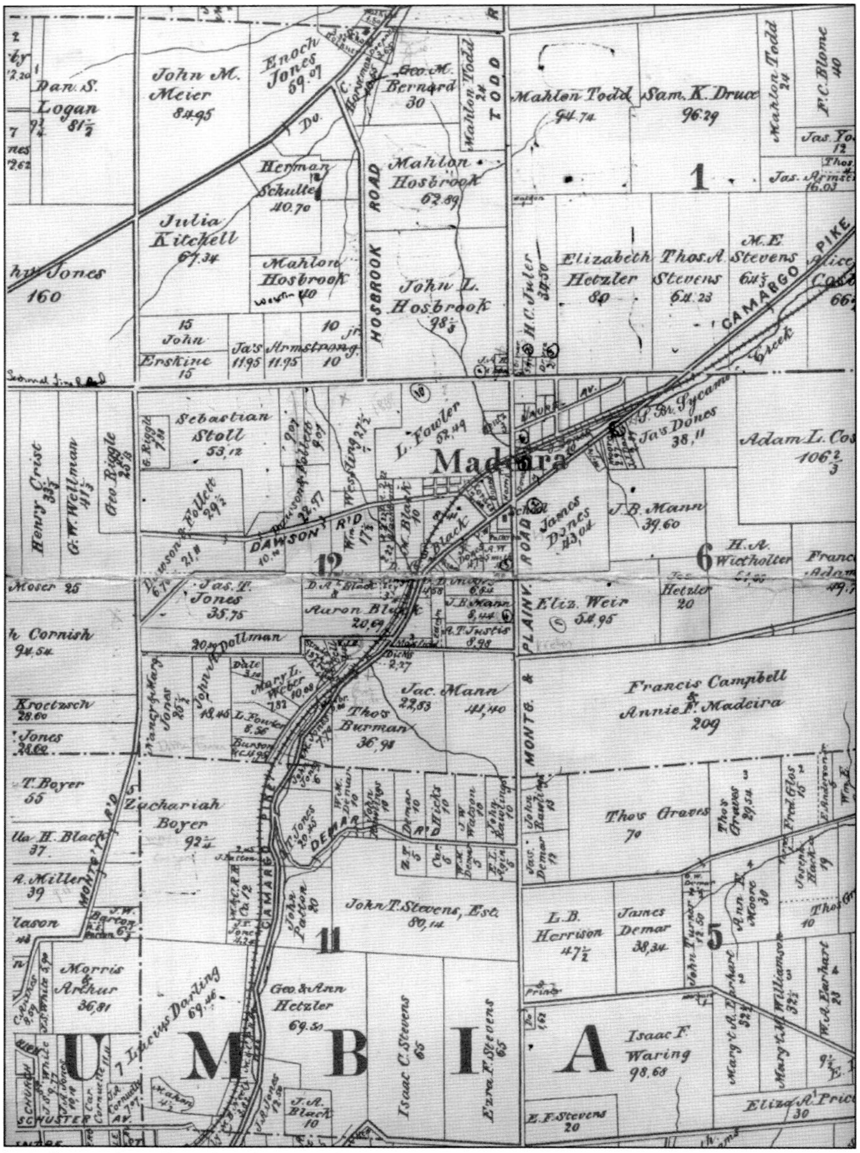

Many of Madeira's founding families are shown on this 1881 map: Dones, Hosbrook, Kitchell, Hetzler, Fowler, DeMar, Black, and Jones. To the east of Montgomery—Plainville Road (today's Miami Avenue)—sits a large lot belonging to Francis Campbell and Annie F. Madeira, who is thought to be a relative of the town's namesake. The railroad that snakes through town made Madeira a suburban home for businessmen working in Cincinnati. (Courtesy Madeira Historical Society.)

On the cover: A *c.* 1910 Sunday school class of the Madeira Presbyterian Church poses for a group portrait. From left to right are (first row) William Knight, unidentified, unidentified, Bill Rapp; (second row) Mildred Stenway, Thelma DeMar, Louise Ray, unidentified, Bernice Senae, unidentified, Naomi Bain; (third row) Oscar Meyer, Catherine Aikin, Mary Burns, Rachel Clark, Cleo Hosbrook, Thelma Siler, and Mary Graves; (fourth row) teachers Nell Curtis and Fanny Curtis. The complete photograph with more names is shown on page 32. (Courtesy Madeira-Silverwood Presbyterian Church.)

IMAGES
of America

MADEIRA

Stephan Johnson and Cheryl Bauer

ARCADIA
PUBLISHING

ISBN 978-0-7385-7816-3

Published by Arcadia Publishing
Charleston, South Carolina

Printed in the United States of America

Library of Congress Control Number: 2009937347

For all general information contact Arcadia Publishing at:
Telephone 843-853-2070
Fax 843-853-0044
E-mail sales@arcadiapublishing.com
For customer service and orders:
Toll-Free 1-888-313-2665

Visit us on the Internet at www.arcadiapublishing.com

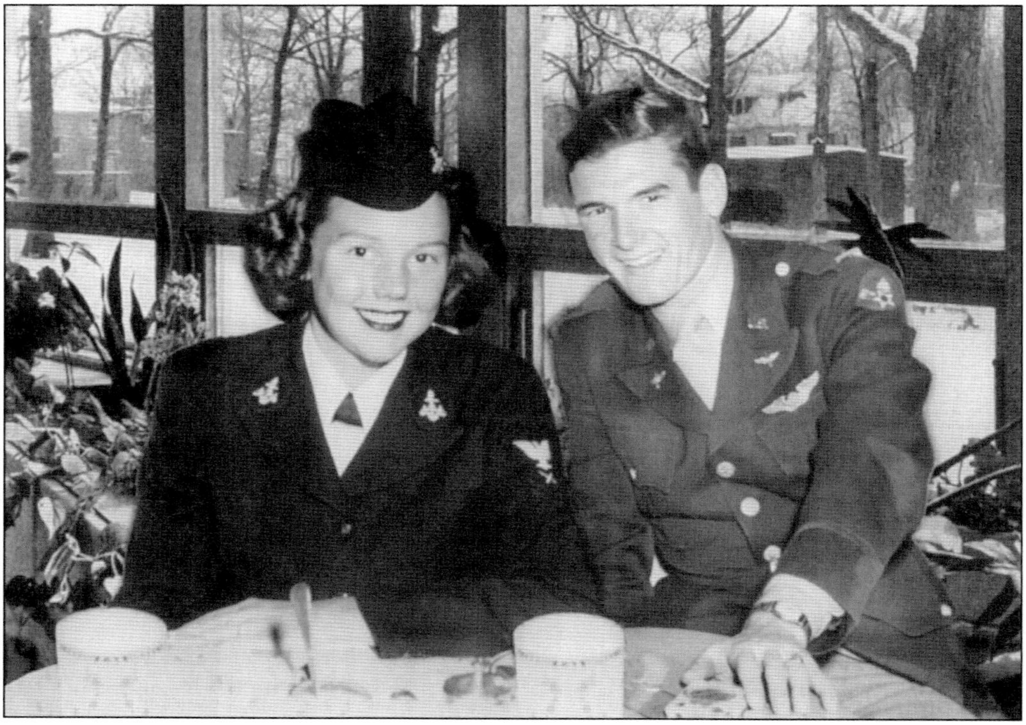

This book is dedicated to my mom and dad,
Doris and Robert D. Johnson.

CONTENTS

Acknowledgments

Madeira is fortunate to have many people who have cherished and preserved community history over the generations, as well as a historical society that is committed to sharing that history with the public. Numerous people have assisted in gathering these images to celebrate the centennial of Madeira's incorporation, and our thanks go to each of them.

Special thanks go to Madeira Historical Society curator Dona Brock, former mayor Daniel D. McDonald, and family historian Roger Ward, who each spent many hours sharing information and images for this book. We are grateful, for their efforts have enriched this book immeasurably by making Madeira's past come alive for future generations.

We thank Lt. Chris Zumbiel for his contributions on the Madeira Police Department and Capt. Clarence Smith and Larry A. Van Pelt for sharing the history of the Madeira and Indian Hill Fire Company. Our appreciation also goes to Jane Bavely, Veda Blevins of the Madeira–Silverwood Presbyterian Church, Marcia Fackler of Connections Christian Church, James Giles, Doris and Norbert L. Henke, Karen Maier of Frisch's Big Boy Restaurants, Madeira city manager Thomas Moeller, Diane Nichols of Madeira City Schools, Douglas Oppenheimer of the Madeira Historical Society, Susie Quinn of St. Gertrude Church, Holly Perin Richard, and Joseph E. Schirmer.

Randy McNutt has our deepest gratitude for hours of scanning and sharpening the images in this book, as well as his unlimited support and enthusiasm. We also wish to thank Melissa Basilone, our editor at Arcadia Publishing, who said "yes" to a Madeira book.

Introduction

Since the late 1700s, Madeira has evolved from a handful of frontier farms into one of Hamilton County's loveliest small cities. For people who were raised there, who moved there, and who visit there, Madeira represents home and history.

For Revolutionary War veterans who began arriving in the late 1780s, the region held danger and promise. As a part of the vast Northwest Territory in 1787, the Ohio country was an untamed place where a sudden fever or a wrong turn in a snowstorm could mean death. It was also a place where people who were committed to hard work and sacrifice created homes and a community that has endured.

When land mogul Judge John Cleves Symmes began selling parcels and sections of his Symmes purchase in the late 1780s, the buyers primarily planned to establish family farms. Daniel Bates, David Black, Peter Crist, Jacob Hetzler, John Hosbrook, John Jones, Calvin Kitchell, John Mann, and Willis Pearson Jr. are reported to have settled in the region by 1800. Survival was not a certainty. "The wolves and panthers were specially troublesome here in the old days, while the deer devoured the wheat," noted Fords' 1881 *History of Hamilton County*. "Bear hunts were quite common."

Pioneers also had to be aware of Native Americans who lived there after being edged out of the Mill Creek Valley in the early 1800s. "Madeira pioneers along the entire Indian Hill—for Madeira is on the north side of the hill—did not dare sleep soundly up to the [1820s]," wrote *Madeira Journal* publisher Lawrence Bonham in 1932. Madeira's relationship with people of the Miami tribe, as well as other Native Americans, is still evidenced by many streets named for them. Early settlers' family names are represented in Dones Avenue, Fowler Avenue, and Hosbrook Road.

Through the years, a hidden part of Madeira stood along side the familiar one. Longtime residents pointed it out to the younger generations. Those memories go back to when ice-skaters glided on Hosbrook Pond, moviegoers enjoyed double features at the Camargo Theater, and children amassed treasures at the Miami 5¢ to $5 Store. This book celebrates the hidden Madeira through archival images from the community's earliest days to 1970.

Madeira was only a small collection of farms until the Marietta and Cincinnati (M and C) Railroad opened a freight station along its new tracks in 1866. In its *Historic Inventory of Hamilton County*, published in 1991, the Miami Purchase Association identified 11 remaining farmhouses from the community's settlement period. In addition to livestock and grain crops, the area became known for its apple and pear orchards and its vineyards.

When the M and C depot opened, it was named Madeira, after John Madeira, a Chillicothe man who was the railroad's treasurer and a property owner in the area. John L. Hosbrook and John D. Moore began to lay out the village in 1871. Previously constructed roads—Montgomery, Plainville (modern Miami Avenue), Madison, and Camargo Turnpike—brought farmers and businessmen to the freight station, and a community began to grow around it.

Muchmore and Son general store was the primary business by 1874, when land agent Richard Nelson wrote a book called *Suburban Homes* to attract people into moving into communities along the M and C line. The two-story brick store housed the owners' business and residence. Madeira's post office, created in 1867, operated there with E. G. Muchmore as postmaster. The Independent Order of Odd Fellows, a fraternal organization, met there, as did at least two church groups.

John Dones lived and ran a store at the corner of the turnpike and Plainville Road. James Thompson operated a belting manufacturing business near the train station. The Methodist Episcopal Church, a 30-foot-by-40-foot frame building, was completed in the summer of 1873. The rest of the village consisted of several homes on large lots filled with gardens, orchards, barns, and outbuildings. In 1875, a brick, two-story schoolhouse was built at the southwest corner of Miami Avenue and Camargo Turnpike.

Development increased with the coming of the Cincinnati and Columbus electric interurban streetcar line in 1906, Madeira's incorporation in 1910, a new schoolhouse in 1912, Cincinnati water service in 1925, paving of Miami Avenue in 1927, and official formation of the Madeira and Vicinity Volunteer Fire Company that same year. Between 1910 and 1930, the village's population increased from 500 to 1,165.

By 1932, Madeira had a high school and elementary school. Presbyterians and Catholics had established sanctuaries. A public library branch served patrons out of the municipal building. Bonham wrote that businesses included his newspaper, a department store, hardware store, beauty parlor, delicatessen, three barbershops, six oil stations, two coal companies, a bank, two grocery stores, two real estate offices, and a building and loan.

In 1942, the Madeira Police Department was formally created, replacing the services of elected marshals and appointed deputy marshals. By the mid-1940s, the fire department was primarily serving Madeira and Indian Hill, so it took on its present name of the Madeira and Indian Hill Fire Company.

Madeira celebrated 50 years of incorporation in 1960 with a population of 6,500. It was a thriving suburb of independent business owners, growing schools, and pleasant tree-lined residential streets. The Madeira Swim Club opened, as did a new post office. The new public library branch opened.

During the 1960s, new businesses began to appear around town. City leaders worked on keeping important businesses in town and improving streets and the infrastructure. Police and fire department services expanded. School additions and renovations kept pace with the growing population. Congregations of the Church of Christ and Baptist denominations became active.

Madeira annexed the South Kenwood area in 1970, giving the city its current boundaries. Madeira committed itself to being a family community by decreeing that most residential zoning would be for single-family housing, a decision that was upheld by the Ohio Supreme Court in 1978. By 1985, the city's population reached about 9,400.

Madeira has continued to garner state and national praise for its family-friendly environment and outstanding schools. In 2008, *Business Week* magazine listed Madeira as the 40th best city to raise children in the United States. *U.S. News and World Report* awarded Madeira City Schools a silver medal that same year for having one of the top public high schools in the country. The Ohio Department of Education awarded Madeira City Schools their 10th consecutive Excellent with Distinction rating for the 2008–2009 school year, noting that Madeira High School had the third-highest mean ACT scores in Ohio. Reading scores of third and fourth graders at Madeira Elementary were ranked number one in the state.

Efforts to preserve the city's heritage received a boost in 1998, when Mrs. Bruce (Elizabeth) Miller bequeathed her home on Miami Avenue to the historical society. The 1922 Sears, Roebuck, and Company catalogue house is now the site for the group's collections and periodic open houses. In 2009, the first wedding was held on the property, linking the past and future.

As the city prepares to observe the centennial of its incorporation in 2010, the population stands at around 9,040. Vibrant and welcoming, Madeira continues to be one of the most desirable places to live in Hamilton County.

One

Homegrown

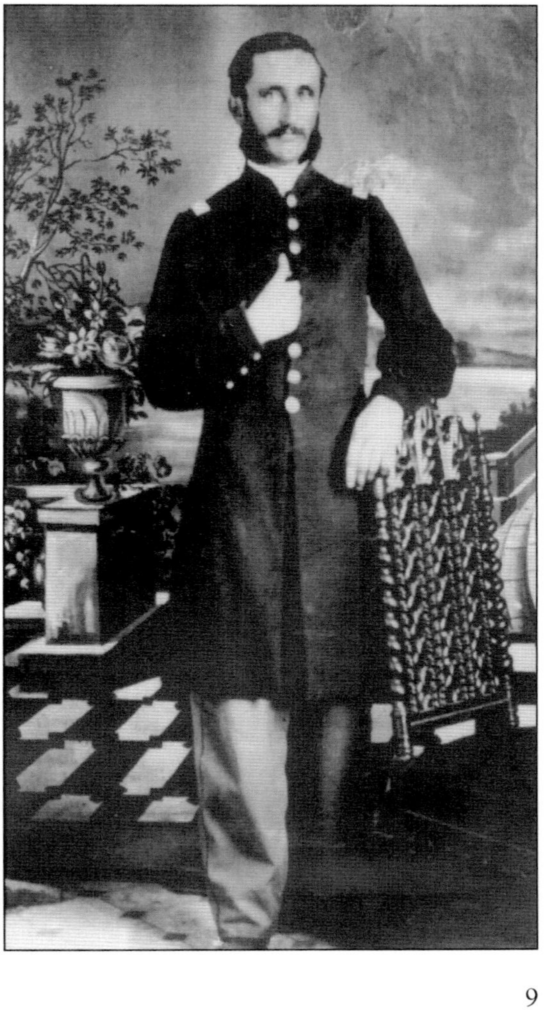

Founded by Revolutionary War veterans, many of Madeira's next generation went on to fight in the Civil War. James DeMar, who lived on Miami Avenue with his wife, Laura (née Hennes), and their four children after the war, fought in the 83rd Ohio Volunteer Infantry, as did his brothers Isaac and John. John was wounded at Vicksburg in 1863 and returned home to die. On April 9, 1865—the day General Lee surrendered at Appomattox—the other two brothers were engaged in a battle near Blakely, Alabama. Isaac was shot in the head "and died like a true soldier, nobly fighting for the cause he loved," James wrote to his parents. With his letter, James enclosed a lock of Isaac's hair and a promise to try to have him reinterred in Ohio once the war ended. James was a captain by the war's end. (Courtesy Madeira Historical Society.)

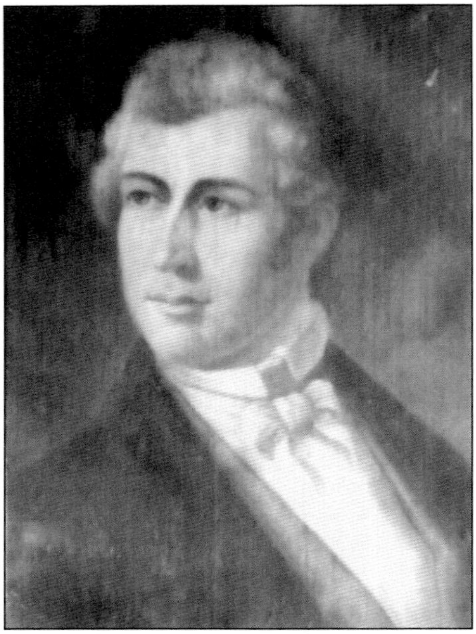

The community received the name Madeira in 1866 when the Marietta and Cincinnati Railroad laid tracks through the region. The village is named for John Madeira, treasurer of the railroad. Madeira owned a Chillicothe hotel and later a tract of wooded land in the Madeira area. (Courtesy Madeira Historical Society.)

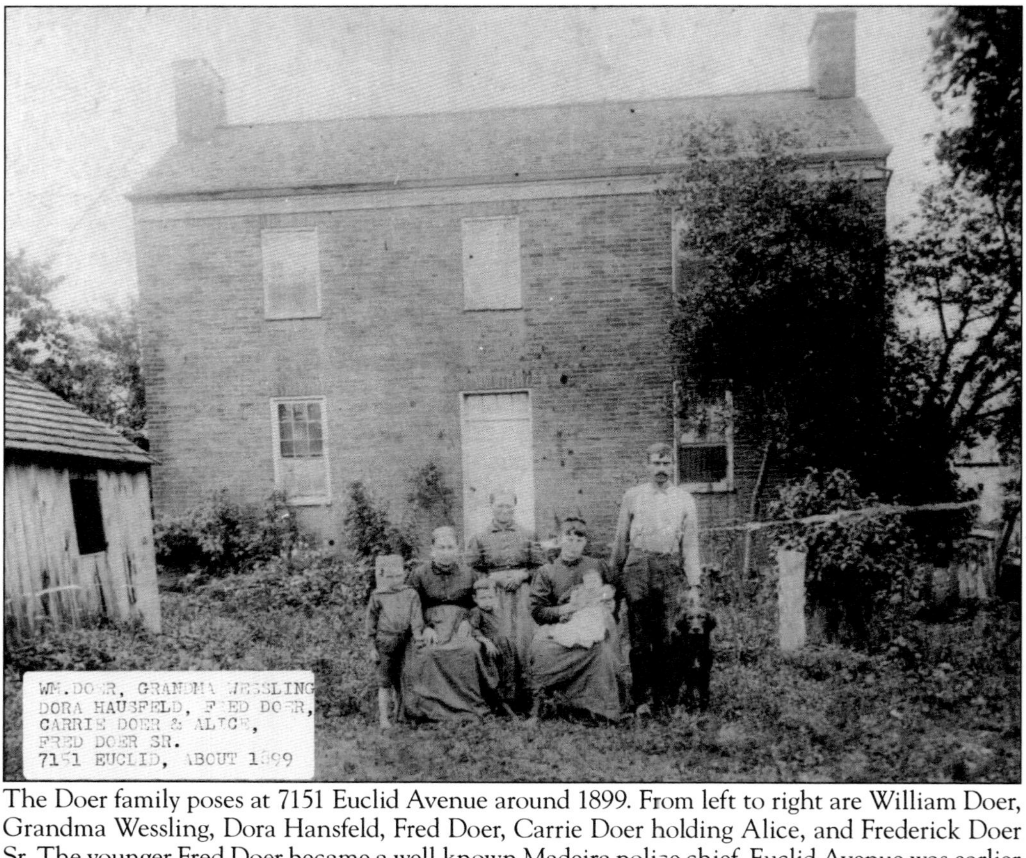

The Doer family poses at 7151 Euclid Avenue around 1899. From left to right are William Doer, Grandma Wessling, Dora Hansfeld, Fred Doer, Carrie Doer holding Alice, and Frederick Doer Sr. The younger Fred Doer became a well-known Madeira police chief. Euclid Avenue was earlier known as Bond Street. (Courtesy Madeira Historical Society.)

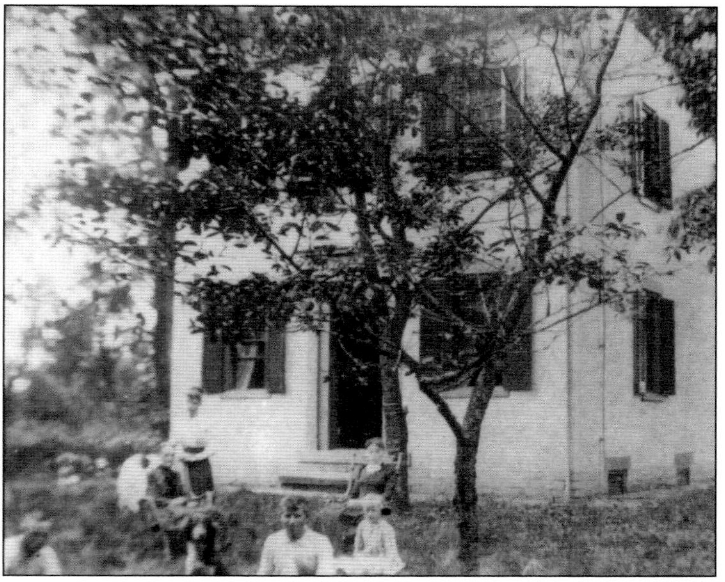

Leonard Fowler built this home in the 1850s at the corner of what is now Summit and Euclid Avenues. Fowler, an Englishman by birth, acquired 56 acres surrounding his home. Most of the property was subdivided into Madeira Heights about 1900. Fowler was a farmer and turnpike contractor who also served as township trustee and treasurer. His daughter Alice married into the Hosbrooks, one of Madeira's first families. (Courtesy Madeira Historical Society.)

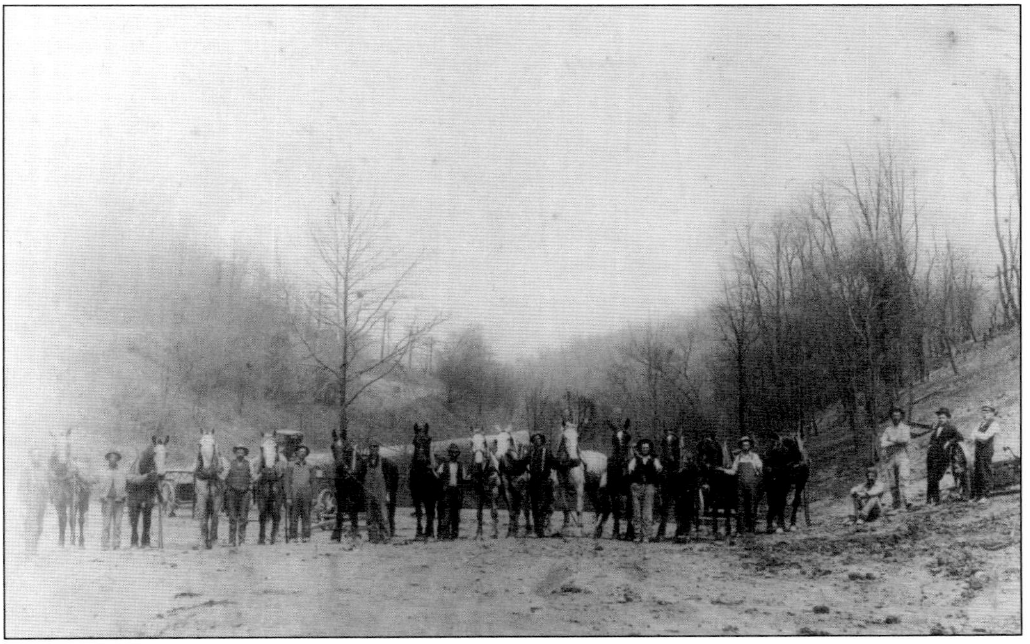

Around 1915, this team of men and mules worked to install culverts replacing two bridges on Camargo Road, then unpaved. People in the picture include, in no particular order, Frederick Doer Sr., Oscar Fischer, Joseph Williams, and Humphrey Rich; the others are unidentified. (Courtesy Madeira Historical Society.)

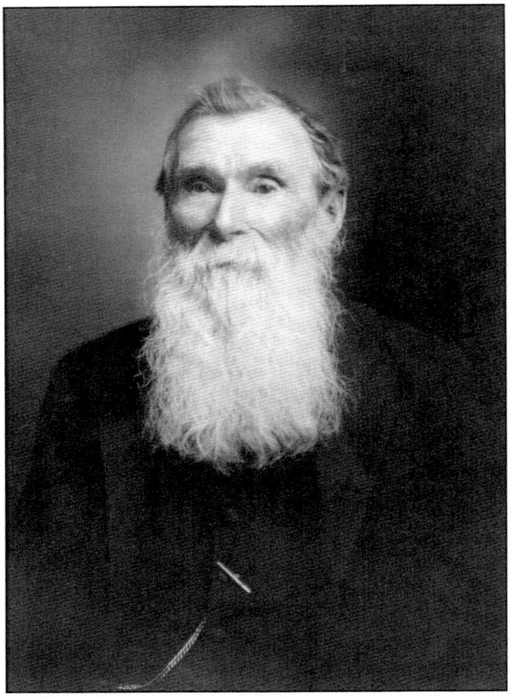

Joseph A. Muchmore served with the civilian volunteers known as the Squirrel Hunters during the Civil War. The volunteers mobilized to protect greater Cincinnati from Confederate invasions. *Madeira Milestones* notes that Morgan's Raiders did pass through northern sections of Madeira in 1863, taking horses and bridles from several residents. (Courtesy Madeira Historical Society.)

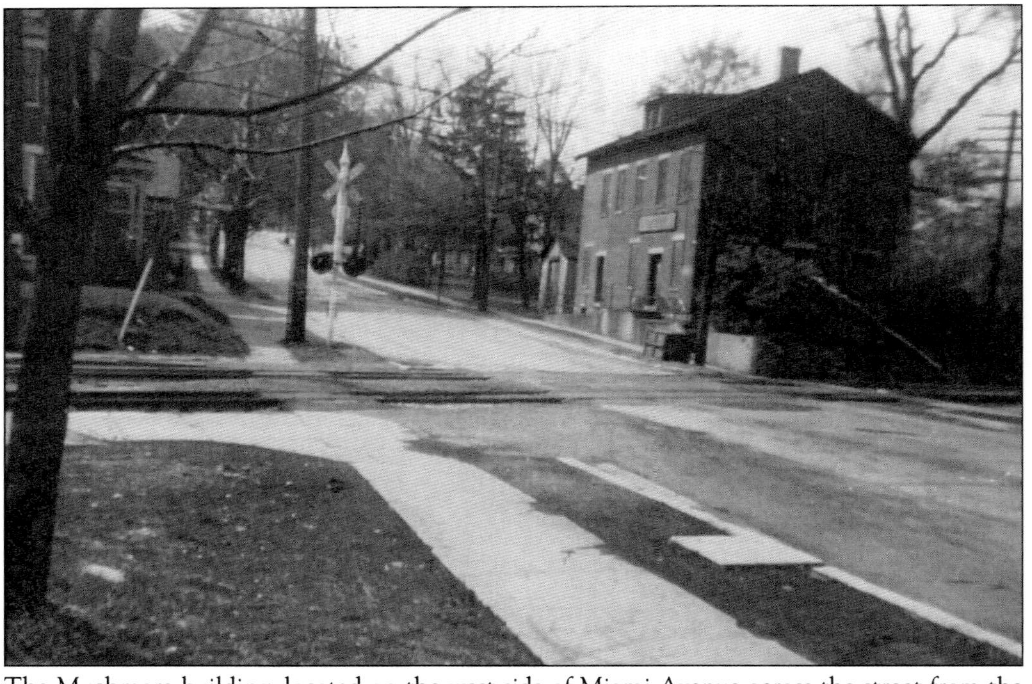

The Muchmore building, located on the west side of Miami Avenue across the street from the current location of Coffee Please, was the site of most community social occasions for decades. Elias Guerin Muchmore opened a dry goods store in the building around 1855. The Odd Fellows Lodge and Madeira Lyceum used the upper floors for their programs before the building was razed in 1944. (Courtesy Madeira Historical Society.)

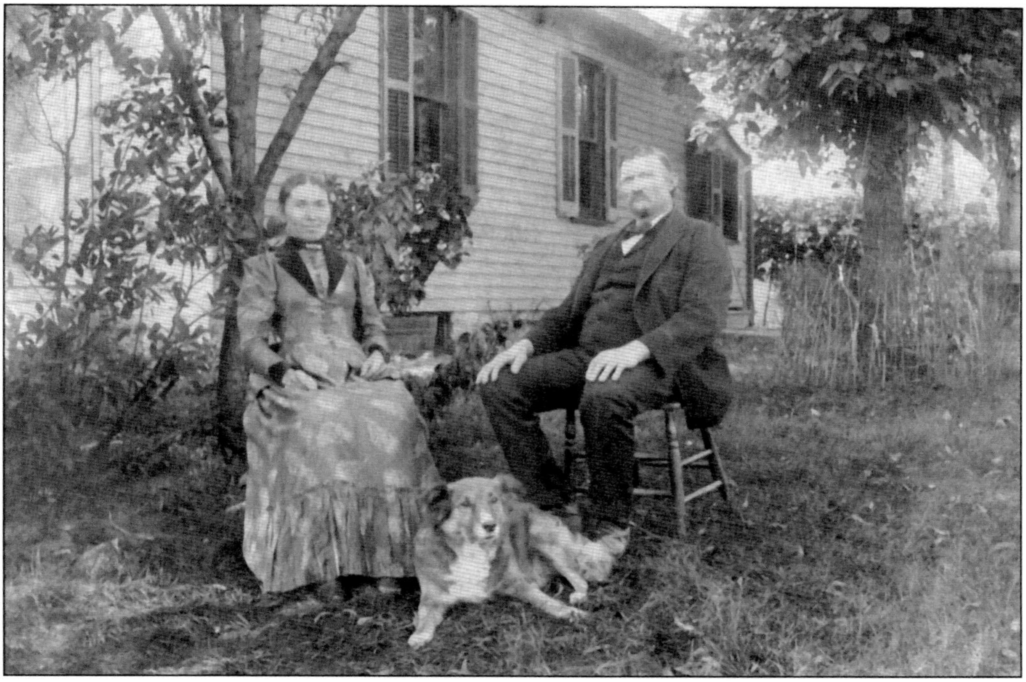

Susan and John Watson sit in front of their home around 1900. In a diary that he kept from roughly 1864 to 1898, Watson recalled working for many of Madeira's prominent families, commenting on their quirks and character as well as his wages, including husking corn for the Druse family for $1 a day. Susan cared for a needy child in the 1880s before foster care was available. (Courtesy Roger Ward.)

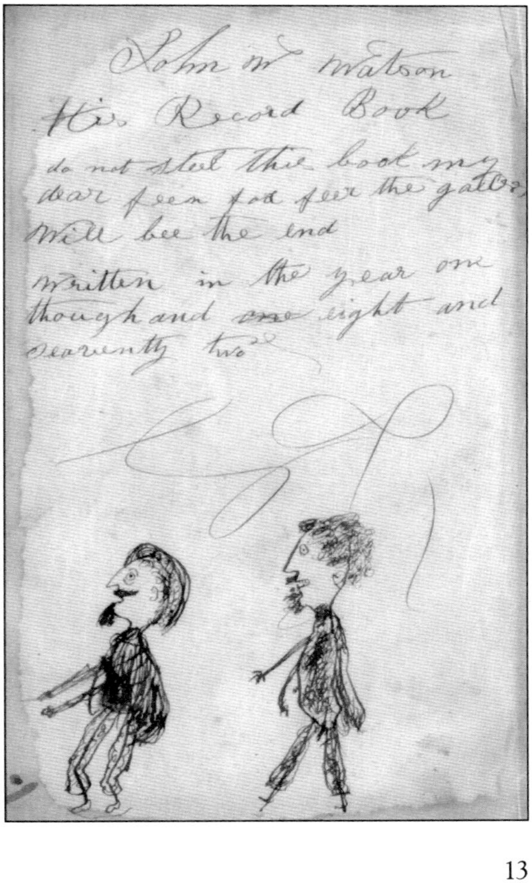

John W Watson
His Record Book
do not steel this book my
dear feen fod feer the galos
Will bee the end
written in the year one
though and ~~one~~ eight and
seaventy two

Victorian doodles decorate John Watson's 19th-century diary. He recorded his lost days of work for 1864, noting a few days lost to playing baseball, a day of loafing, and a half day to hearing Clement Vallandigham, the Peace Democrat gubernatorial candidate who had earlier been banished from the country by President Lincoln as a subversive. (Courtesy Roger Ward.)

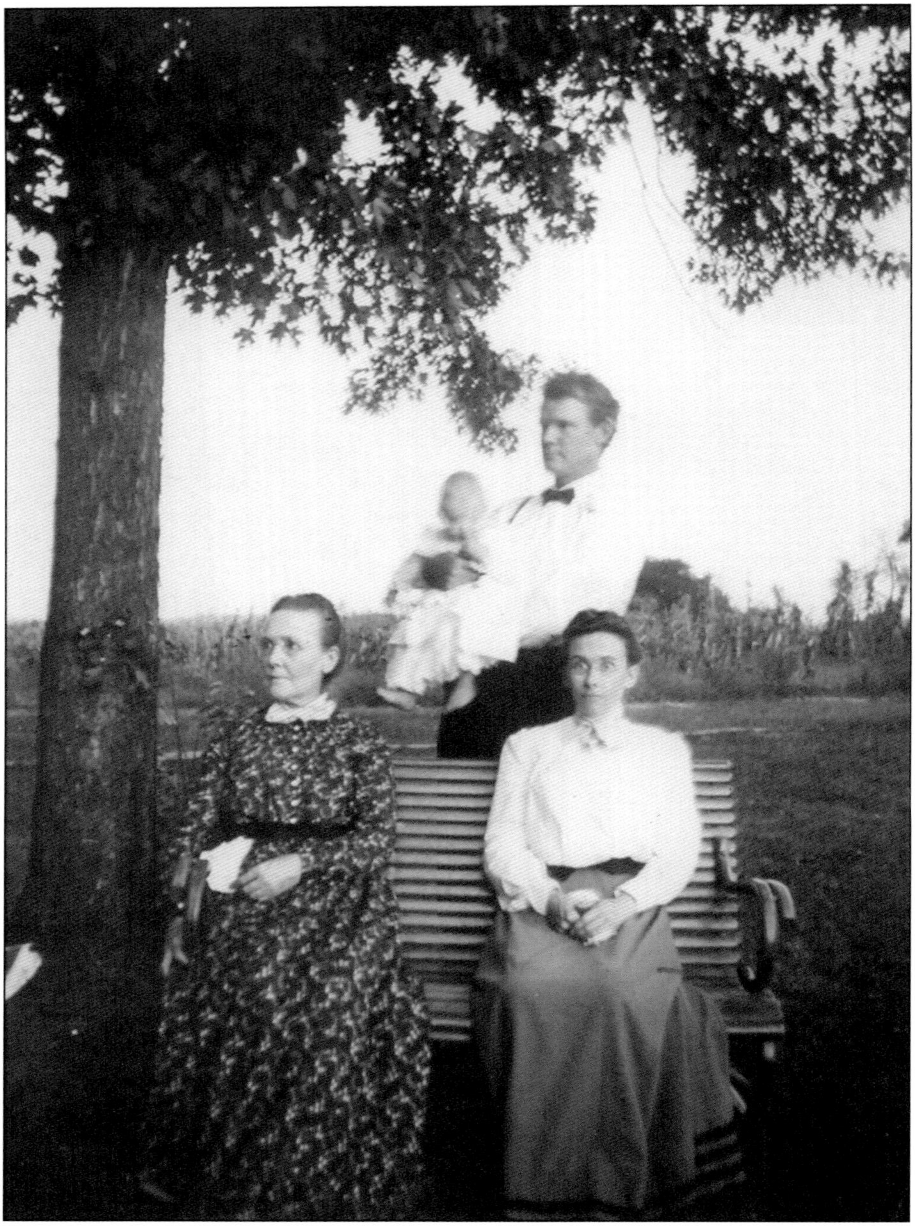

Two of Madeira's early families—the Hosbrooks and the Muchmores—were united through the marriage of Charles J. Hosbrook and Maude Muchmore. Here the couple poses with their daughter Cleo and her grandmother, Viola Hosbrook. John Hosbrook, originally from New Jersey, settled in the area in 1794–1795. His son Daniel purchased land in the vicinity in 1807. As an adult, Daniel traveled out to the nearby community of Columbia one frigid winter day to obtain salt. On his way home, he took a wrong turn in the heavily wooded territory and became lost. His frozen corpse was later discovered just a few rods from his home, according to the 1874 *Suburban Homes*. The Hosbrooks were related by marriage to the Bates and Kitchell families, other early settlers. Hosbrook Road is one of the early streets that retains its original name. (Courtesy Madeira Historical Society.)

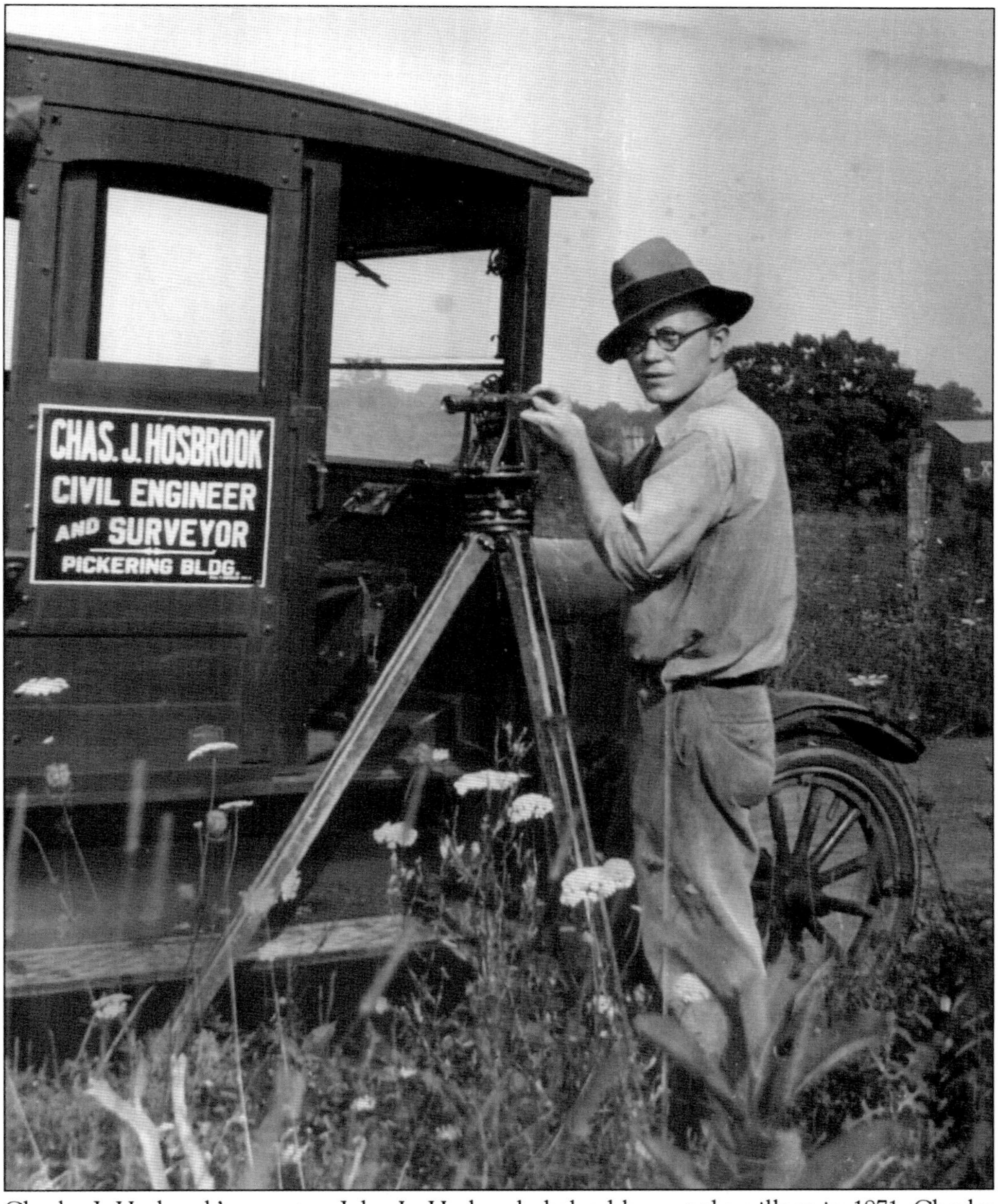

Charles J. Hosbrook's ancestor, John L. Hosbrook, helped lay out the village in 1871. Charles (shown here) took up similar work, becoming a surveyor and eventually being hired as Madeira's first village engineer, helping to shape the community's streets and infrastructure so it could grow. Charles's father, D. S. Hosbrook, was county surveyor and county engineer from 1873 to 1879 for Hamilton County, Ohio. He also served as city engineer for St. Bernard and Reading, Ohio. Another relative, J. A. Hosbrook, was appointed as a special engineer for Hamilton County, Ohio, in 1878, served on the Madeira Board of Education, and worked as village engineer for nearby Madisonville. (Courtesy Madeira Historical Society.)

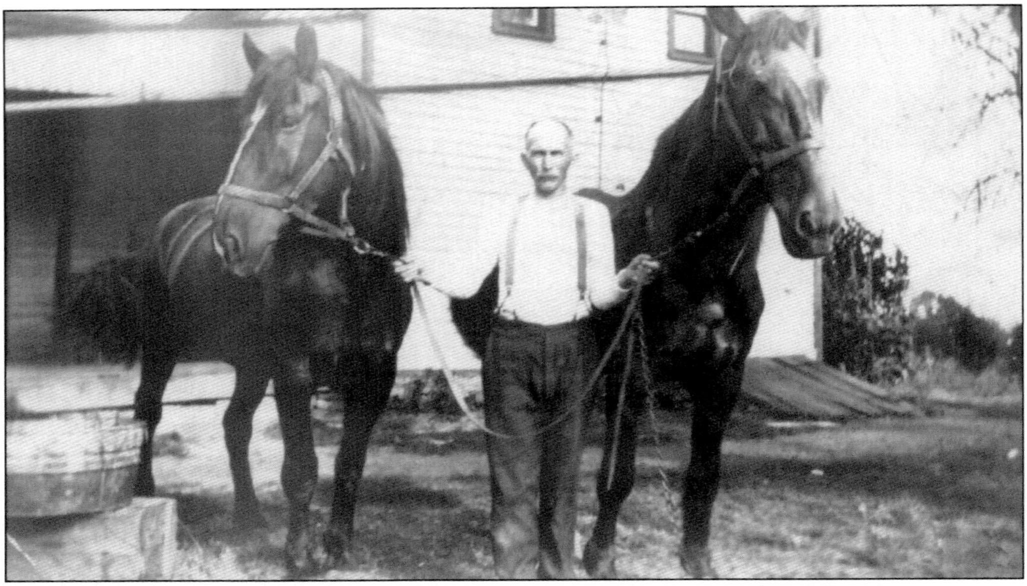

William Henke traveled to the United States from Germany at age 15 with his three sisters to seek his fortune. Sponsored by an Oakley family, Henke became a laborer and then a streetcar conductor. After a doctor advised him to leave the urban pollution, he and his wife, Wilhelmine, bought 43 acres on Stoney Lane off of McCullum Road. They raised six children on the family farm there. (Courtesy Doris and Norbert L. Henke.)

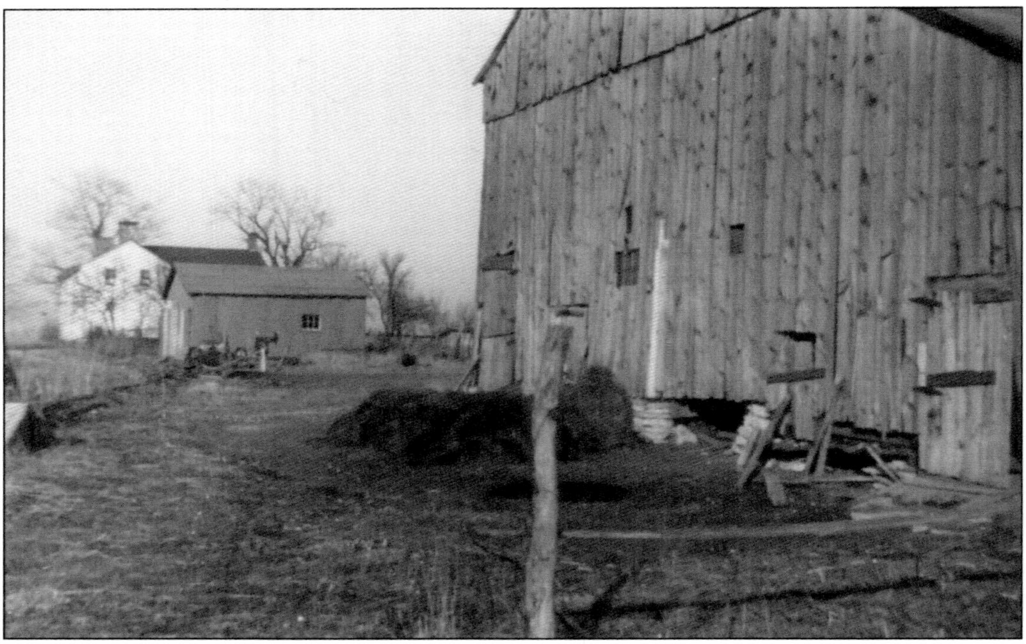

The Henkes had a truck farm and orchard and raised chickens, pigs, and cows on the farm. They took seasonal produce to downtown Cincinnati weekly with a two-horse platform wagon and later to William's old Evanston neighborhood where he had first lived after marrying. Shown here are the Henke farmhouse, barn, and outbuildings on Stoney Lane. (Courtesy Doris and Norbert L. Henke.)

Two

GOING PLACES

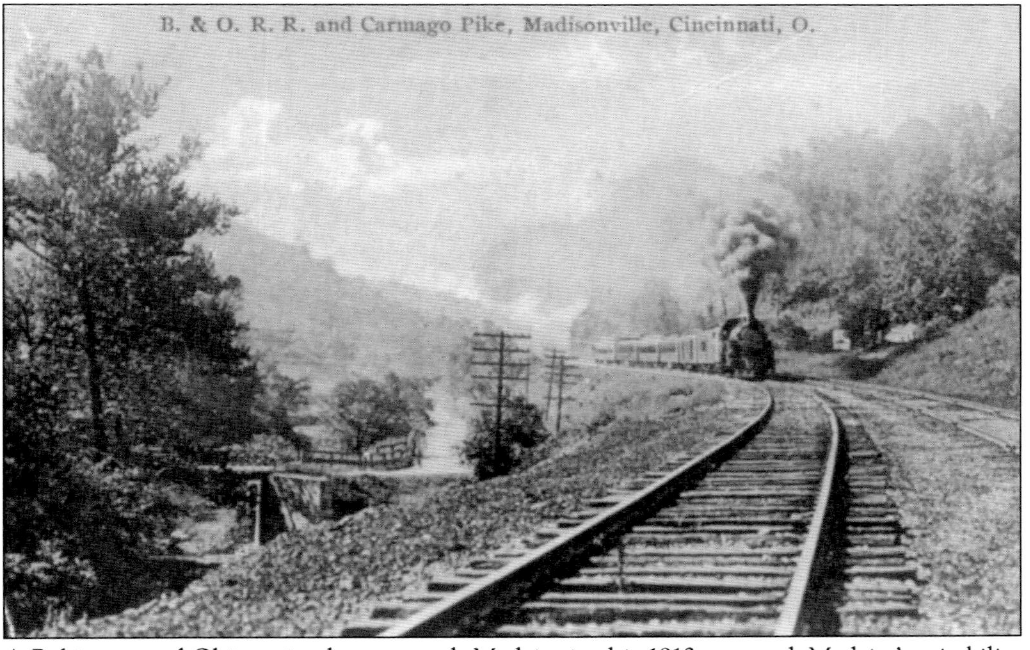

A Baltimore and Ohio train chugs towards Madeira in this 1913 postcard. Madeira's suitability as a freight station and water stop prompted the Marietta and Cincinnati railroad owners to built a depot there. They completed tracks linking Loveland and Norwood. The town began to grow around the depot, which brought both businessmen and residents to the area. The M and C railroad later became the B and O. (Courtesy Madeira Historical Society.)

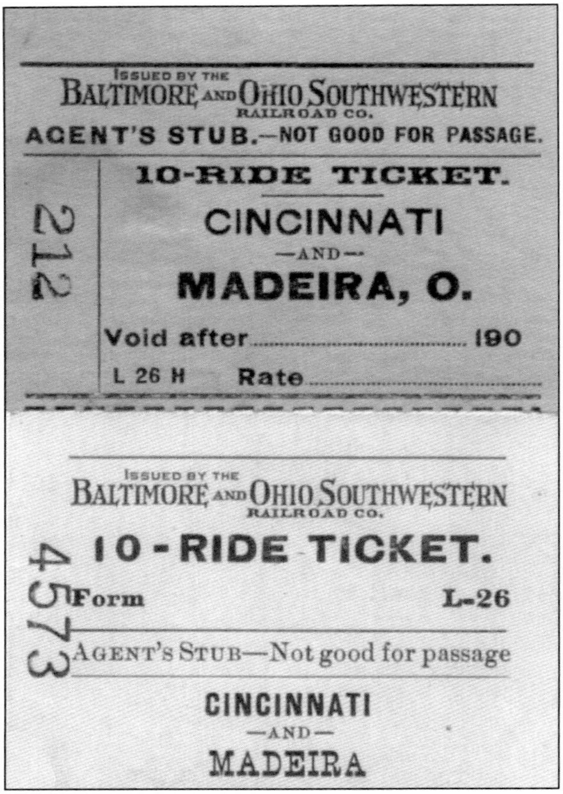

ISSUED BY THE
BALTIMORE AND OHIO SOUTHWESTERN
RAILROAD CO.
AGENT'S STUB.—NOT GOOD FOR PASSAGE.
10-RIDE TICKET.
212
CINCINNATI
—AND—
MADEIRA, O.
Void after 190
L 26 H Rate ....

ISSUED BY THE
BALTIMORE AND OHIO SOUTHWESTERN
RAILROAD CO.
10-RIDE TICKET.
4573
Form L-26
AGENT'S STUB—Not good for passage
CINCINNATI
—AND—
MADEIRA

Students and businessmen commuting to Cincinnati bought 10-ride tickets for the week in the early 1900s. Land agent Richard Nelson wrote in his 1874 *Suburban Homes* that the convenience of the railroad made Madeira perfect for households whose breadwinners worked in Cincinnati. In 1874, property within a five-minute walk of the station sold for \$300 to \$800 per acre, or \$3 to \$5 per foot. (Courtesy Madeira Historical Society.)

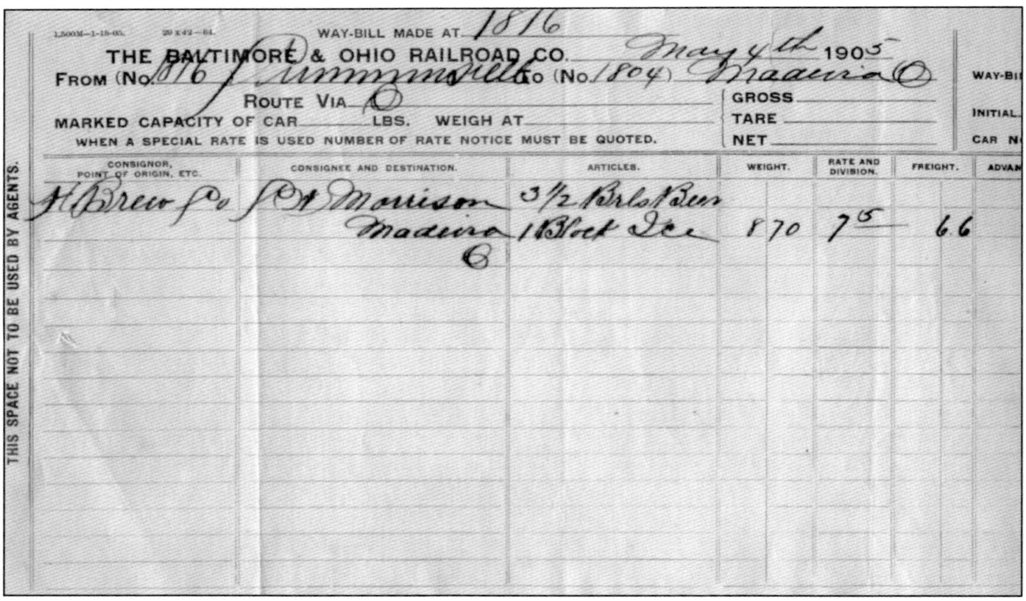

WAY-BILL MADE AT 1816
THE BALTIMORE & OHIO RAILROAD CO. May 4th 1905
FROM (No. 1816) .... TO (No. 1804) Madeira O
ROUTE VIA ....
MARKED CAPACITY OF CAR .... LBS. WEIGH AT ....
WHEN A SPECIAL RATE IS USED NUMBER OF RATE NOTICE MUST BE QUOTED.
GROSS
TARE
NET
THIS SPACE NOT TO BE USED BY AGENTS.

CONSIGNOR, POINT OF ORIGIN, ETC.	CONSIGNEE AND DESTINATION.	ARTICLES.	WEIGHT.	RATE AND DIVISION.	FREIGHT.
[illegible]	[illegible] Morrison Madeira O	3 1/2 Brls Beer 1 Block Ice	870	75	6.6

American commerce moved by rail in 1905 when this receipt for three and a half barrels of beer and one block of ice was written. The depot was Madeira's center for shipping and receiving goods, sending telegrams, greeting visitors, and exchanging news with acquaintances. (Courtesy Daniel D. McDonald.)

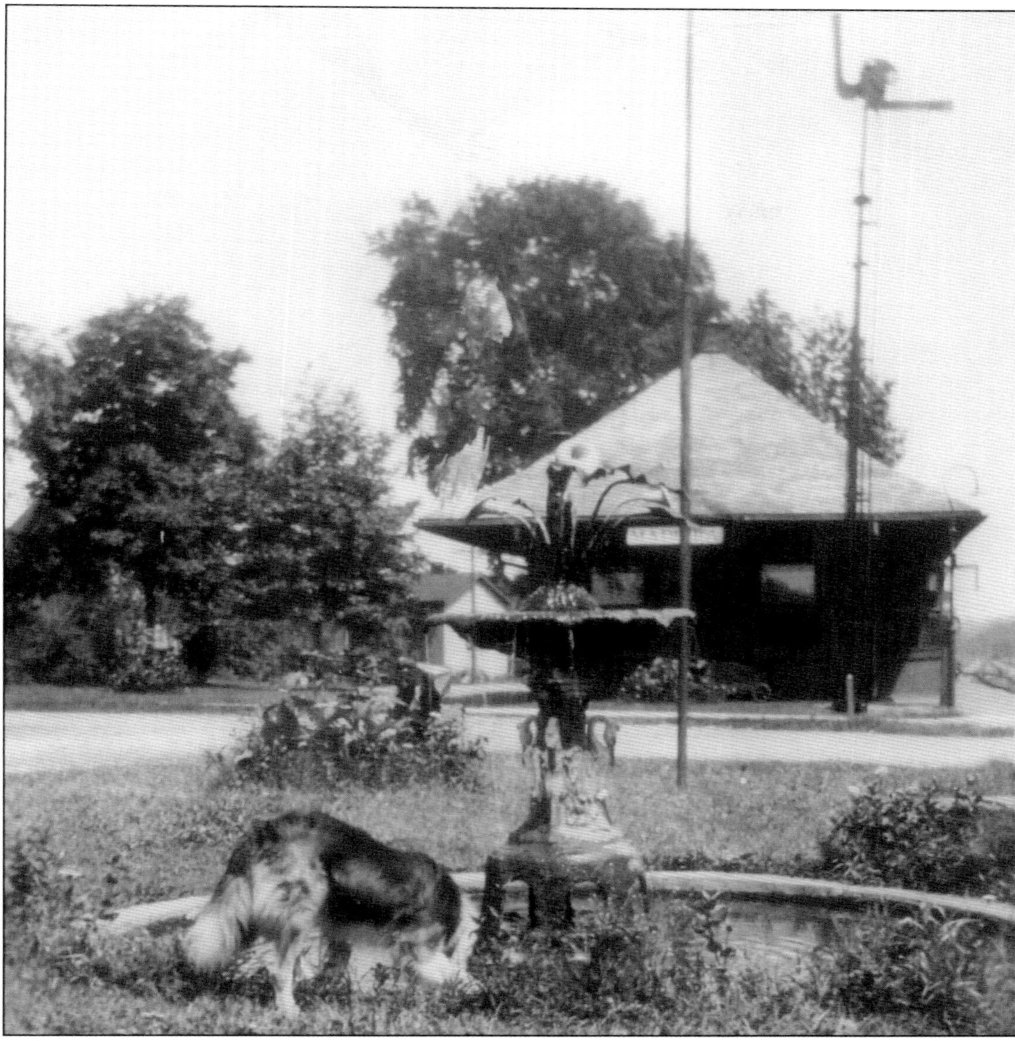

The first passenger station in Madeira was built in 1872 to accommodate passengers of the Marietta and Cincinnati Railroad. This depot, photographed in 1915, stood on the site of the original. "The train depot was open 24 hours a day until the 40s," resident Oscar Meyer told the authors of *Madeira Milestones* in 1985. "Someone was always on duty there, so it was a hangout." By 1960, passenger trains no longer routinely stopped there. Paul Sperry still ran the freight station in 1960. As Madeira celebrated the country's bicentennial, a special train pulled into the station to deliver a Liberty Bell that was purchased by residents and school children to be displayed at the municipal building. An exact replica of the original fountain was installed in 2000. The depot was once home to the Madeira Historical Society. Choo Choo's, a railroad-themed restaurant, occupies the site today. (Courtesy Madeira Historical Society.)

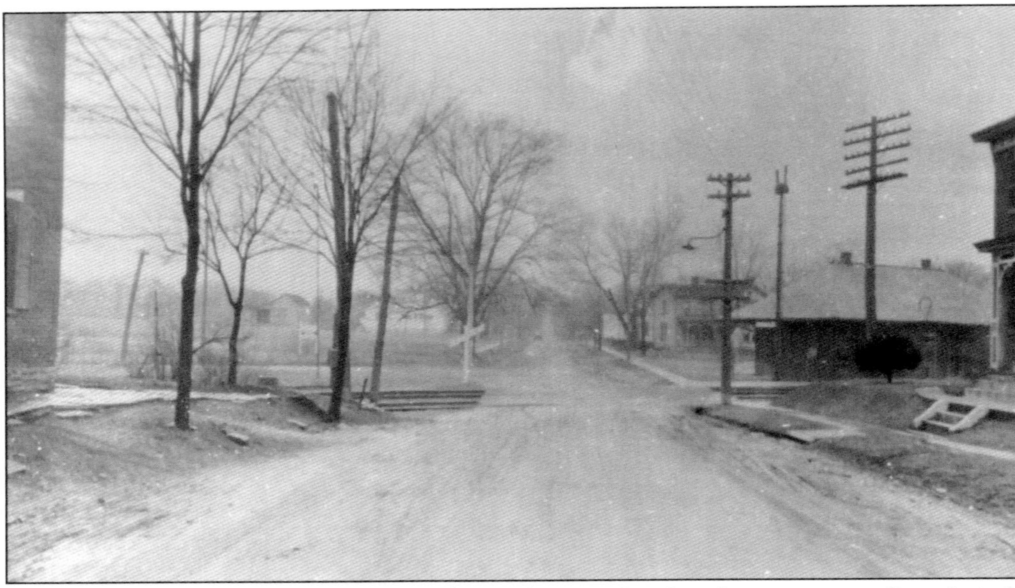

Miami Avenue, named for the Miami Indians who once lived in the area, was still a relatively uncrowded thoroughfare in 1910, but that was about to change with Madeira's incorporation that year. The original road, built in 1832, was called Plainville Road south of Euclid Avenue; the northern portion was called Montgomery Road. (Courtesy Madeira Historical Society.)

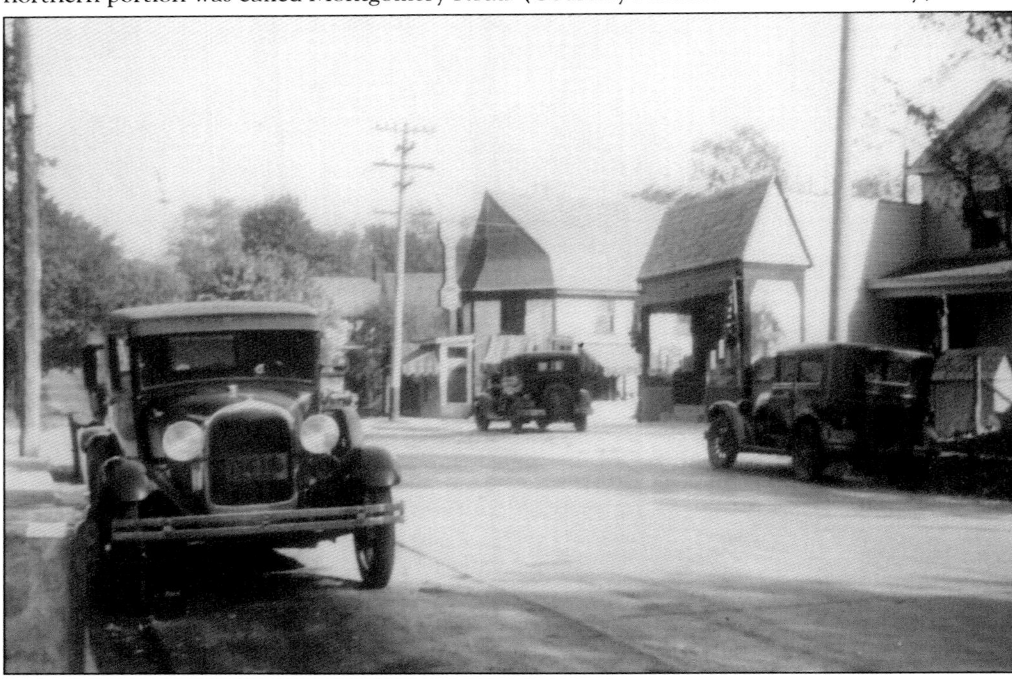

The intersection of Laurel and Miami Avenues was a busy place by the time this photograph was taken in 1936. Even in the midst of the Great Depression, close to two dozen businesses operated in town. More residential growth saw the expansion of the schools as well as public library service when a branch of the Madisonville Library opened on Laurel Avenue in 1931. (Courtesy Madeira Historical Society.)

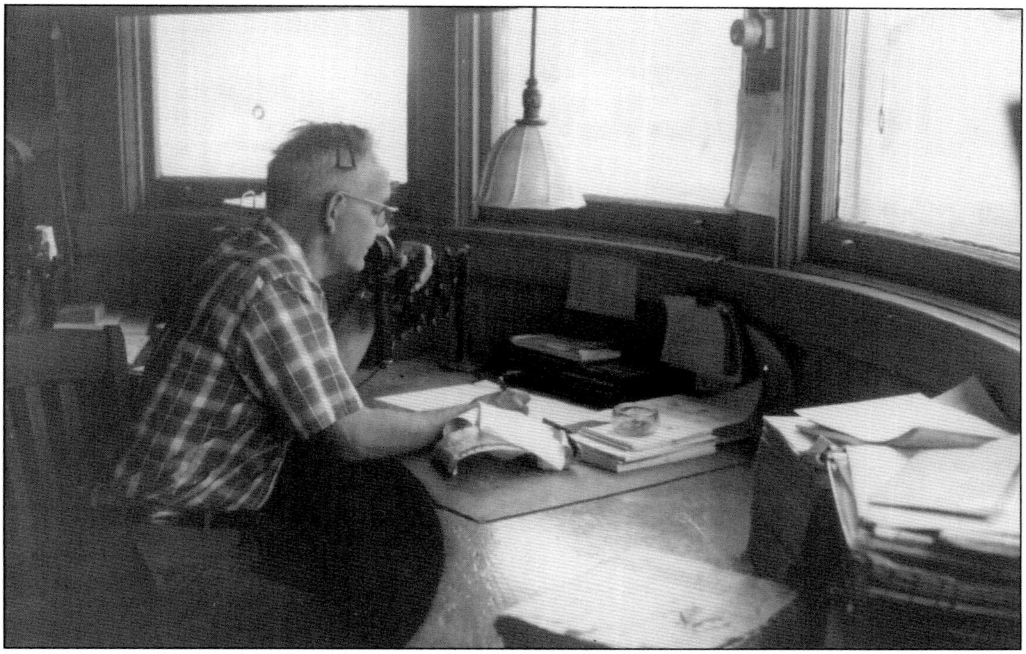

Carrying on the tradition of previous generations, Nelson Stewart dispatches a train at the Madeira depot (now Choo Choo's Restaurant). (Courtesy Madeira Historical Society.)

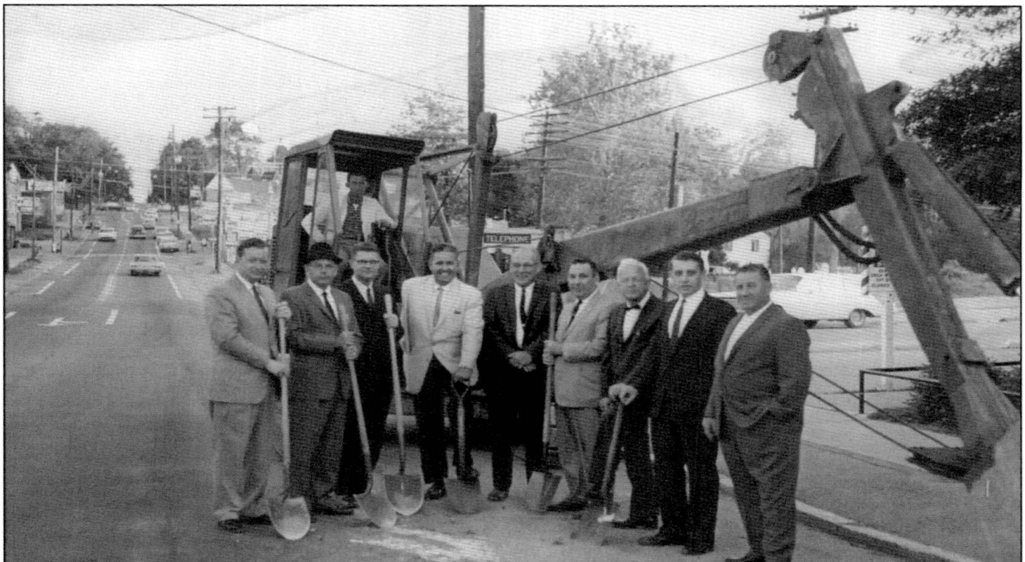

Ground-breaking for Miami Avenue improvements on May 15, 1963, was part of a mission by city government to keep Madeira thriving, along with upgrading of the public sewer system and curbing most secondary streets. From left to right are Mayor Daniel D. McDonald, unidentified, unidentified, councilman Harold Caldwell, councilman Lewis Krehnbrink, unidentified, councilman James B. Long, city manager John Griffin, and unidentified; among the unidentified are project contractor Don Carter, Hamilton County administrator Bud Anderegg, and Carter foreman Bill Grant. Improvements were completed by the end of 1963. (Courtesy Daniel D. McDonald.)

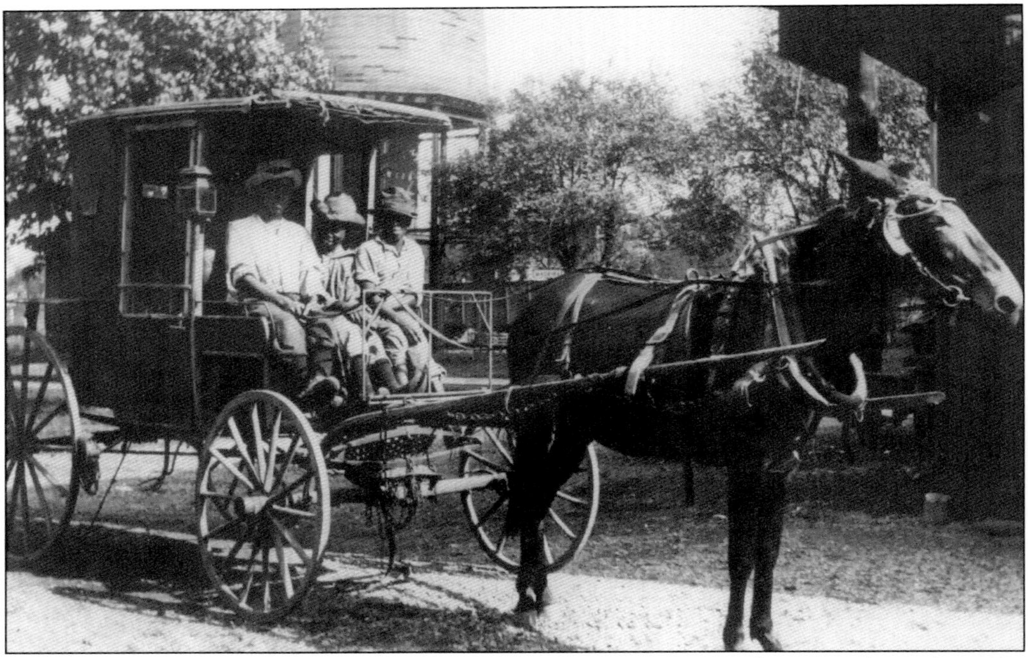

Buggies drawn by horses or mules were still common for getting around town in the early 1900s. The Spaulding family pauses for a photograph around 1900. The railroad water tower is visible in the background. The Spaulding family provided trash collection for the village and lived at the site of today's McDonald Commons Park. (Courtesy Madeira Historical Society.)

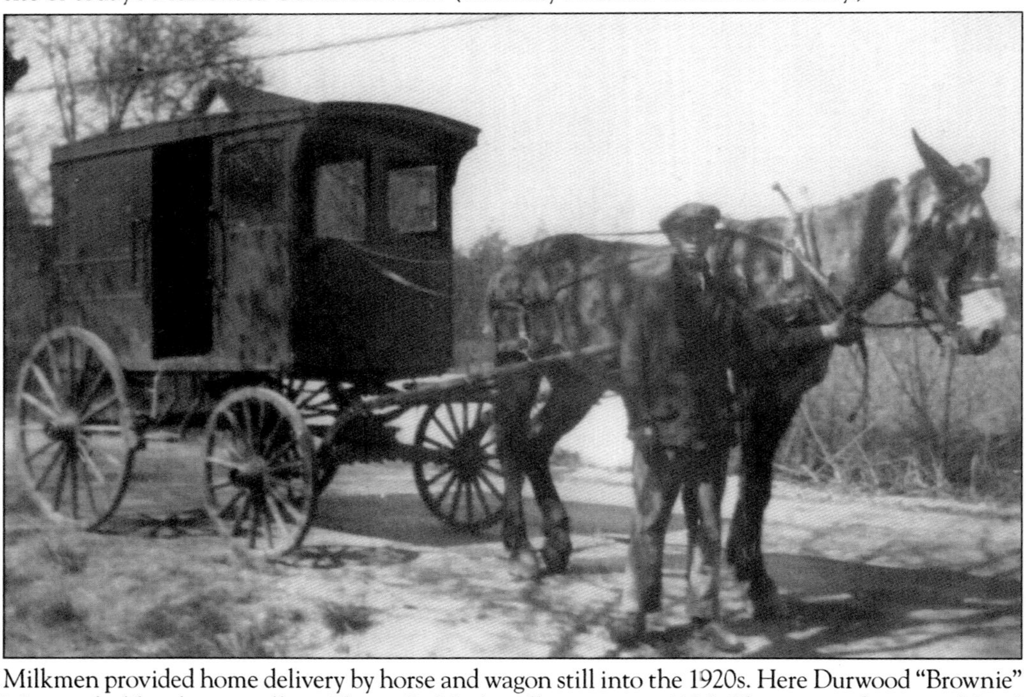

Milkmen provided home delivery by horse and wagon still into the 1920s. Here Durwood "Brownie" Morgan holds a horse pulling Blaine DeMar's milk wagon in 1926. Blaine was the son of Civil War captain James DeMar and his wife, Laura. (Courtesy Madeira Historical Society.)

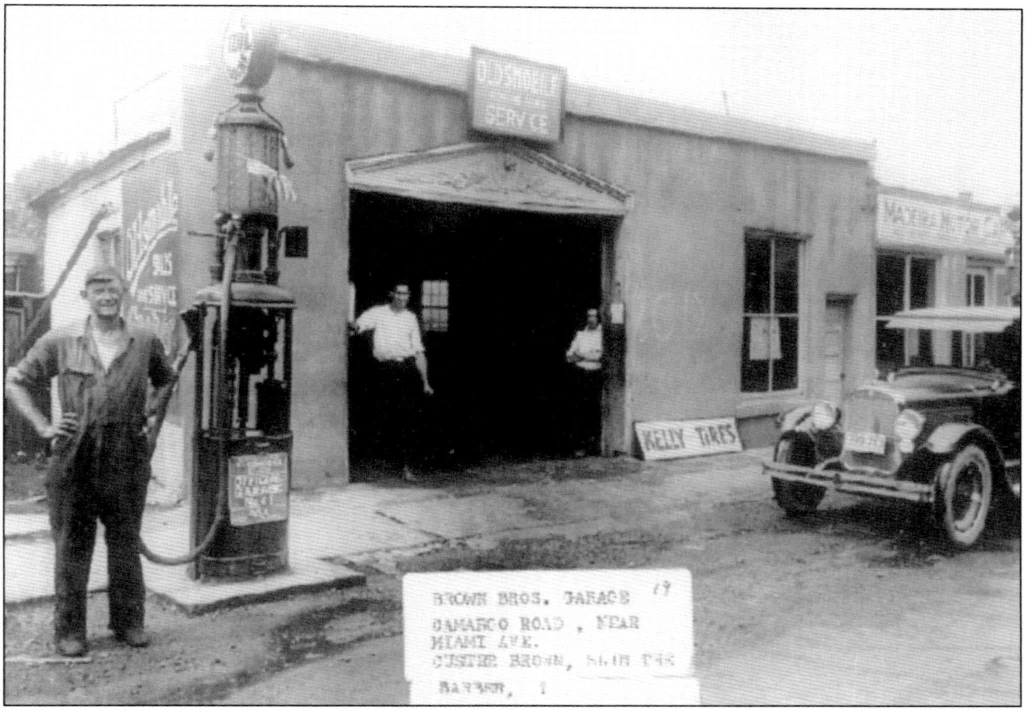

These men pose around 1930 in front of Brown Brothers' Garage on Camargo Road near Miami Avenue back when a gas station was a full-service filling station. From left to right are Custer Brown, "Slim the Barber," and an unidentified man. (Courtesy Madeira Historical Society.)

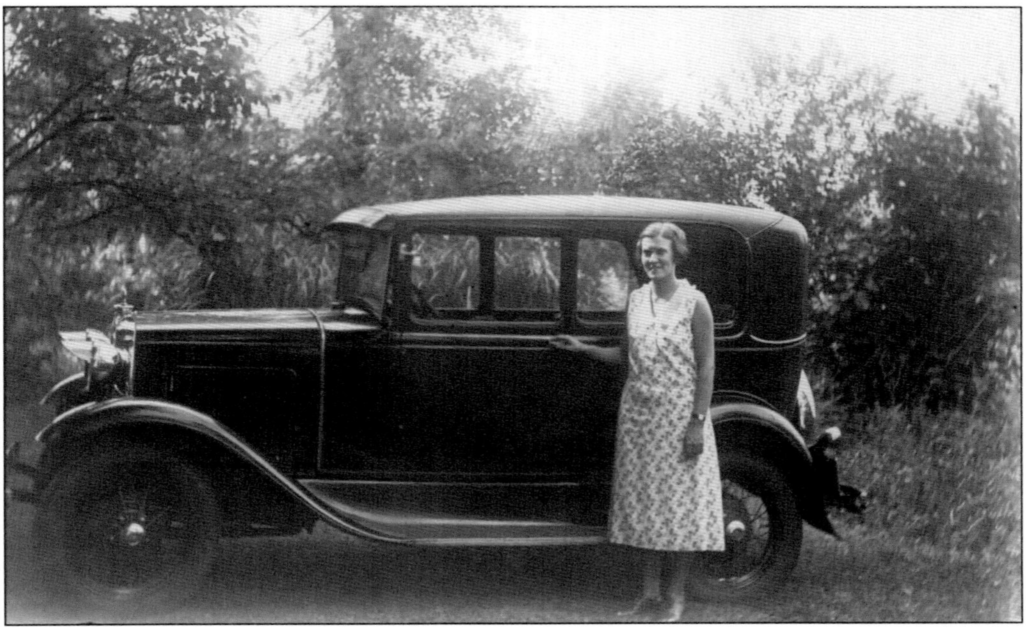
Cleo Hosbrook, daughter of Maude and Charles J. Hosbrook, poses with her 1930 Ford. In 1927, Miami Avenue was rebuilt as a hard surface road, making driving much easier for the increasing number of automobiles in the village. (Courtesy Madeira Historical Society.)

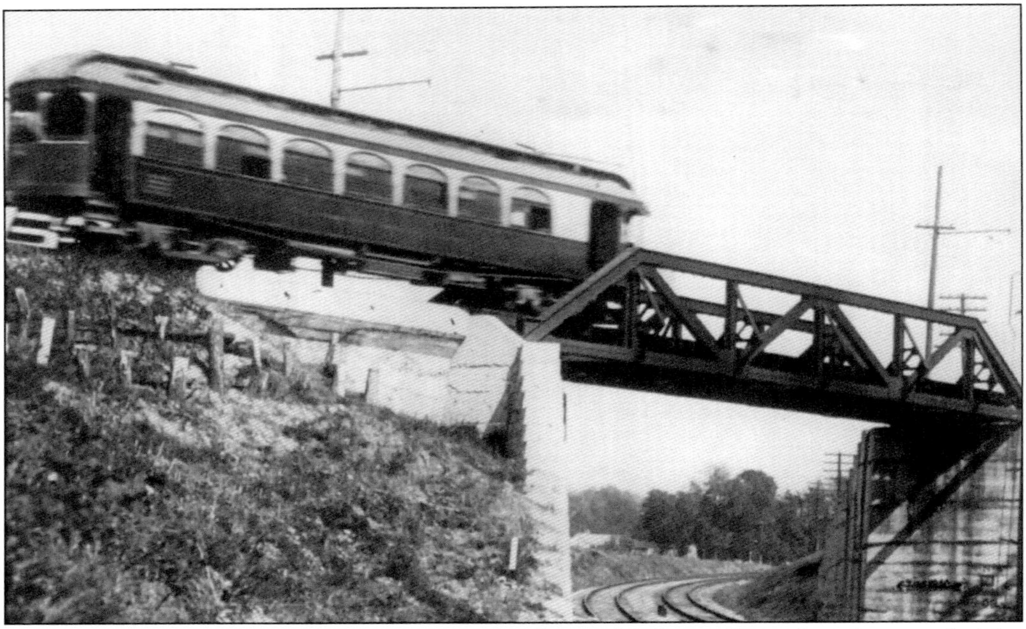

A Madeira traction car speeds over a trestle, heading to Madisonville in this photograph. The Cincinnati and Columbus electric interurban traction car line began serving the community in 1906. People now began relying on the interurban system, called the Swing Line, rather than the trains for daily commuting and trips into Cincinnati. The traction line was discontinued in 1919 as more and more people relied on their own automobiles. (Courtesy of Madeira Historical Society.)

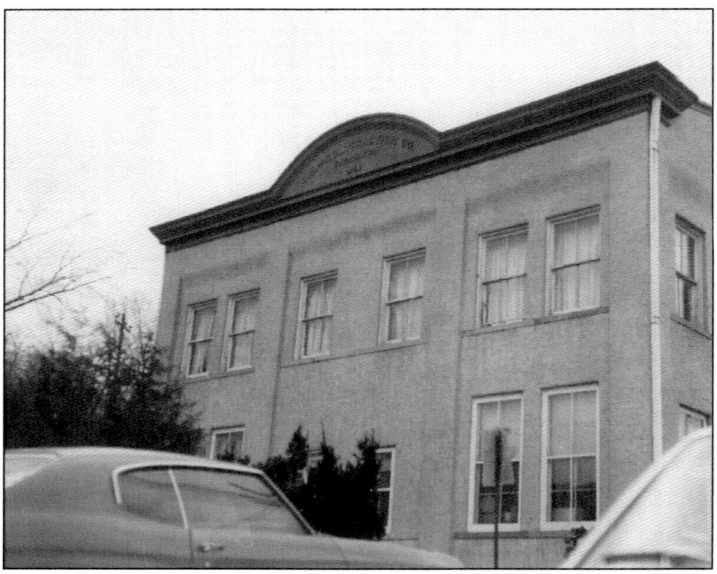

Substation No. 1 for the Swing Line was located at 6912 Miami Avenue, later home to the Madeira and Indian Hill Fire Station. The interurban brought electricity to Madeira. When the last traction car of the day completed its trip, the lights went out all over Madeira, explained Daniel D. McDonald. After the line was abandoned, Madeira contracted with the Union Gas and Electric Company for electric power. (Courtesy Madeira Historical Society.)

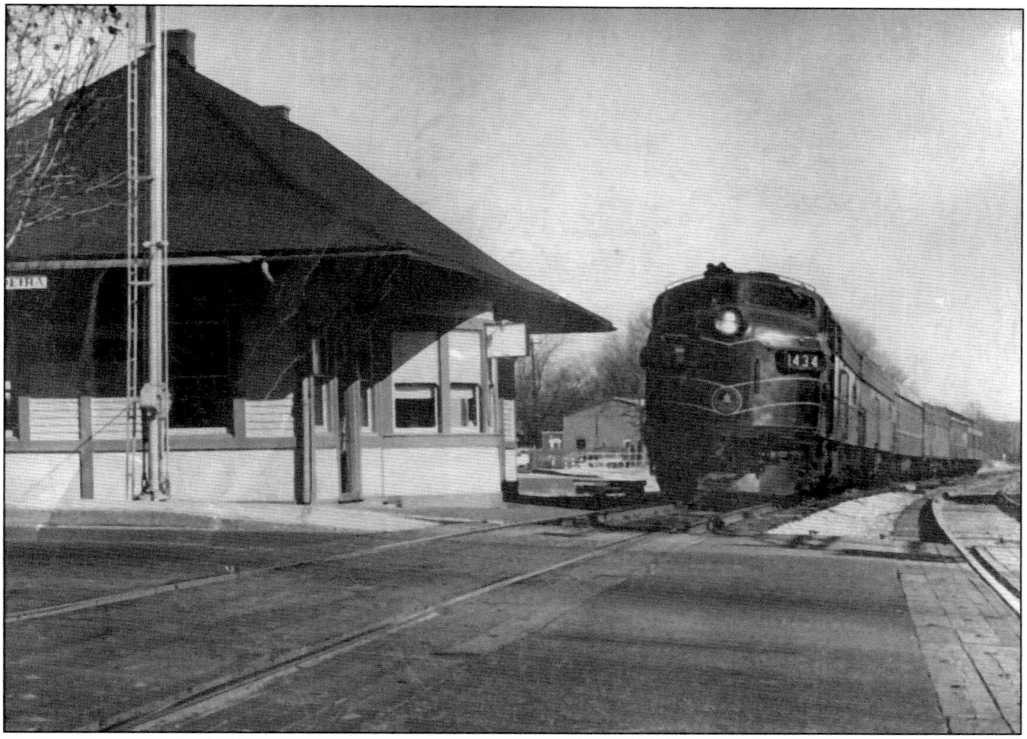

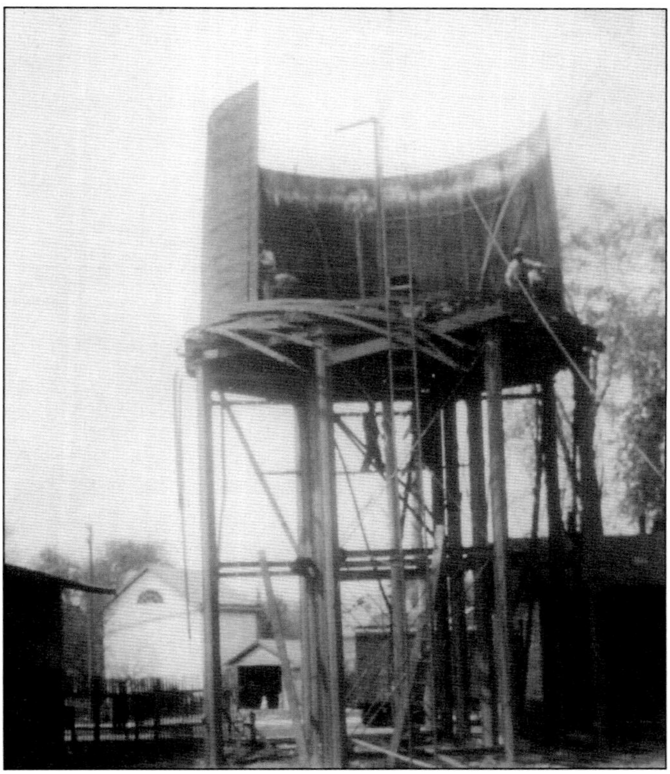

A diesel train (above) pulls into the depot in this undated photograph. With steam locomotives largely bowing out to diesel after World War II, an abundant water supply—the reason Madeira had first been chosen for a depot—was no longer a factor. The old water tower (right) was razed in 1931. By the mid-1950s, there were only 7,718 steam locomotives still operating in the United States as opposed to 17,358 diesels. (Both courtesy Madeira Historical Society.)

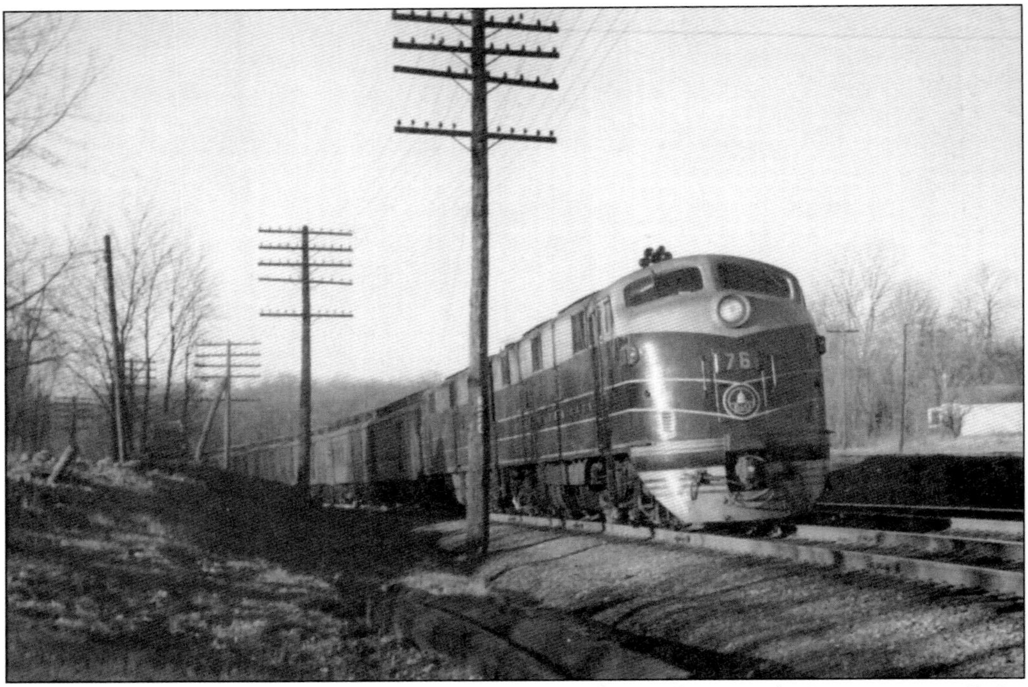

A Baltimore and Ohio train heads to Madeira in this 1952 photograph. Trains were still the most economical and dependable way to move freight then. The capacity of a standard freight car had risen from about 20 tons after the Civil War to 53 tons in 1953. (Courtesy Madeira Historical Society.)

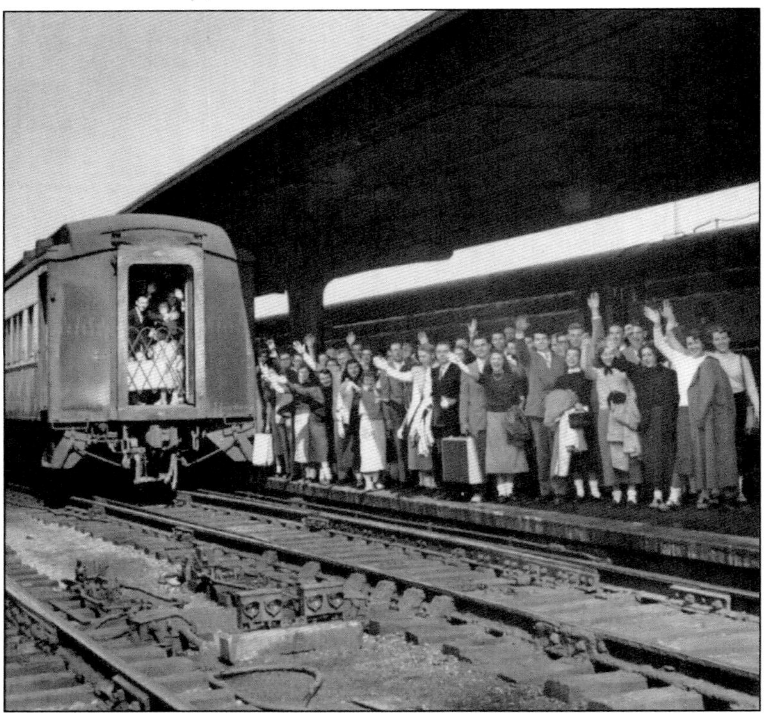

Madeira High School's class of 1952 prepares to board the train for a spring trip to Washington, D.C. Rail travel was common then, but the Federal Highway Act of 1956 was about to change that. The act authorized construction of a 41,000-mile interstate highway system. The interstates, teeming with luxurious, affordable, American-made automobiles, would make road trips the popular choice for many travelers. (Courtesy Madeira City Schools.)

Three

Faith Matters

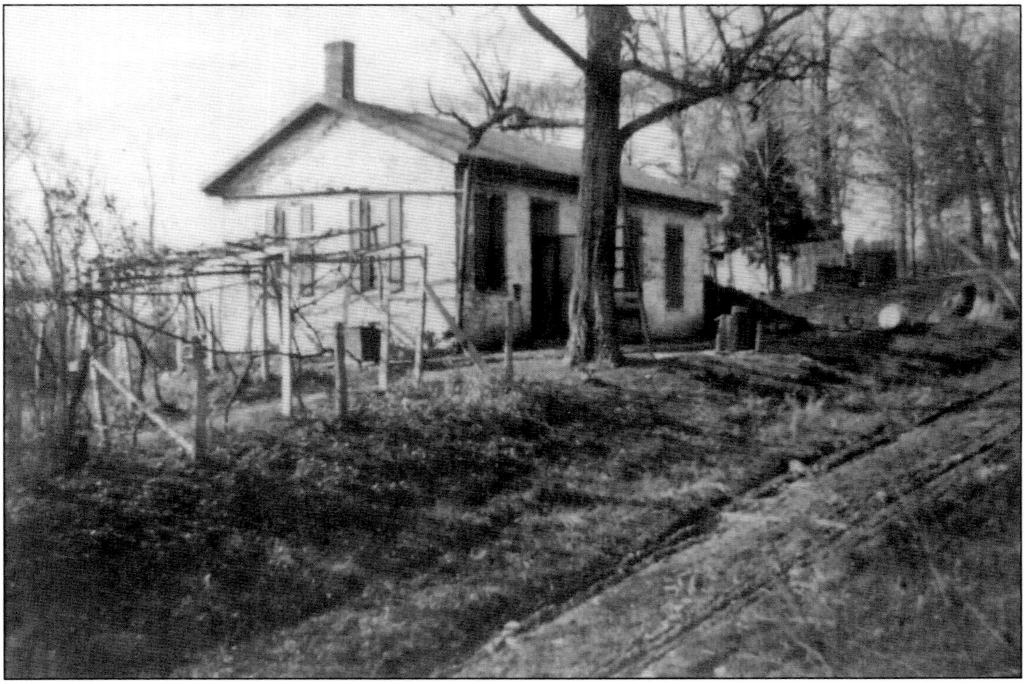

Around 1849, Pioneers began worshipping at the McCullum School, which was built around 1839. The stone building on Shawnee Run Road is the oldest extant structure in Madeira, according to the 1991 *Historic Inventory of Hamilton County*. Oliver Jones, son of pioneer settler John Jones, built the schoolhouse on land acquired from his sister Rebecca Jones McCullum. Nondenominational worship was first held in a log schoolhouse that stood at the corner of what are now Miami and Euclid Avenues. The services were called the Union Sunday School. The Madeira Presbyterian Church and the Madeira Methodist Episcopal Church emerged from this group. (Courtesy Madeira-Silverwood Presbyterian Church.)

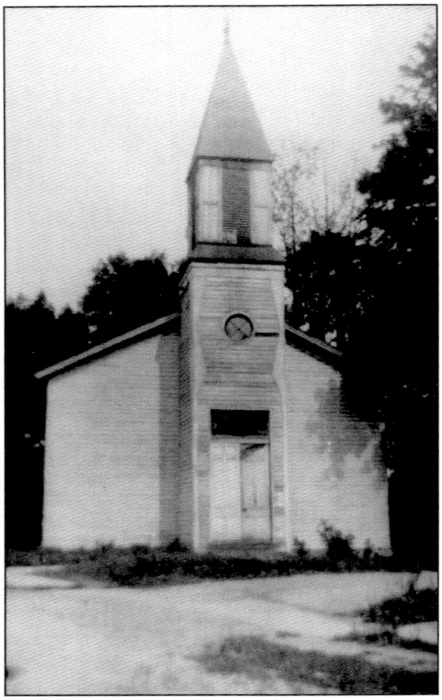

The Methodist Episcopal Church was built at the southeast corner of Laurel Avenue and Center Street in 1873 on a lot that cost $100. Brothers J. B. and Jacob Mann led a group of people to raise the small frame building. A circuit minister, who also served Camp Dennison, Indian Hill, Miamiville, Newtown, and Rossmoyne, held biweekly services in Madeira. Members held Sunday school classes weekly. (Courtesy Madeira Historical Society.)

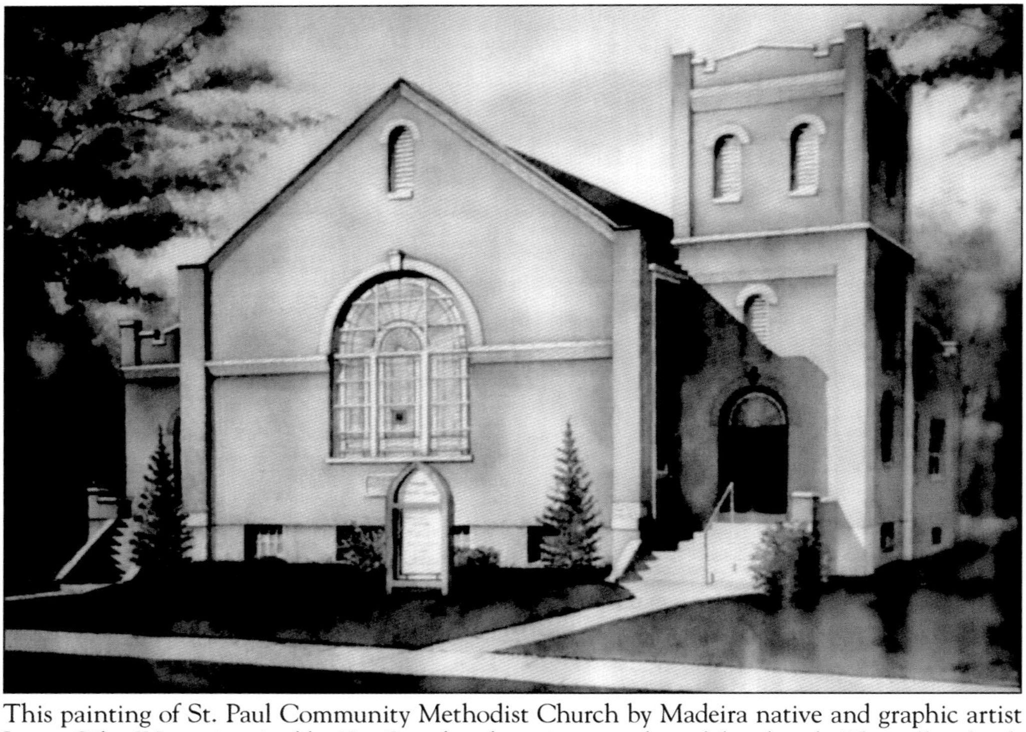

This painting of St. Paul Community Methodist Church by Madeira native and graphic artist James Giles IV was inspired by Kay Storch, a longtime member of the church. The yellow brick building at the southwest corner of Miami and Euclid Avenues was completed in 1928 at a cost of approximately $34,000. (Courtesy St. Paul United Methodist Church.)

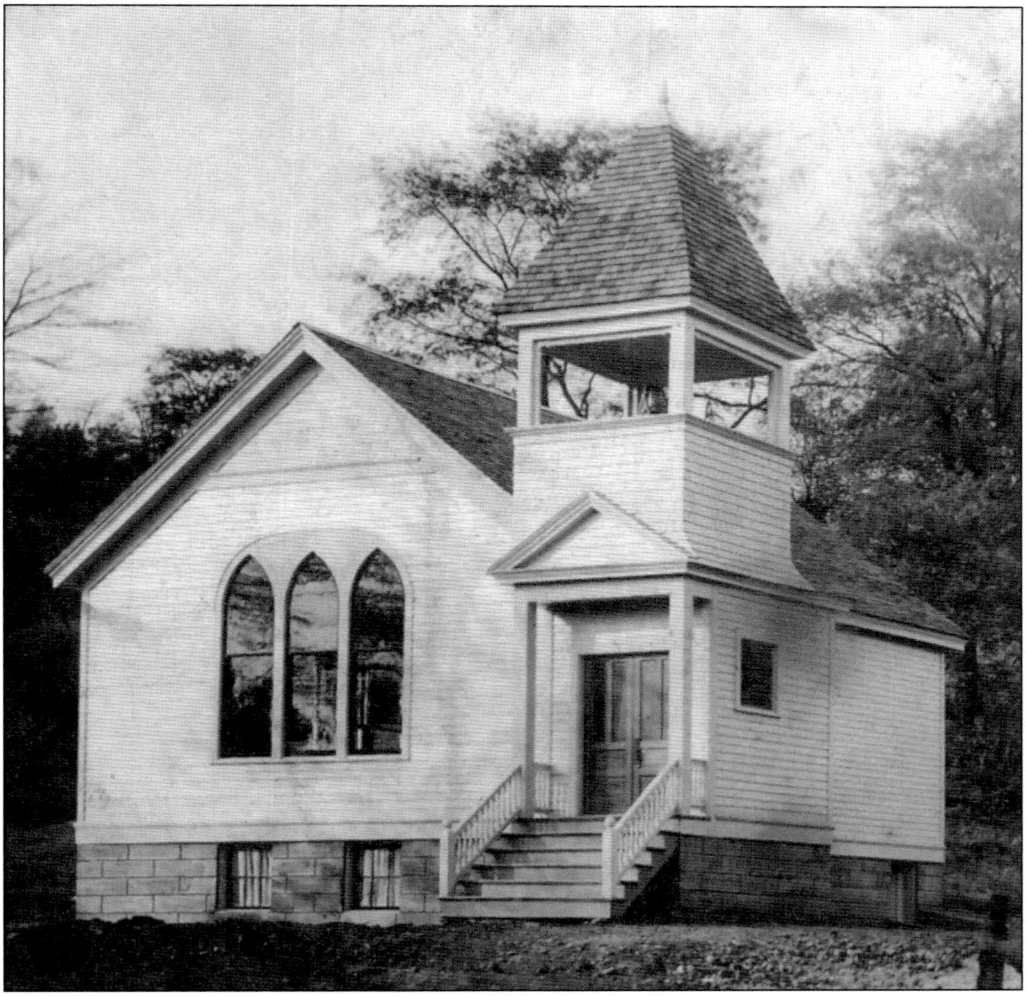

Sunlight gleams on the Madeira Methodist Church in this undated photograph. With different locations and names over the decades, the congregation has worked together to serve the community. Early members included these families: James Dones, William Edmisten, Milo Hetzler, Wesley Hetzler, Jacob Mann, J. B. Mann, John Maxfield, John Moore, Joseph Richardson, Raymond Smith, Marlin Todd, and John Watson. The Ladies Aid Society was organized in 1887, and the first Missionary Society began in 1916. Bequests from Susan and John Watson and Carrie Schuyler in the 1920s helped to build the 1928 church. Men of the congregation donated hundreds of hours to construct the building; on Saturdays, women of the church would prepare meals and serve them to the men at work. The congregation struggled during the Great Depression, but by 1951 membership had grown to 244 and the church received its first full-time pastor, Rev. Daniel Scovanner. Today the congregation worships as St. Paul United Methodist Church at Miami Avenue and East Galbraith Road. (Courtesy Roger Ward.)

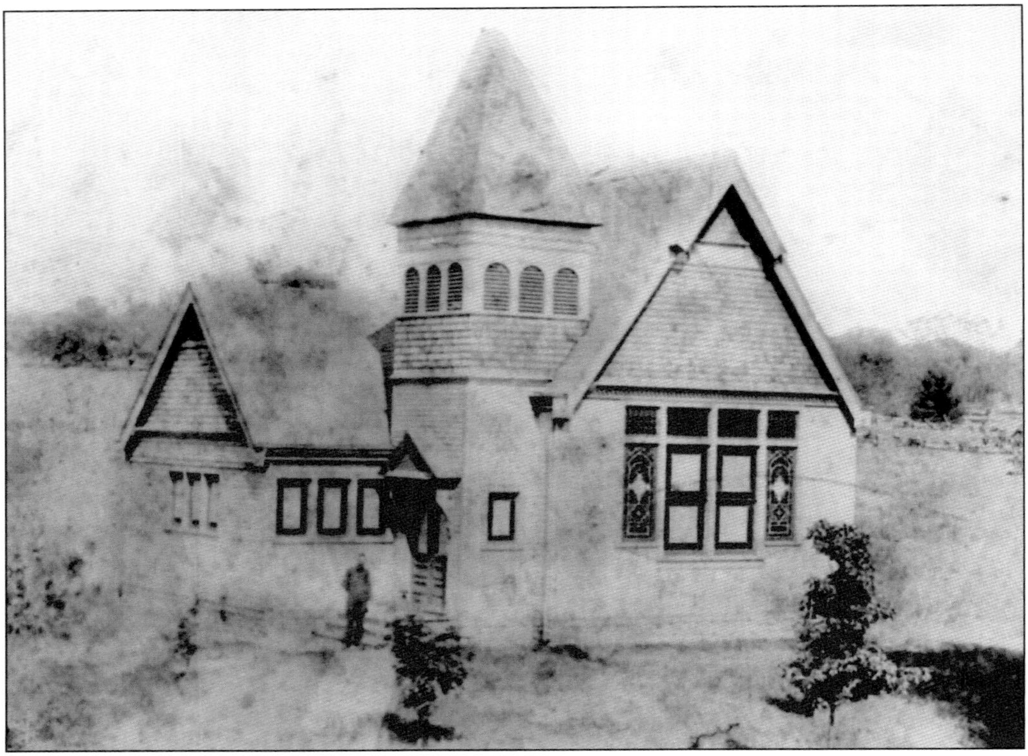

The original Presbyterian Church was completed in 1886 at Laurel and Miami Avenues. It was built of wood and stucco. Prior to construction, Presbyterians had met first at McCullum School and later at Muchmore Hall. (Courtesy Madeira-Silverwood Presbyterian Church.)

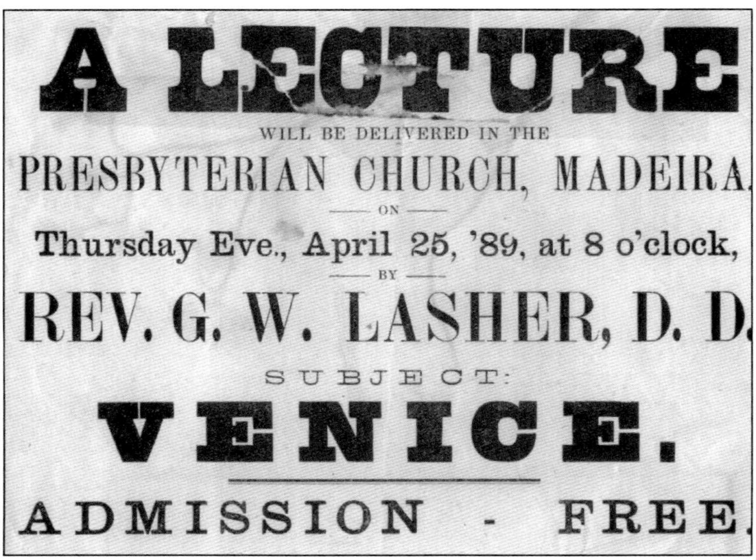

A LECTURE

WILL BE DELIVERED IN THE

PRESBYTERIAN CHURCH, MADEIRA

ON

Thursday Eve., April 25, '89, at 8 o'clock,

BY

REV. G. W. LASHER, D. D.

SUBJECT:

VENICE.

ADMISSION - FREE.

The Presbyterian Church soon became the site of many social events such as music programs, recitals, and lectures like the one announced in this 1889 flyer. (Courtesy Madeira-Silverwood Presbyterian Church.)

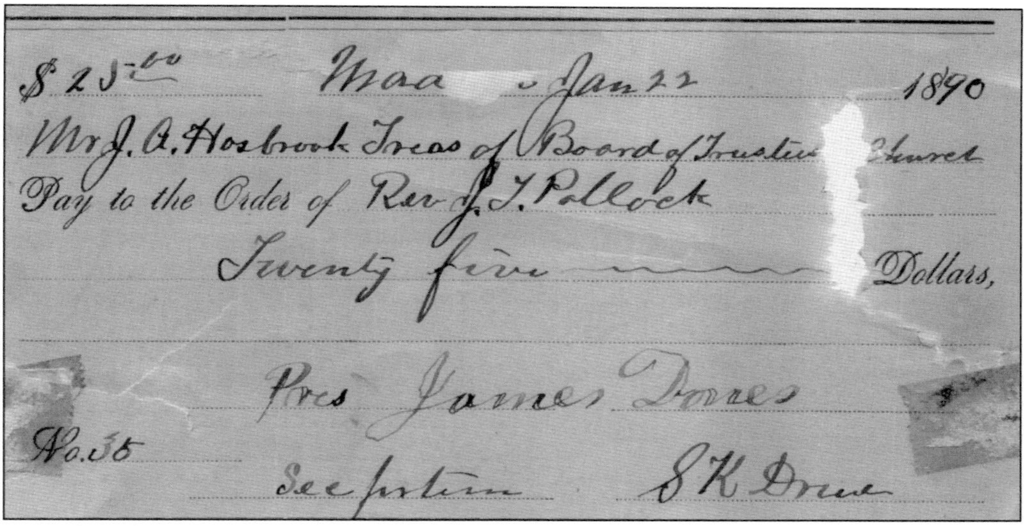
$25.00 Jan 22 1890
Mr J. A. Hosbrook Treas of Board of Trustee
Pay to the Order of Rev J. T. Pollock
Twenty five Dollars,
Pres James
No. 35
Secretary S K Druse

Several Madeira community leaders were members of the early Presbyterian congregation. This 1890 check to Rev. J. T. Pollock, the church's first pastor, bears the names of church treasurer John A. Hosbrook, descendant of early pioneers, and Samuel K. Druse, who later became Madeira's first mayor. (Courtesy Madeira-Silverwood Presbyterian Church.)

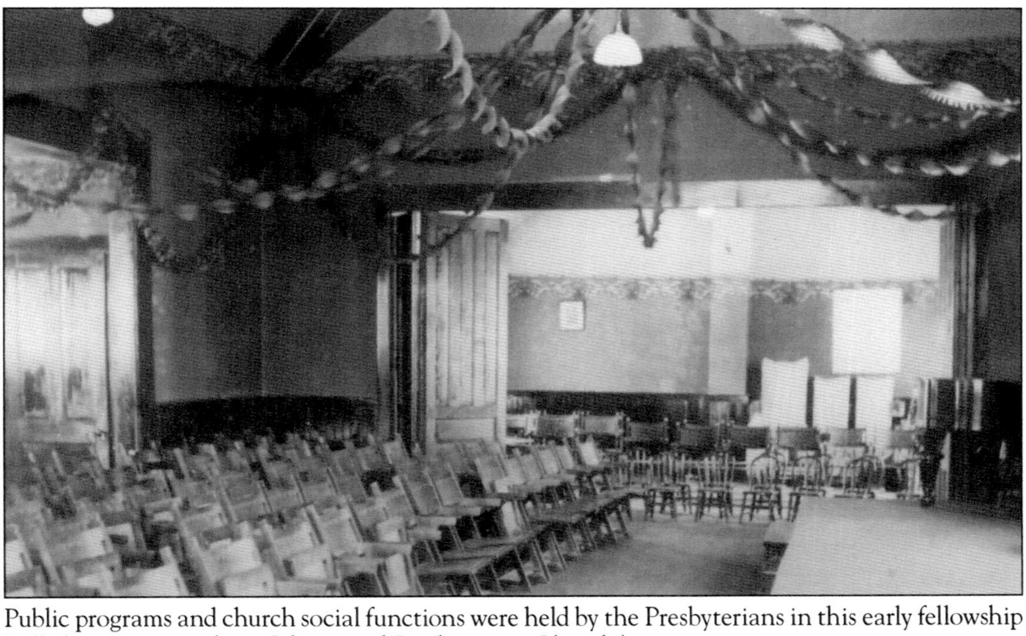

Public programs and church social functions were held by the Presbyterians in this early fellowship hall. (Courtesy Madeira-Silverwood Presbyterian Church.)

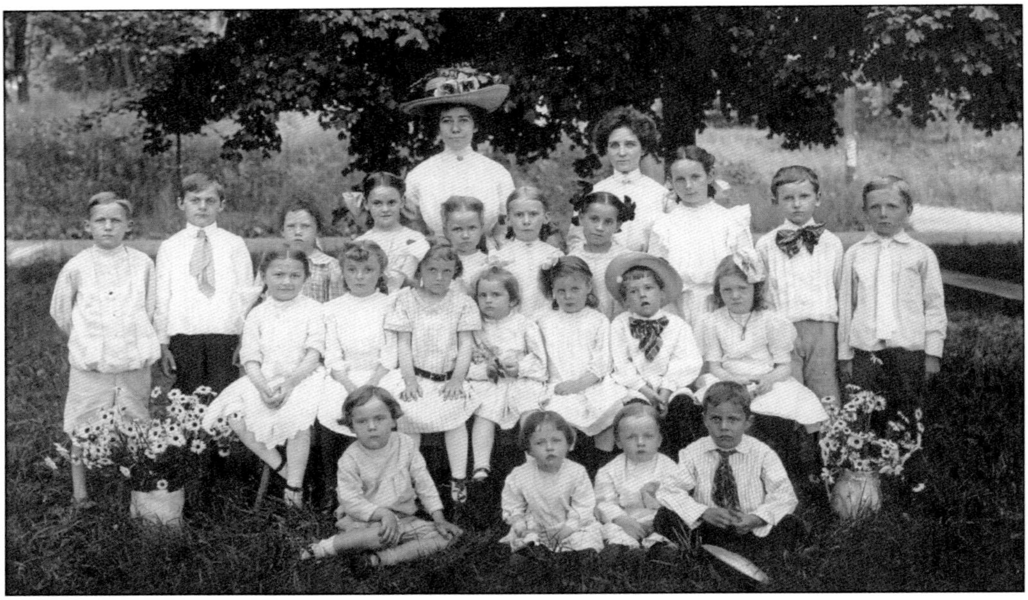

The Presbyterian Sunday school class poses for this photograph around 1910. From left to right are (first row) William Knight, unidentified, unidentified, and Bill Rapp; (second row) Mildred Stenway, Thelma DeMar, Louise Ray, unidentified, Bernice Senae, unidentified, and Naomi Bain; (third row) Telford Sullivan, Oscar Meyer, Catherine Aikin, Mary Burns, Rachel Clark, Cleo Hosbrook, Thelma Siler, Mary Graves, Horace Clark, and Harold DeMar; (fourth row) Nell Curtis and Fanny Curtis. (Courtesy Madeira-Silverwood Presbyterian Church.)

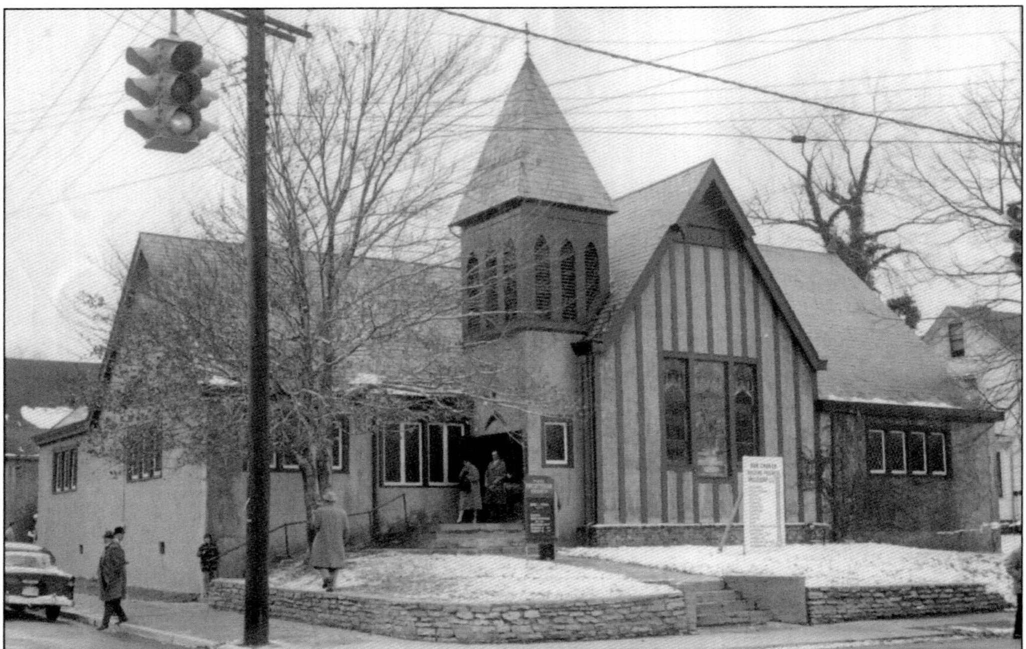

Presbyterian congregants leave church after a Sunday service in 1955. (Courtesy Madeira-Silverwood Presbyterian Church.)

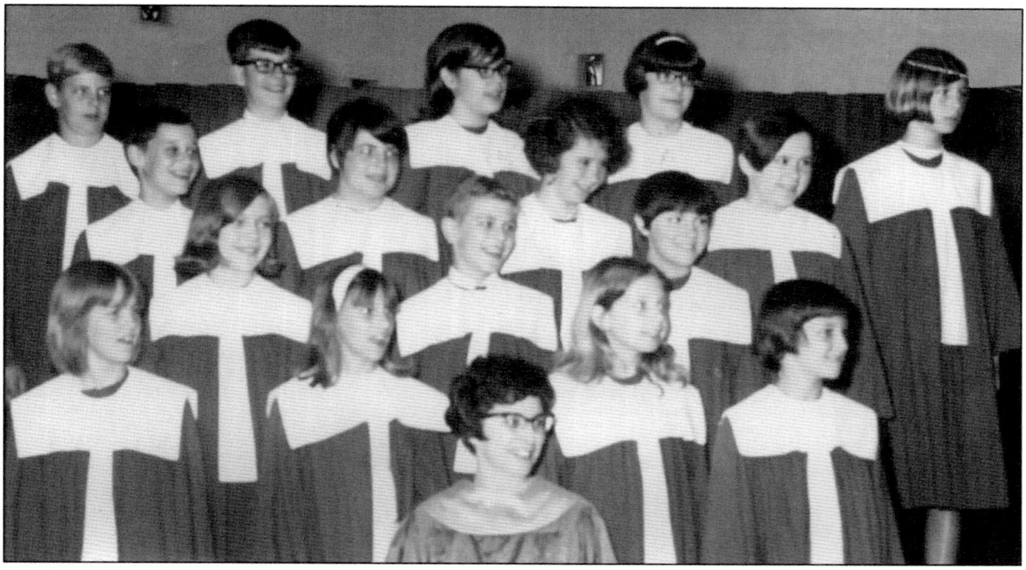

Presbyterians' love of sacred music dates back to John Knox in the 16th century. Singing in the junior choir in 1968 are, from left to right, (first row) Mrs. K. Clark Pester, Terry Kuykendall, Marian Case, Joyce Ertel, and Helen Howard; (second row) Ann Heise, Jim Arthur, and Linda Saum; (third row) Andrew Danzl, Mary Lu Pester, Marlene Snyder, and Chandra Hasty; (fourth row) Paul Rahn, George Wilson, Diane Heitz, Leslie Holmes, and Kathy Kamman. (Courtesy Madeira-Silverwood Presbyterian Church.)

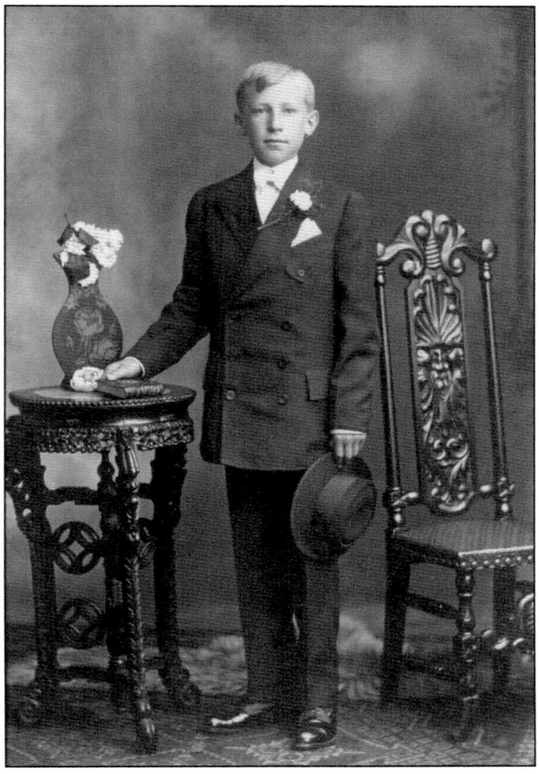

Edward Henke, son of German immigrants William and Wilhelmine (née Dreier) Henke, poses for his church confirmation portrait around 1910. The Henkes attended St. Paul Lutheran Church in Madisonville. As an adult, Edward helped on the family farm and worked at the Norwood Allis Chalmers plant. He married Minnie Emilie Kroeger in 1926 and they raised their children—Norbert, Daniel, and Melba—in Madeira. (Courtesy Doris and Norbert L. Henke.)

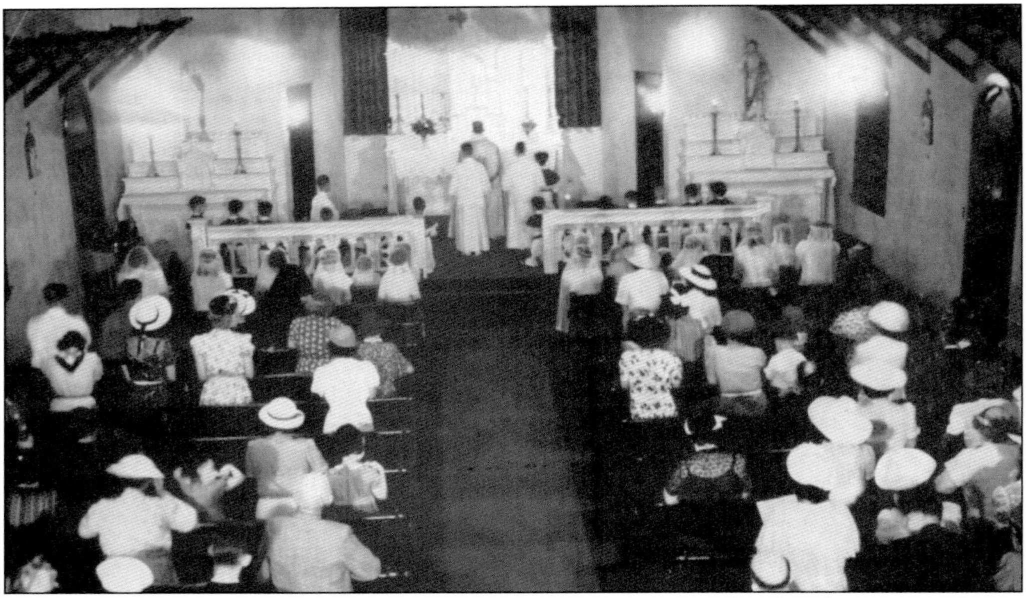

Young people prepare to make their first communion at St. Gertrude Church in 1952. The St. Gertrude mission was established in Madeira in 1923, the church completed in 1925, and the first Mass celebrated on February 8, 1925. (Courtesy St. Gertrude Church.)

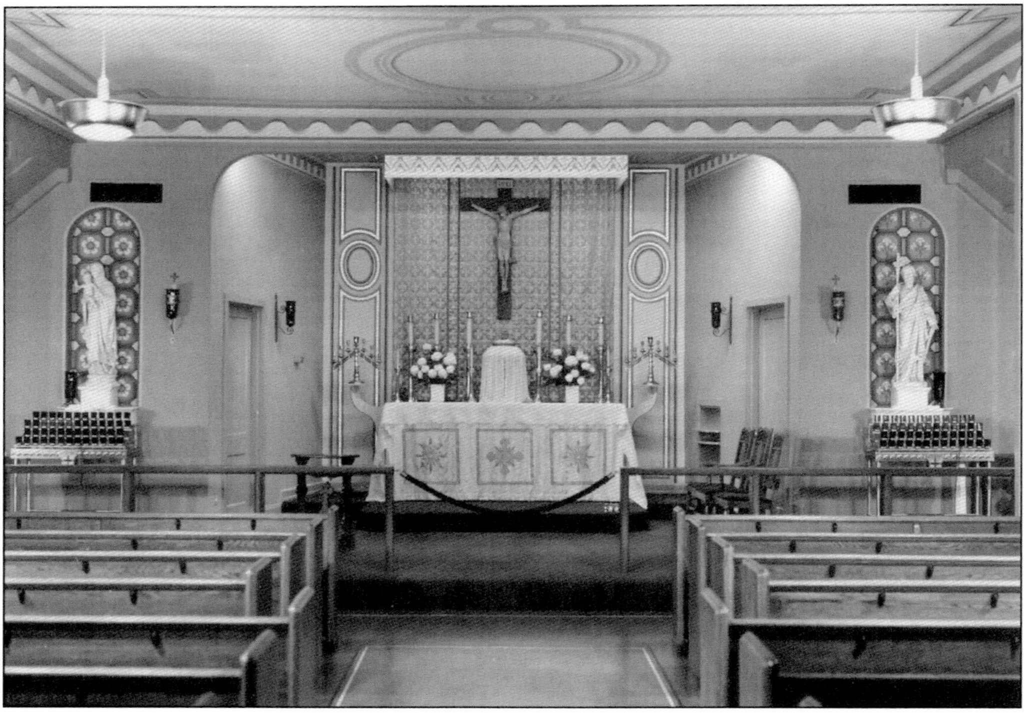

The pews in St. Gertrude's old sanctuary were originally from St. Andrew Church in Milford. They were ice-skated across the Little Miami River one winter to be installed at St. Gertrude. Every pew was filled in the 1950s as membership blossomed from 395 families in 1950 to 800 families in 1956. (Courtesy St. Gertrude Church.)

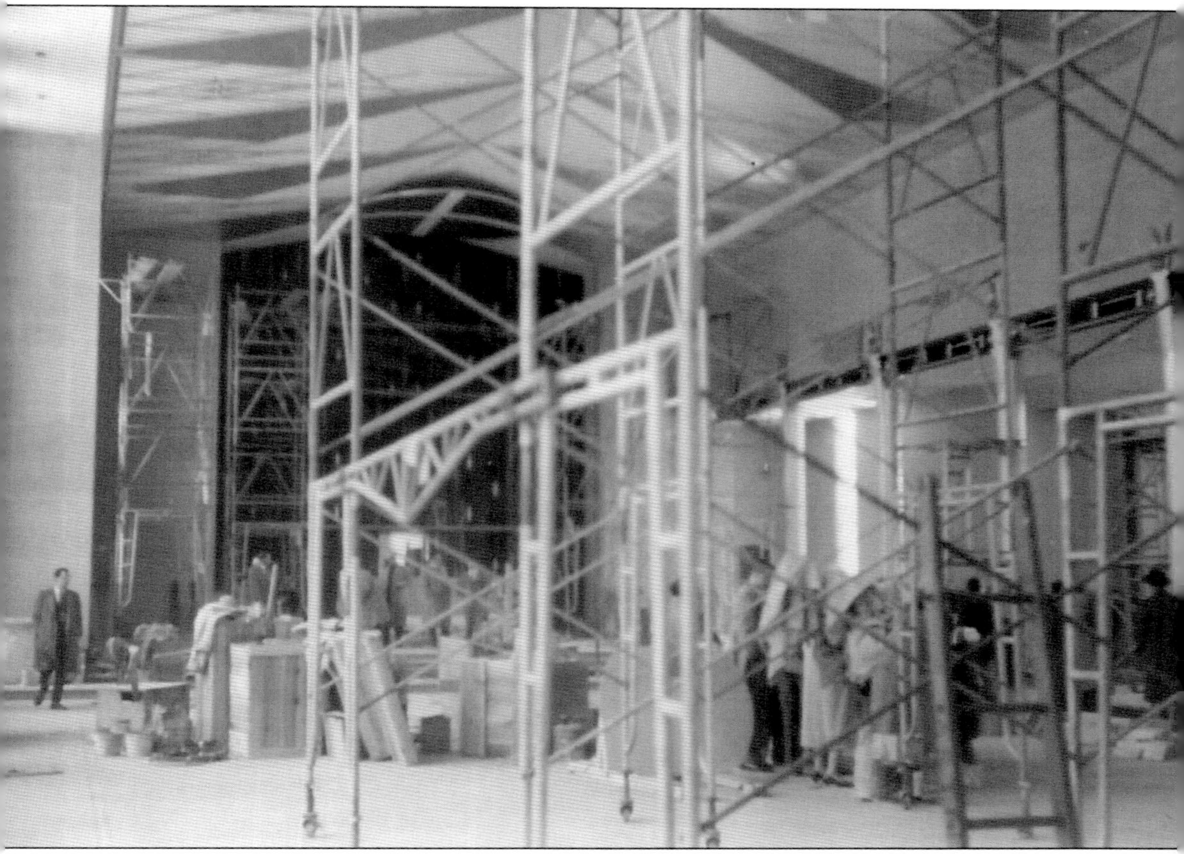

Plans for a new church began in 1958 as St. Gertrude's was holding 10 masses each Sunday to accommodate all parishioners. Fr. James G. Joyce, O. P., began a building fund campaign that year. The cornerstone was laid on Palm Sunday, April 10, 1960, and the church was dedicated on April 16, 1961. Fr. Paul E. Rodgers, O. P., is credited with laying the foundation for the church's expansion in 1955 when he acquired additional property to insure that the church and parish school would be located together. Father Rodgers was pastor there from 1943 to 1956. (Courtesy St. Gertrude Church.)

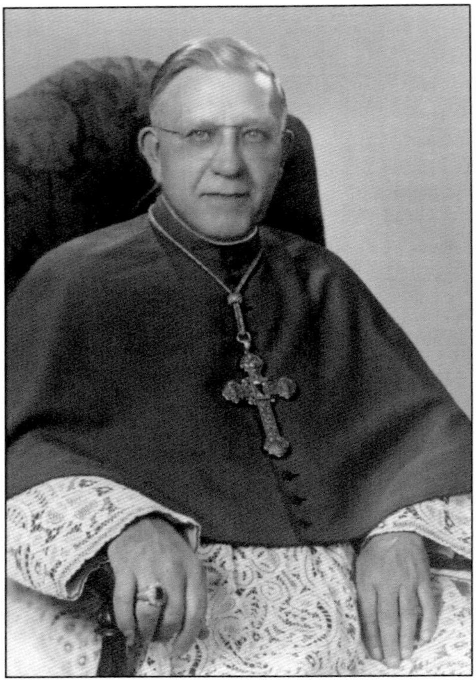

Fr. Joseph Albers was St. Gertrude's first pastor. He led the parish through 1926. He later was named bishop of Lansing, Michigan. (Courtesy St. Gertrude Church.)

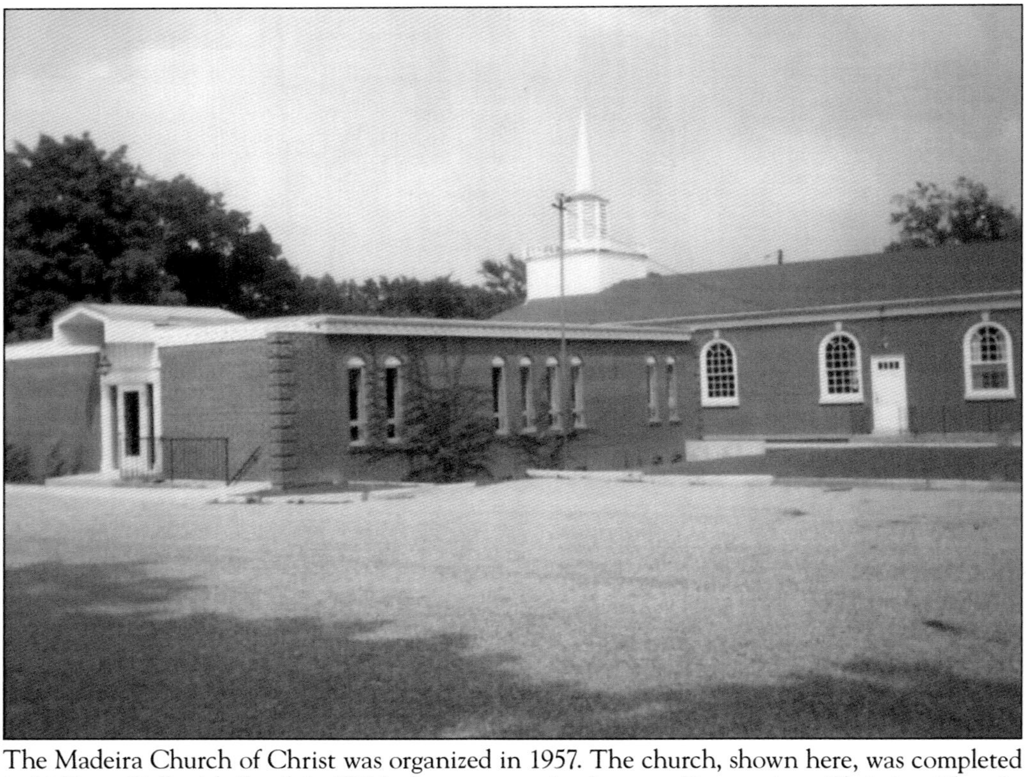

The Madeira Church of Christ was organized in 1957. The church, shown here, was completed in 1960 on Galbraith Road. In 2006, the congregation became Connections Christian Church. (Courtesy Connections Christian Church.)

Four

The Sporting Life

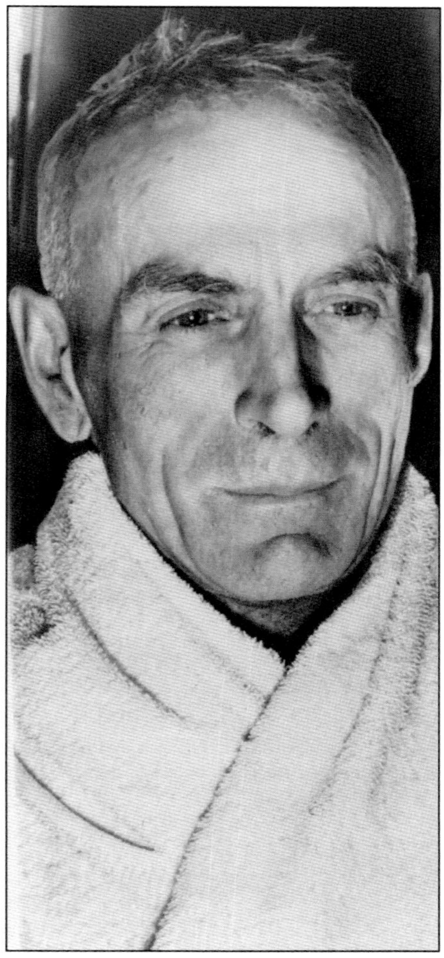

Clarence DeMar is Madeira's best-kept secret celebrity. A holder of numerous records for the Boston Marathon and a three-time Olympics participant, DeMar was born in Madeira on June 7, 1888. A Cincinnati newspaper once wrote that he could run down a jackrabbit when he was a boy on Indian Hill. He started walking to school in Madisonville at age seven. He had over a mile to go and found it "much more pleasant to dog-trot than to walk," DeMar wrote in *Marathon*, his 1937 autobiography. After his father died, DeMar helped his mother support five younger siblings by walking 10 to 20 miles a day to sell pins, needles, thread, and soap. "The DeMars have always been a rather rugged family," he wrote. The family moved to Massachusetts when he was 10. (Courtesy Library of Congress.)

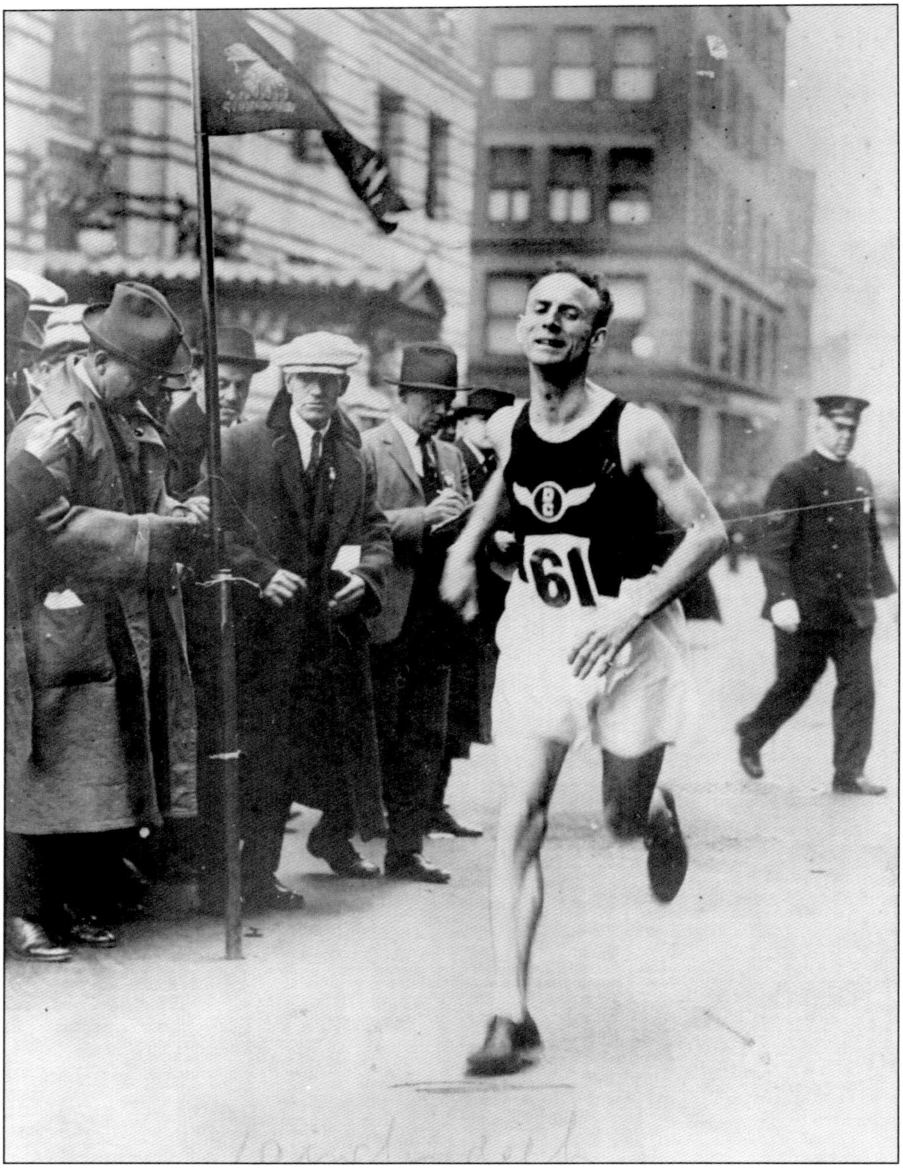

"Clarence DeMar was as heroic in his sport as Bobby Jones, Bill Tilden, and Jack Dempsey were in theirs," wrote Colman McCarthy in the 1981 reissue of DeMar's autobiography. In this 1924 photograph, DeMar runs through Boston's commercial district during the Boston Marathon. During his first Boston Marathon in 1911, DeMar not only won, but he also set a new record by completing the race in about three minutes less than the previous record holder. He ran 34 Boston Marathons in all, winning a record-breaking seven times, and finishing 17 times in the top three. DeMar represented the United States in the 1912, 1924, and 1928 Olympic games; he placed third in the Olympic marathon in 1924. Despite his success and fame, DeMar always sought to maintain a balance between athletics and daily life. He worked as a compositor in a print shop, led a Boy Scout troop, and taught Sunday school at his Baptist church in Melrose, Massachusetts. He died in 1959. Today an annual marathon in New Hampshire is named for DeMar. (Courtesy Library of Congress.)

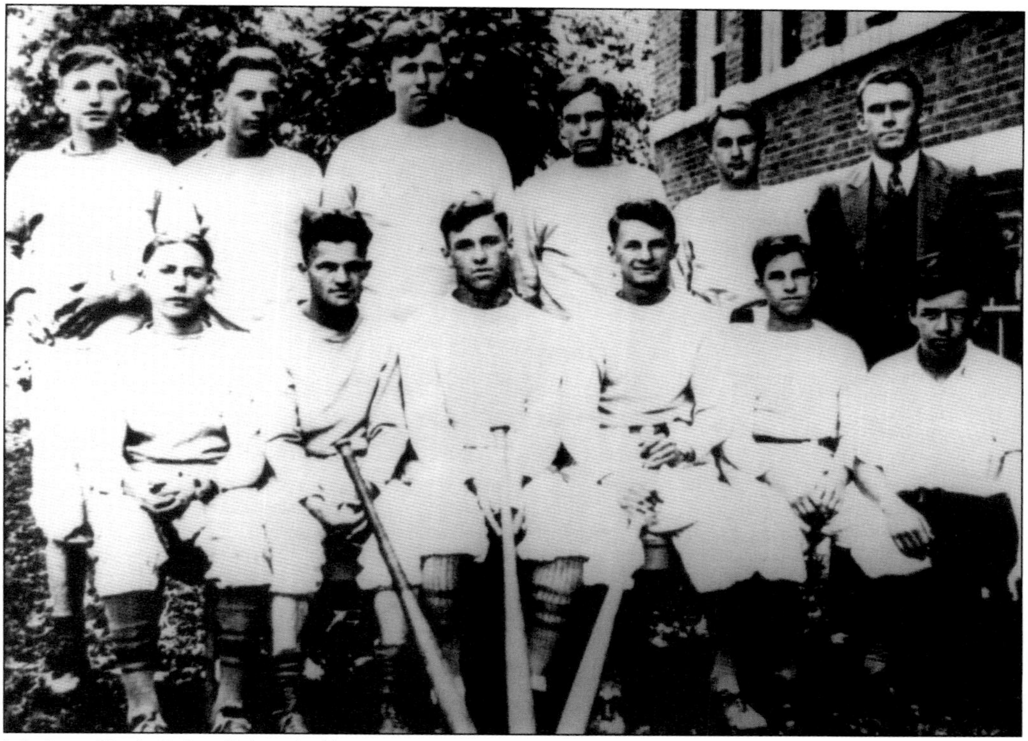

Madeira High School's baseball team poses for a team picture in 1934. From left to right are (first row) Paul Ballman, George Arey, Martin Strifler, Serward Scull, Cliff Lay, and Williard Frie; (second row) Stanley Adams, Ted Browning, Warren Judd, Hubert Young, Barney Scull, and ? Judd. (Courtesy Madeira Historical Society.)

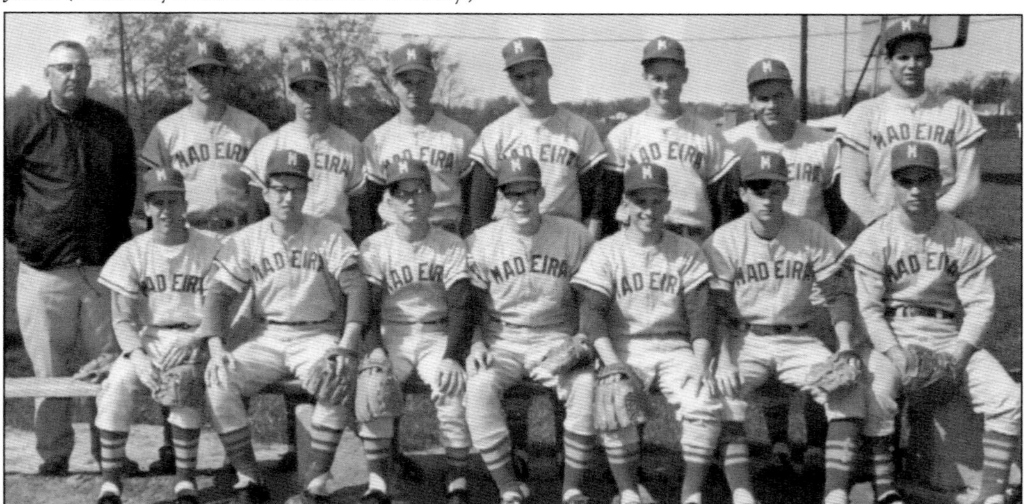

The 1967 Madeira High School baseball team continues the Mustang tradition behind Captains Steve Salt and Bill Trefzger. From left to right are (first row) Mike Hayden, Larry Sheakley, Ken Wippel, Greg Ely, Barry Fite, Scott Bradshaw, and Steve Salt; (second row) Coach Leslie "Doc" Voshell, Randy Tanner, Wayne Elliot, Mike Gregg, John Jones, Terry Hartley, Bill Sims, and Bill Trefzger; Tom Hayman was not present for the photograph. (Courtesy Madeira City Schools.)

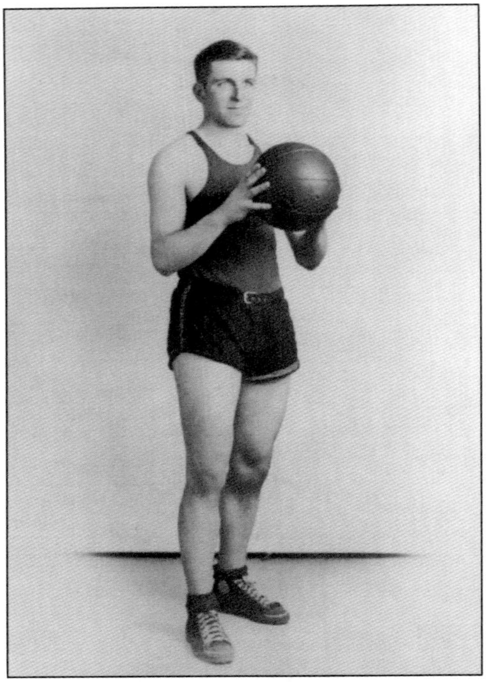

James C. Perin, in the class of 1930 at Madeira High School, poses in his basketball uniform. He also played baseball for Madeira but is most remembered for serving on the Madeira Board of Education from 1942 to 1974. Upon his retirement from the board, the school at Miami Avenue and Camargo Road was named for him. Perin was a civil engineer for Messer Construction Company and was involved in many community issues. (Courtesy Holly Perin Richard.)

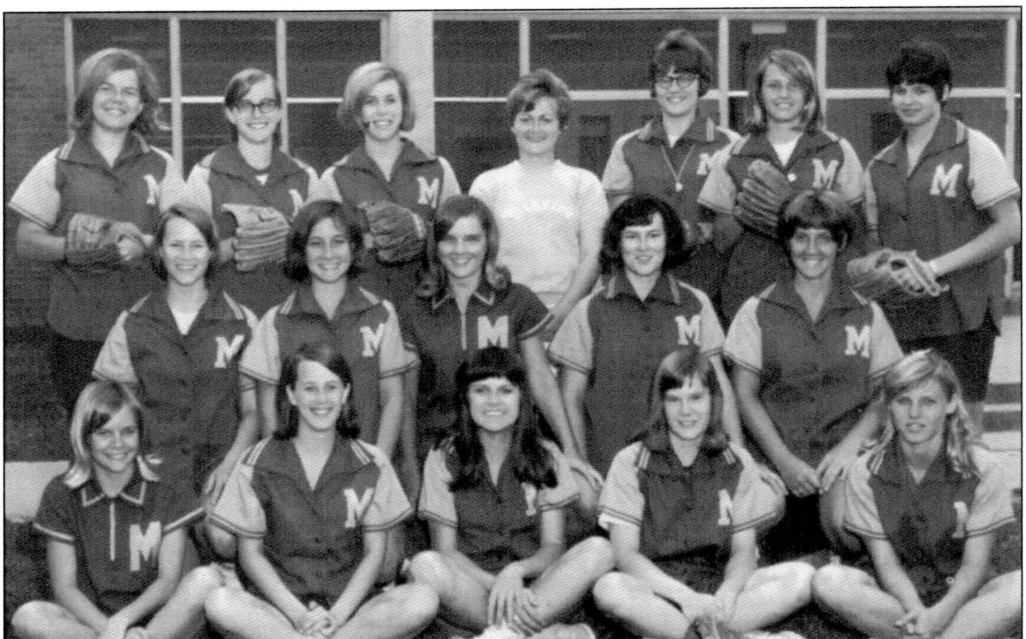

The 1967 Madeira High girls softball team won two-thirds of their games and was captained by pitcher Judy Kidder. From left to right are (first row) Amy Hurst, Joy Godwin, Debby Spears, Dora Fitzsimmons, and Donna Keller; (second row) Barb Fredrickson, Debby Lindner, Suzanne Sommers, Nancy Radcliffe, and Margie Pember; (third row) Marybeth Stimac, Terri Huiet, Judy Kidder, coach Claire Piskor, Patty King, Bonnie Patten, and Rhonda Morgan; Karen Medert was also on the team. (Courtesy Madeira City Schools.)

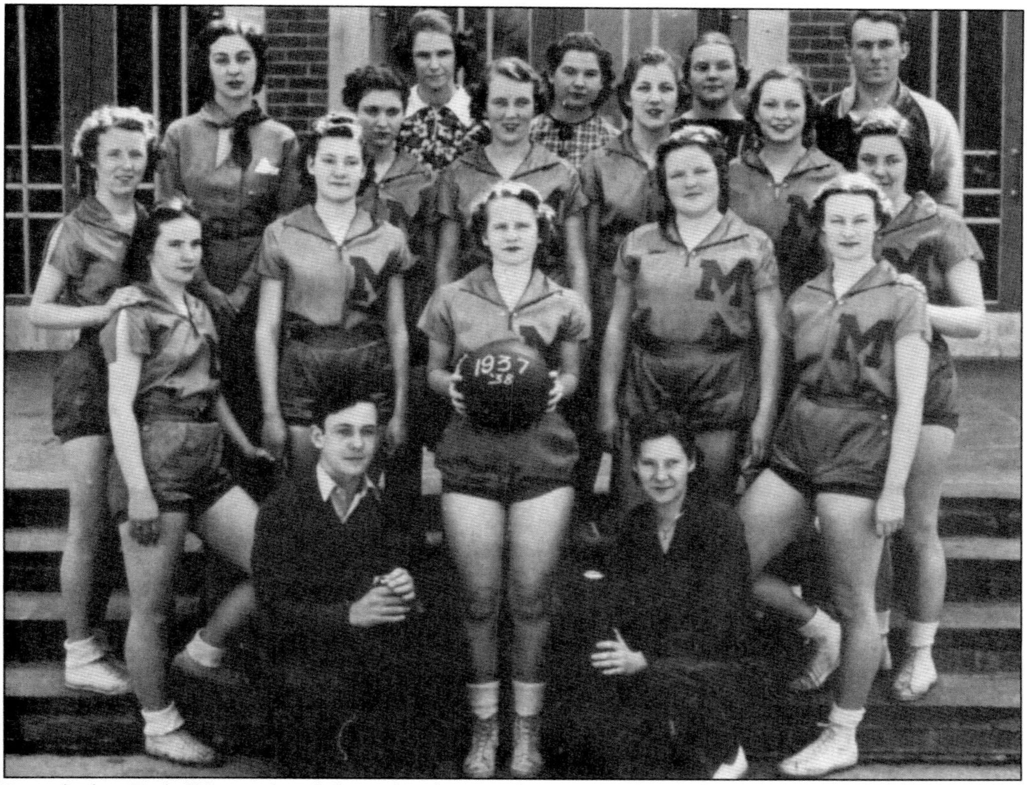

Long before Title IX mandated that schools provide more equitable treatment for women's athletics, the Lady Mustangs were playing basketball. The 1937 squad included (kneeling) cheerleaders Roger Perkis and Margaret Hanning; left to right (first row) Vange Korte, Betty Jane Hanning, Elizabeth Wehrman, Margaret McGinnis, and captain Virginia Teal; (second row) Thelma Bergen, Agnes Wood, Rita Bergen, captain Marion DeMar, Pauline Nevin, and Elsie Griewe; (third row) ? Fagaly and managers Dorothy Macht, Jean Putnam, Mary Jean Teal, and Aaron Gerrard. (Courtesy Madeira City Schools.)

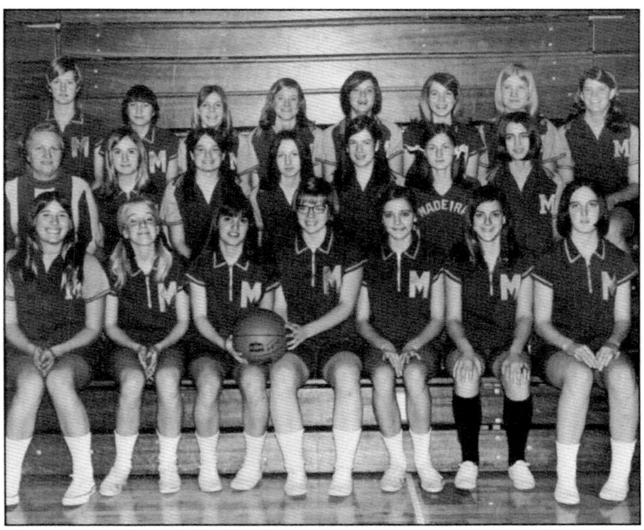

Madeira's junior varsity basketball team for the 1969–1970 school year included, from left to right, (first row) Kim Wipple, Debbie Schuebeler, Sharon Allman, Karen Miller, Donna Henke, Coleen Cordano, and Beth Hodgkins; (second row) coach Nadine Wilson, Patty Scott, Kim Morgan, Debbie Holzaur, Cynthia Faux, Dana Burton, and Debbie Patten; (third row) Barb Acomb, Barb Gill, Lorie Trefzger, Janis Jordan, Pam Linder, Jan Gibson, Lurline Fineran, and Judy Hungerland. (Courtesy Madeira City Schools.)

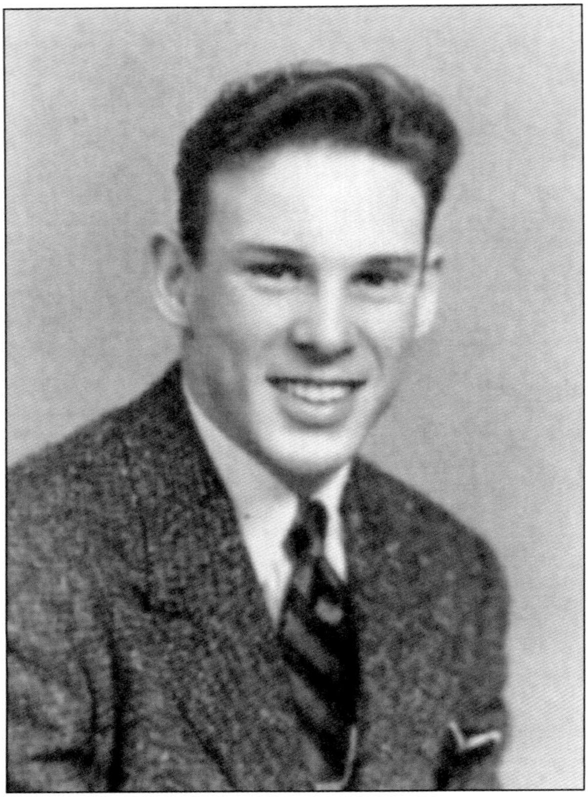

Richard Knight's nickname at Madeira High School was "Doc," and his most notable characteristic was his laugh. In 1941 and 1942, he placed first in his track events at state. (Courtesy Madeira City Schools.)

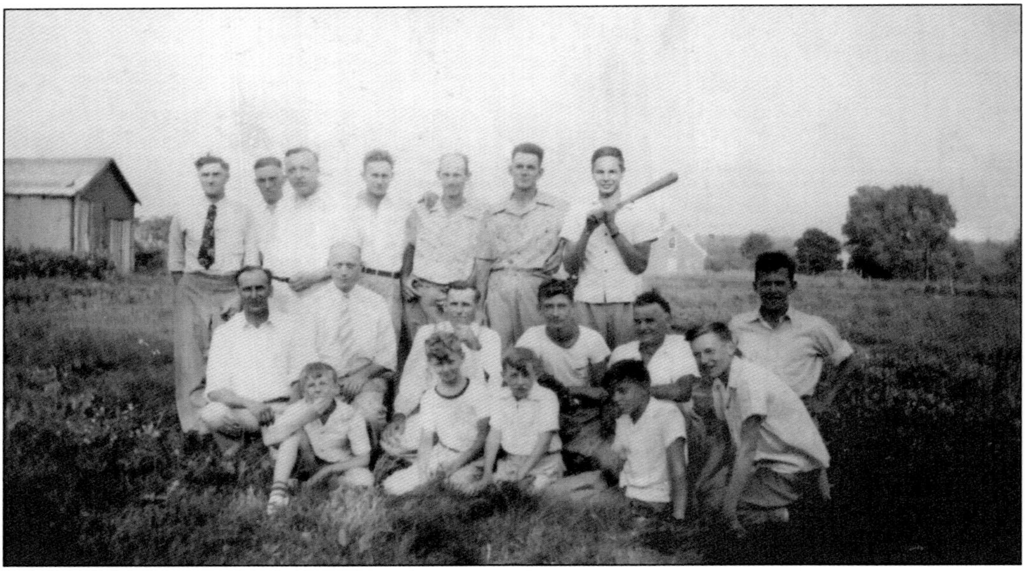

This group gathered at the William Henke farm on Stoney Lane on July 5, 1942, to play baseball. From left to right are (first row) Bill Henke, Donald Henke, Daniel Henke, Paul Krummel, and Norbert L. Henke; (second row) Albert Henke, Walter Krummel, Carl Aulen, Richard Henke, Bill Uchtman, and Harold Henke; (third row) Fred Meier, Harry Jess, Bill Henke, unidentified, Harold Meier, George Beekley, and Bill Powell. (Courtesy Doris and Norbert L. Henke.)

Nadine Wilson coached girls athletics at Madeira High for many years. She was inducted into the Madeira High School Athletic Hall of Fame in its inaugural year, 1991, along with Les "Doc" Voshell, Perry Ancona, William Klenk, Walter Farrington, and James C. Perin. (Courtesy Madeira City Schools.)

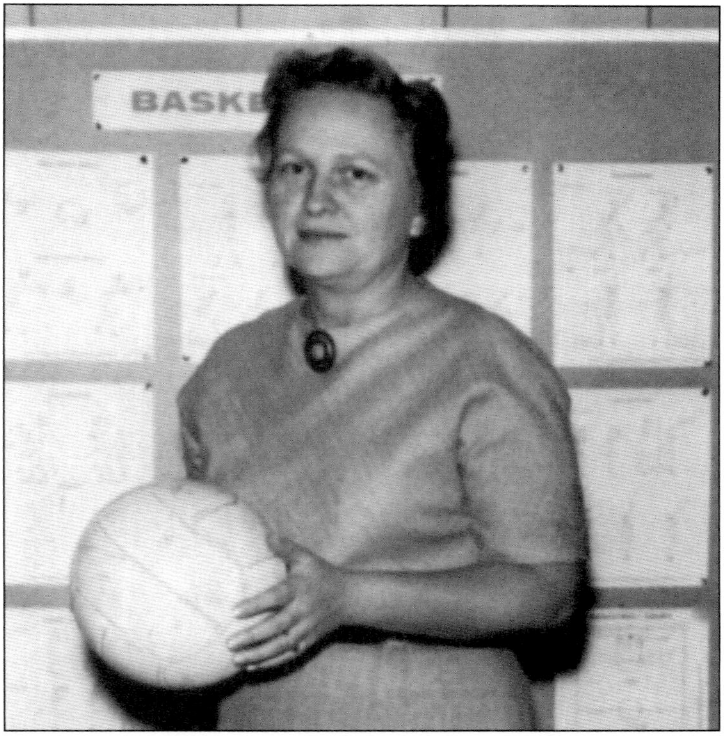

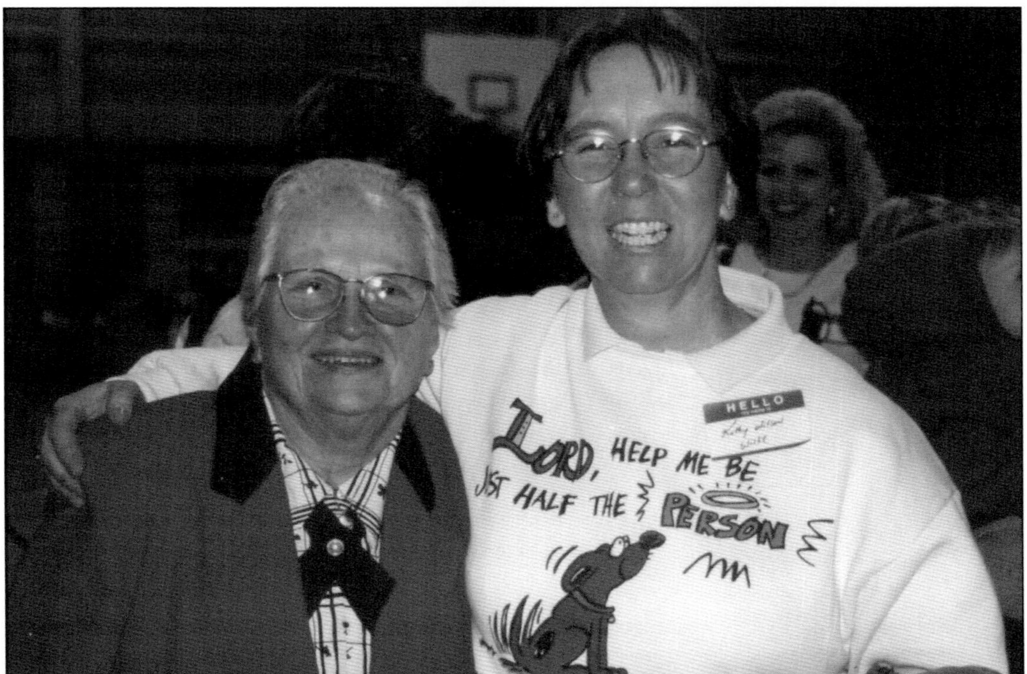

Nadine Wilson visits with former student Kathy Wilson (no relation), who played volleyball and basketball and ran track at Madeira. (Courtesy Madeira City Schools.)

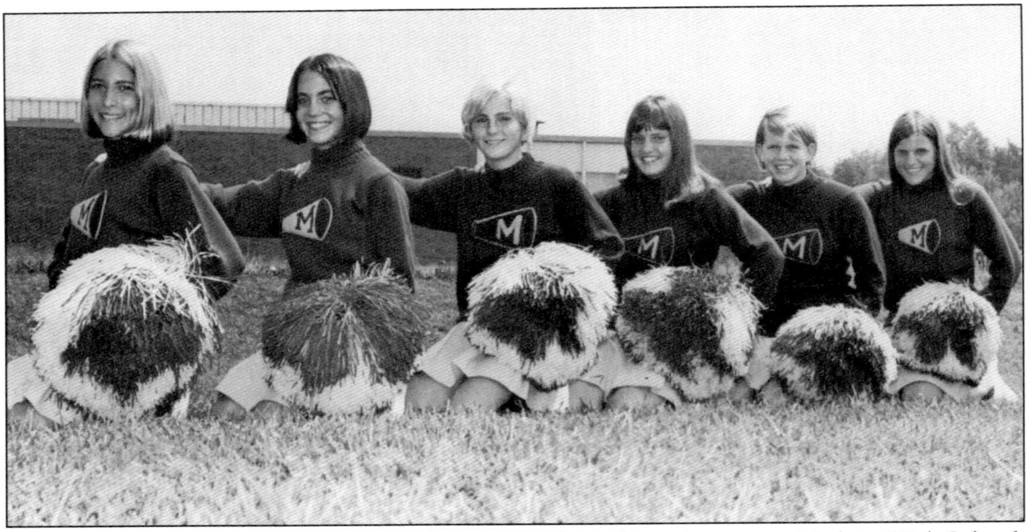

Cheerleaders have encouraged teams and supporters throughout the years at Madeira High School. The 1969–1970 squad included, from left to right, Beth Davis, Candy Trainer, Nancy Peterson, Sharon Allman, Emmy Bradshaw, and Jann Estebo. (Courtesy Madeira City Schools.)

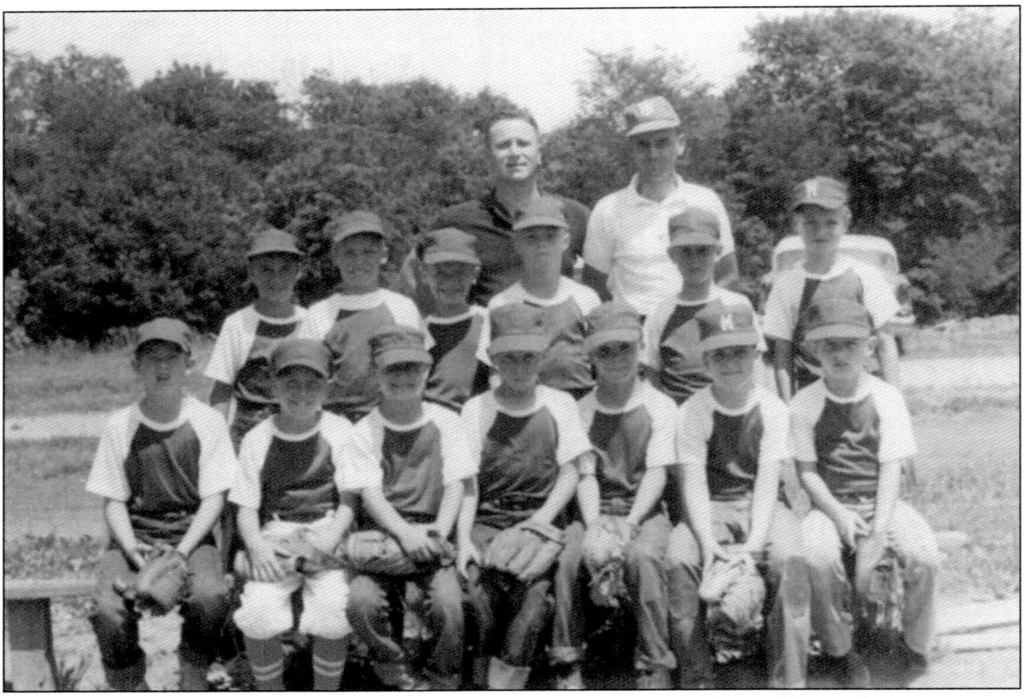

Thousands of Madeira youngsters have participated in little-league baseball over the generations. Clyde Wilcoxson (back left) and William P. Kincaid (back right) coached this little-league team in 1960. Kincaid's son Steven is the boy to the far left in the second row. (Courtesy Mildred Kincaid.)

Five

ON THE BEAT

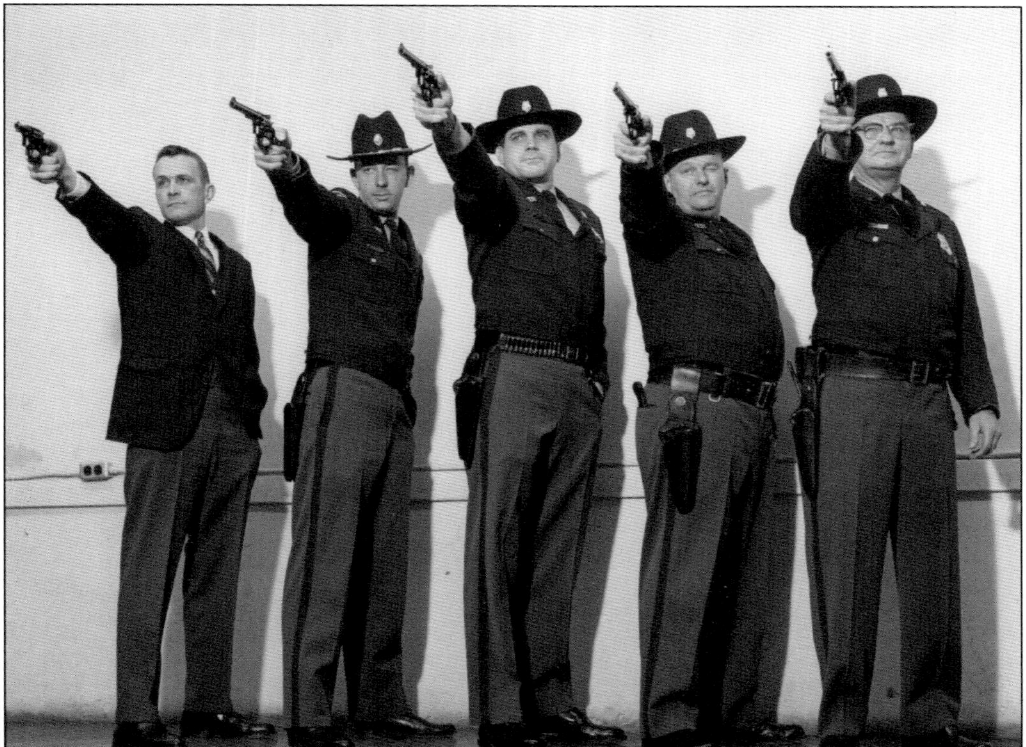

Members of the Madeira Police Department pose for a publicity shot in 1964. The department had placed high in a pistol marksmanship match sponsored by the Hamilton County Police Association and Fraternal Order of Police the previous year, according to an article in the *Cincinnati Telephone Bulletin* (April/May 1964). From left to right are Chief Thomas Gerth; officers John Geary, Donald Wallace, and Russell Ward; and Capt. Norwood Bowman. Arthur Smith was the relief man for the department at the time. (Courtesy Madeira Patrolmen's Benevolent Association.)

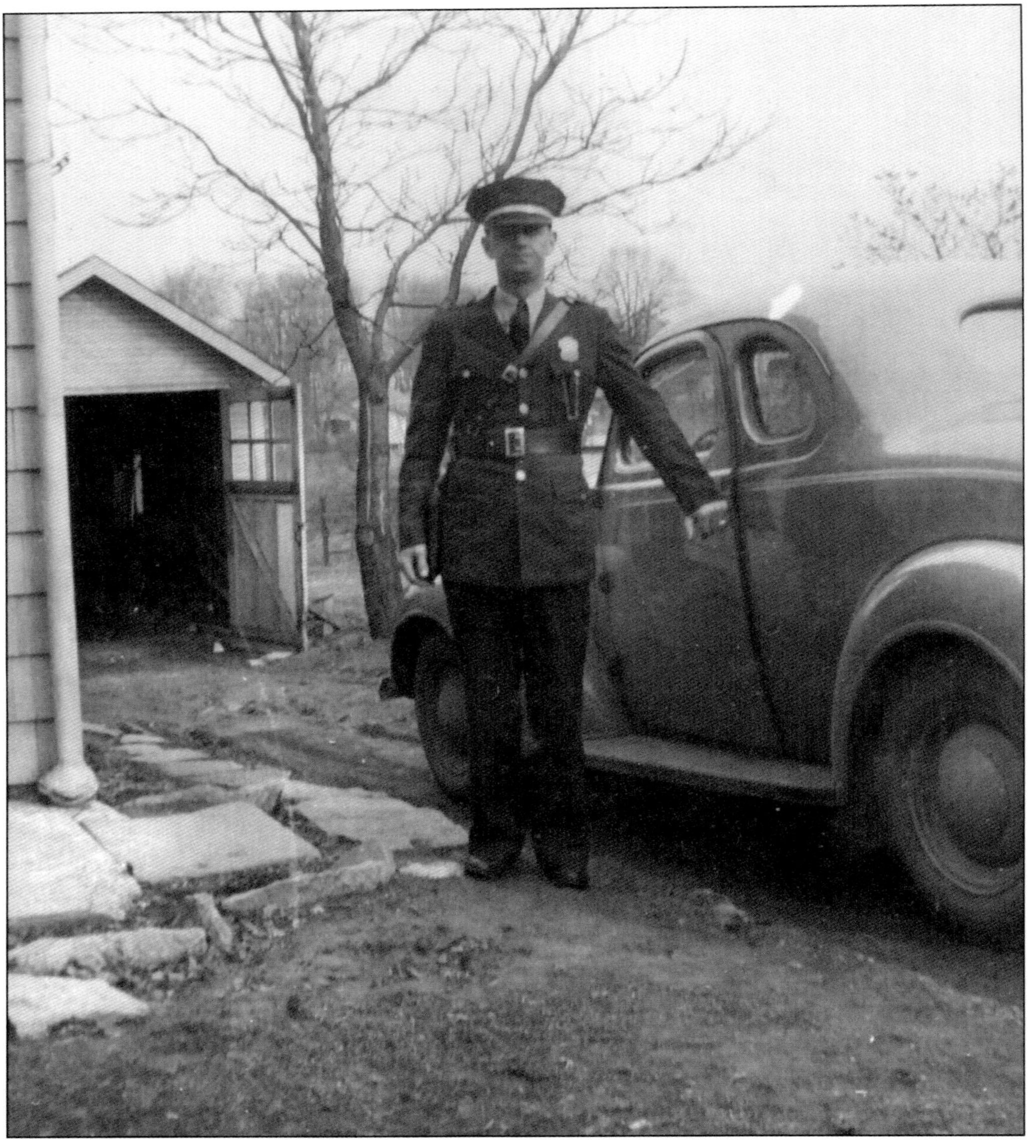

Thomas C. Fesmire was appointed chief of the village's new police department in 1942 at the age of 39. Madeira's population at that time was approximately 2,700. Prior to 1942, residents were protected by a series of elected town marshals and appointed deputy marshals. Fesmire was a North Carolina native who resided in Madeira by 1930. He worked as a machinist for the steam railroads before he entered law enforcement. Chief Fesmire served until 1947. (Courtesy Madeira Historical Society.)

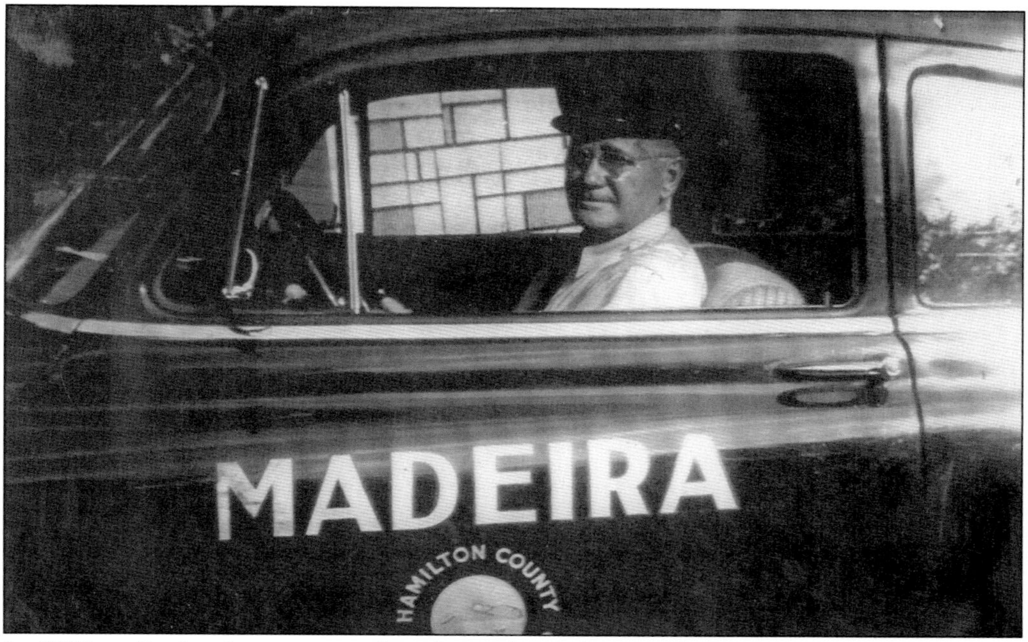

Lt. William Fey heads out to patrol in this undated photograph. Fey was nicknamed "Tag 'em Willie" for being quite conscientious writing traffic citations. (Courtesy Madeira Patrolmen's Benevolent Association.)

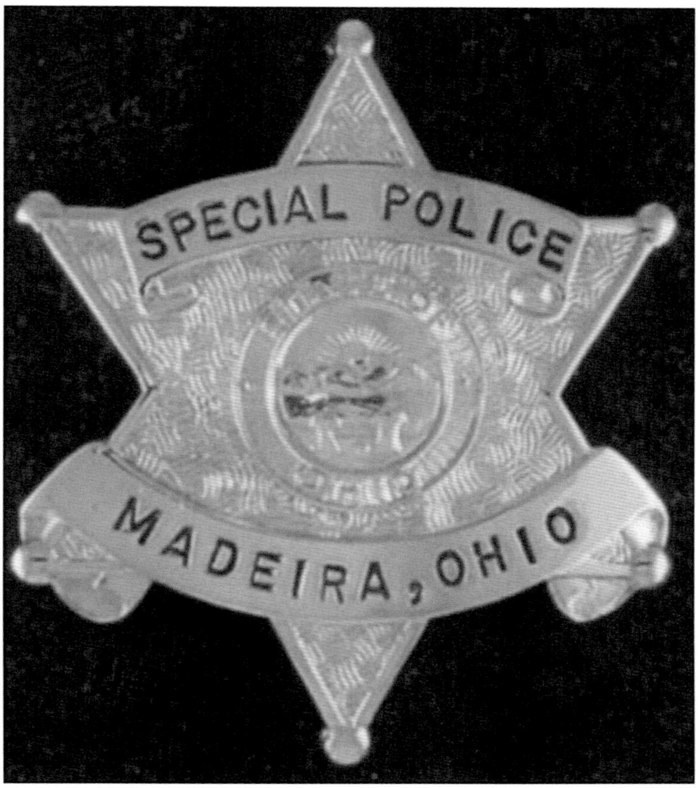

This special police badge was worn by a part-time officer who worked Sundays in the 1950s. (Courtesy Madeira Patrolmen's Benevolent Society.)

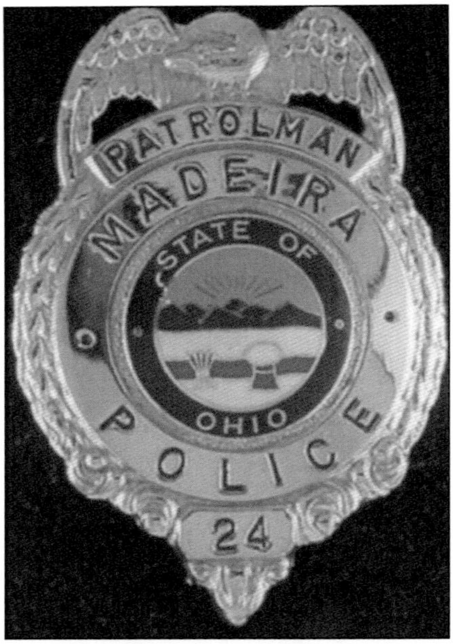

This badge was worn by full-time, regular patrolmen of the Madeira Police Department. The badge features the officer's number and the seal of the state of Ohio. (Courtesy Madeira Patrolmen's Benevolent Association.)

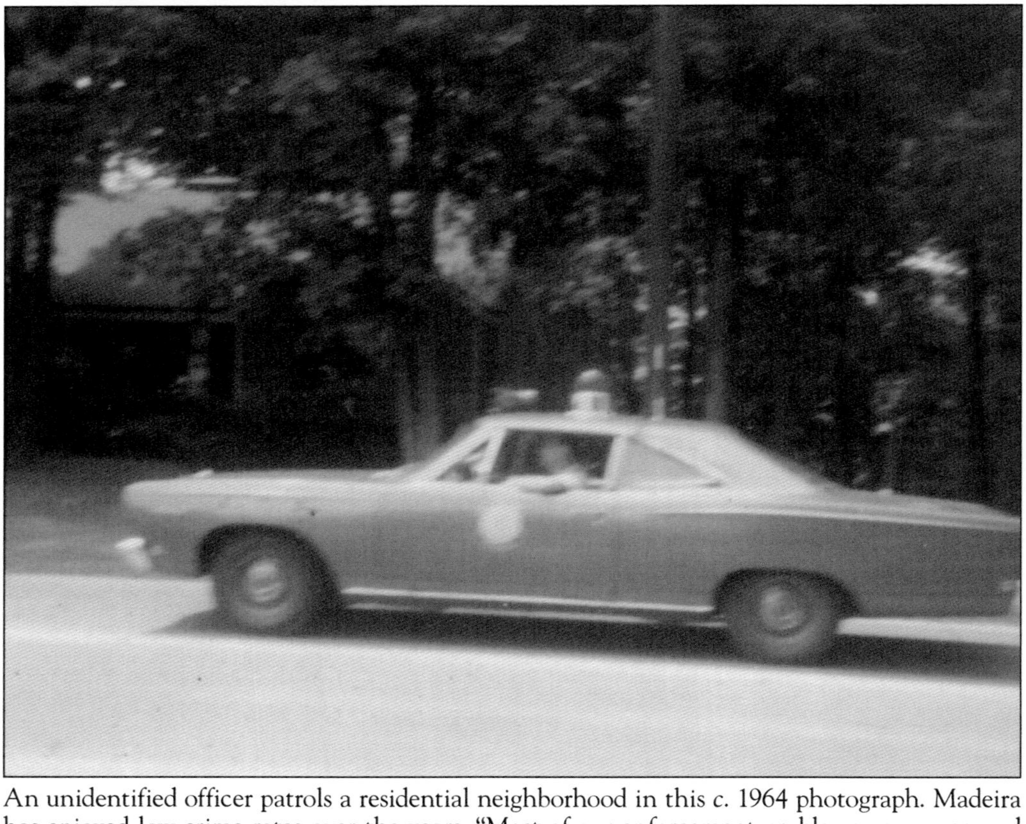

An unidentified officer patrols a residential neighborhood in this *c.* 1964 photograph. Madeira has enjoyed low crime rates over the years. "Most of our enforcement problems are concerned with traffic and larceny," Chief Thomas Gerth told a writer for the *Cincinnati Telephone Bulletin* in 1964. (Courtesy Madeira Patrolmen's Benevolent Association.)

Fred Doer became Madeira's second police chief in 1947 and served in that office until 1962, seeing the department and the community through many changes. When he became chief, he had one deputy, built his own radio for receiving calls, and used his own transportation. By 1954, the department had four full-time officers and two vehicles and calls were dispatched through the new Hamilton County Communications Center. (Courtesy Madeira Patrolmen's Benevolent Association.)

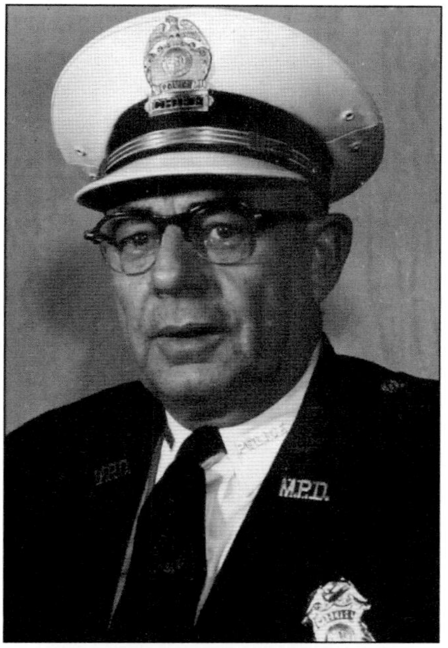

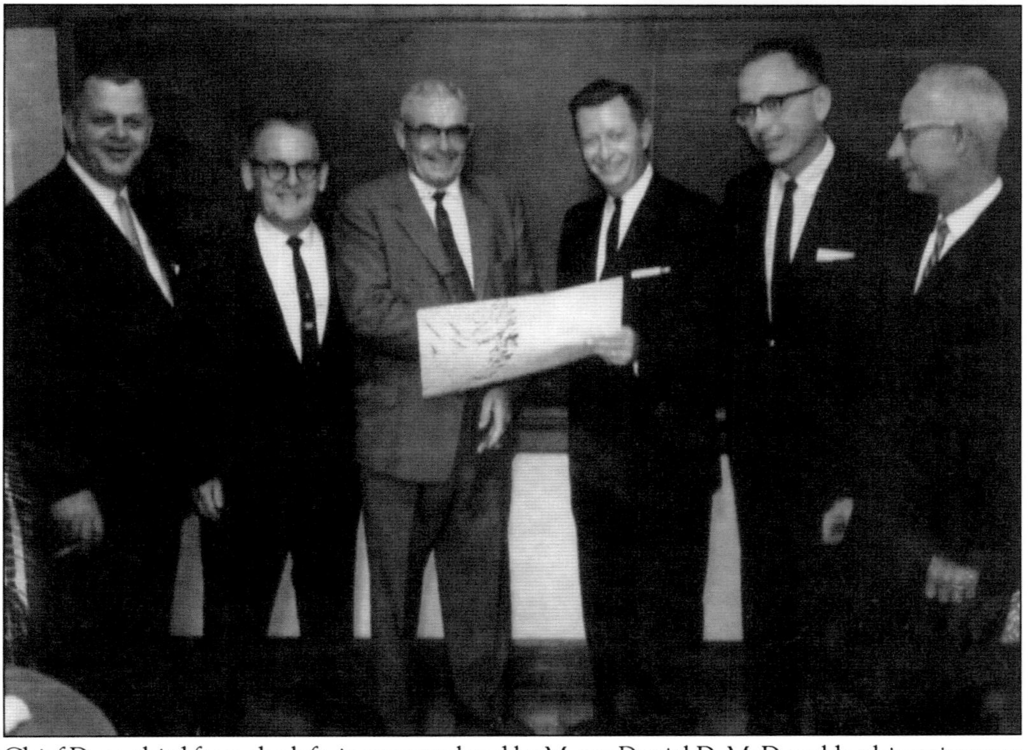

Chief Doer, third from the left, is congratulated by Mayor Daniel D. McDonald at his retirement in 1962; former mayor Russell Patten (1958–1959) is at the far right. From the 1950s through the early 1960s, Doer worked to equip and train police personnel in photography, fingerprinting, and basic first aid, according to the Madeira Police Department web site. He also saw Madeira through the transition from village to city in 1959. (Courtesy Daniel D. McDonald.)

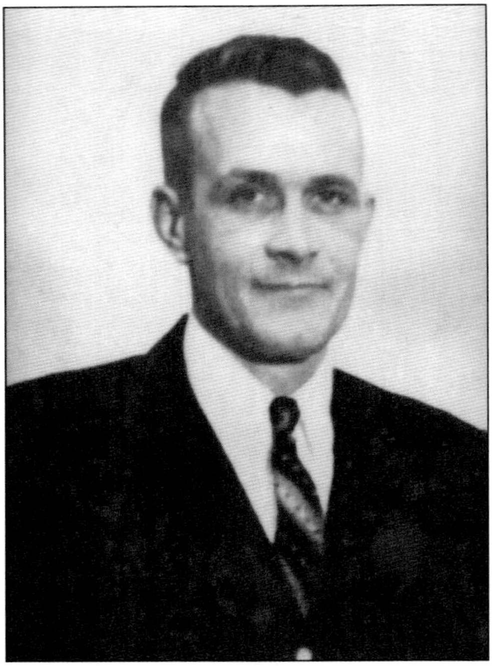

Thomas Gerth served as police chief from 1962 to 1967. He helped establish a teletype network that allowed all police departments in Hamilton County to receive vital information simultaneously, according to a *Cincinnati Telephone Bulletin* article. The network was an important technological advancement of the time. Gerth served with the Amberly Village Police Department before coming to Madeira. (Courtesy Madeira Patrolmen's Benevolent Association.)

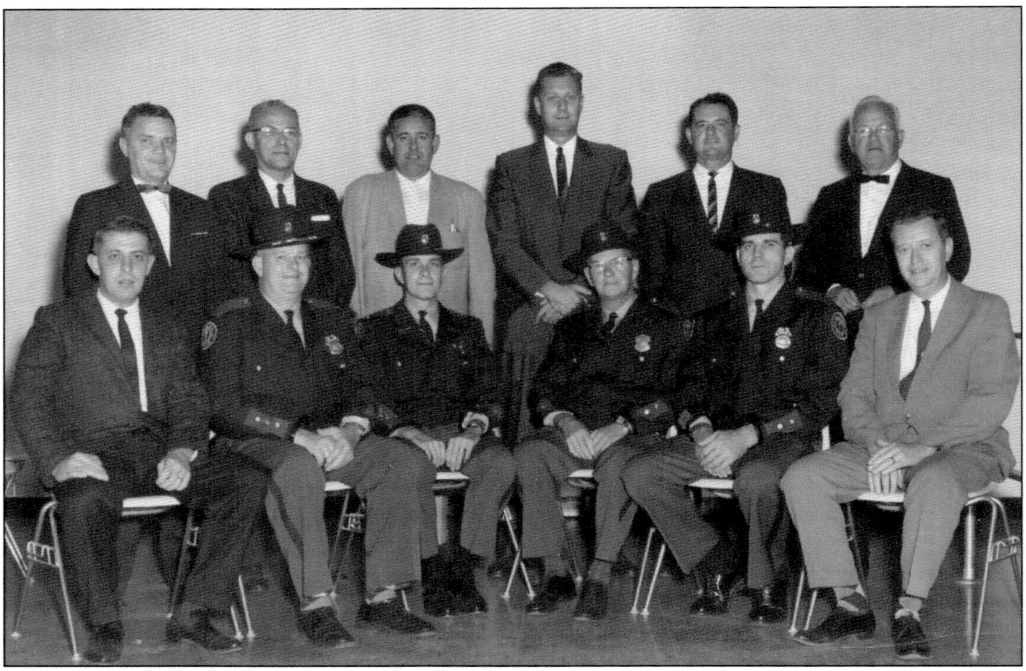

In 1963, Madeira was recognized by the American Automobile Association for 17 years without a pedestrian traffic fatality. Shown in this 1964 photograph are, from left to right, (first row) city manager John Griffin, officer Russell Ward, officer John Geary, Capt. Norwood Bowman, Chief Donald Wallace, and Mayor Daniel D. McDonald; (second row) councilmen Allen Reed, Lewis Krebrink, Harold Coldwell, Carl Thornton, Thomas O'Molley, and James Lowrey. (Courtesy Madeira Patrolmen's Benevolent Association.)

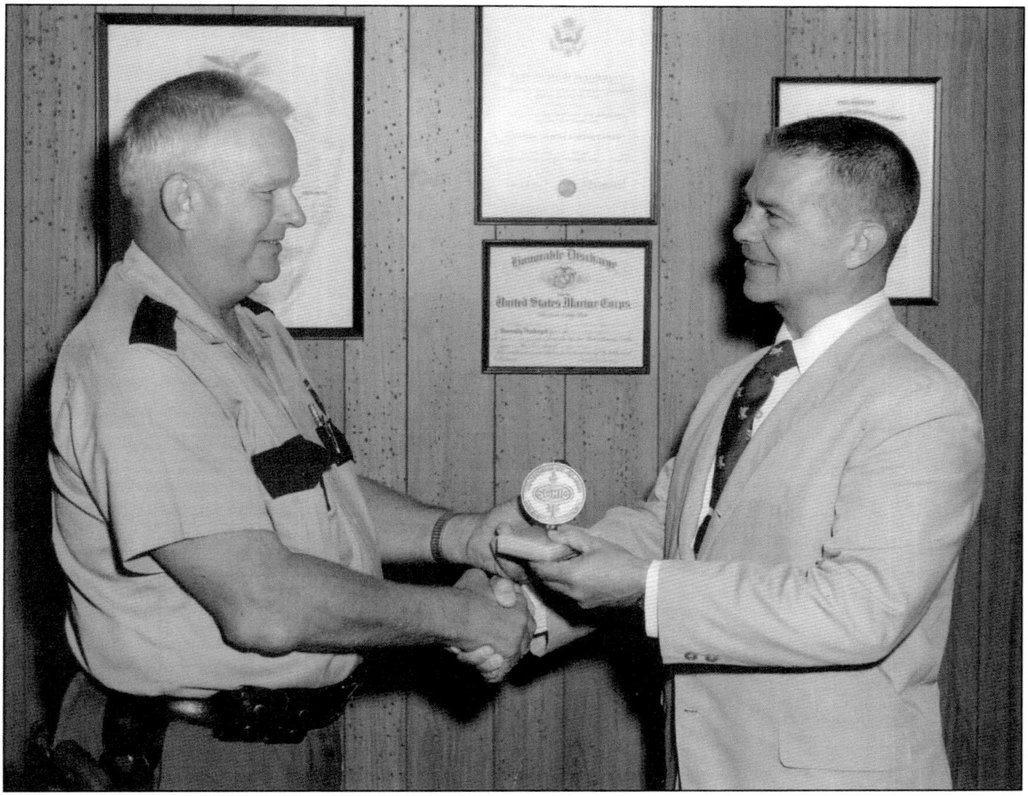

City manager George Babe presents officer Russell Ward with an award from the Standard Oil Company in 1968. Ward foiled a burglary of the Madeira Sohio gas station and arrested three suspects on June 11, 1968. (Courtesy Madeira Patrolmen's Benevolent Association.)

The police department and the city had experienced much change by September 1983, when officer Russell Ward was photographed at the corner of Miami and Laurel Avenues. Madeira's population in 1980 peaked at 9,341, and by the mid-1980s the department had 11 officers. The building to the left with the shoe-repair sign behind Ward doubled as the first police station and a post office. (Courtesy Madeira Patrolmen's Benevolent Association.)

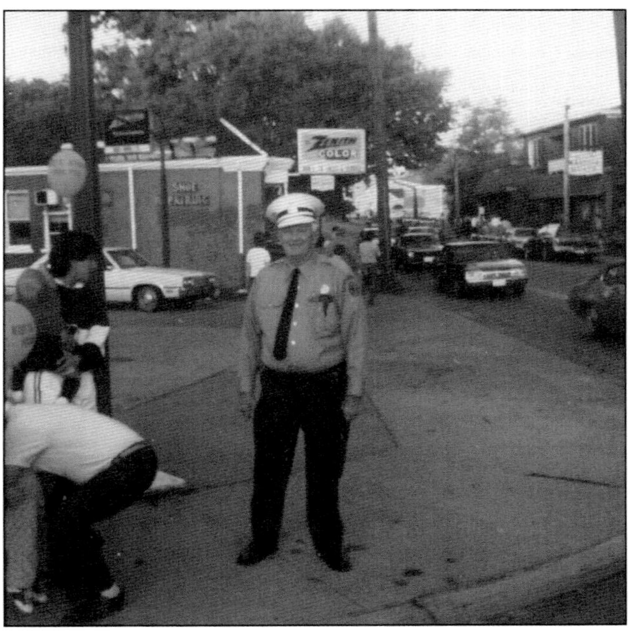

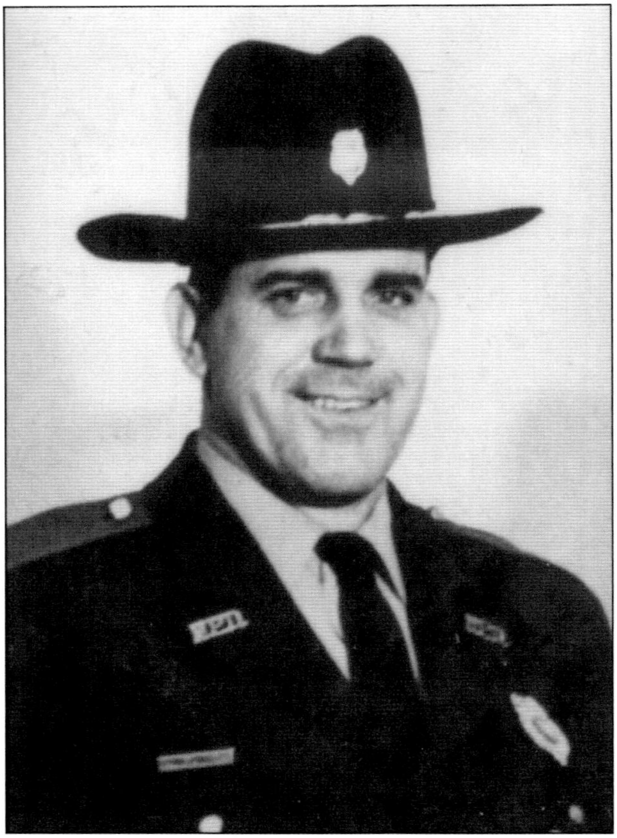

Donald Wallace became chief of police in 1967. During his tenure, the department nearly doubled in size to 10 full-time officers. The growth was greatly influenced by the annexation of the South Kenwood portion of Columbia Township in 1970. Wallace died in office in 1971 of Hodgkin's disease. (Courtesy Madeira Patrolmen's Benevolent Association.)

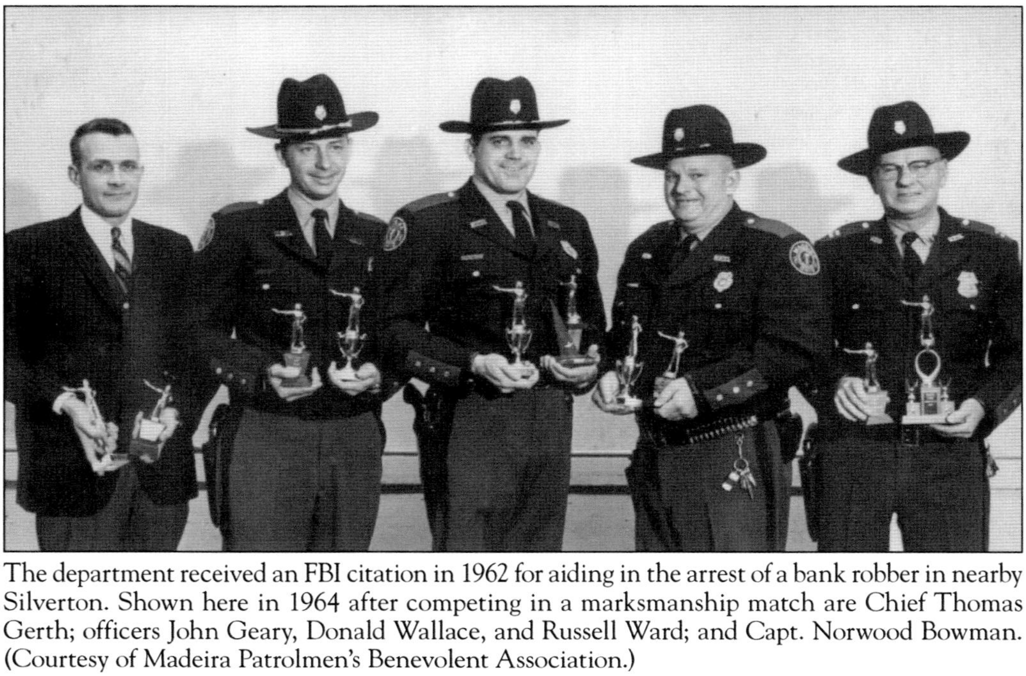

The department received an FBI citation in 1962 for aiding in the arrest of a bank robber in nearby Silverton. Shown here in 1964 after competing in a marksmanship match are Chief Thomas Gerth; officers John Geary, Donald Wallace, and Russell Ward; and Capt. Norwood Bowman. (Courtesy of Madeira Patrolmen's Benevolent Association.)

Six

PUTTING OUT FIRES

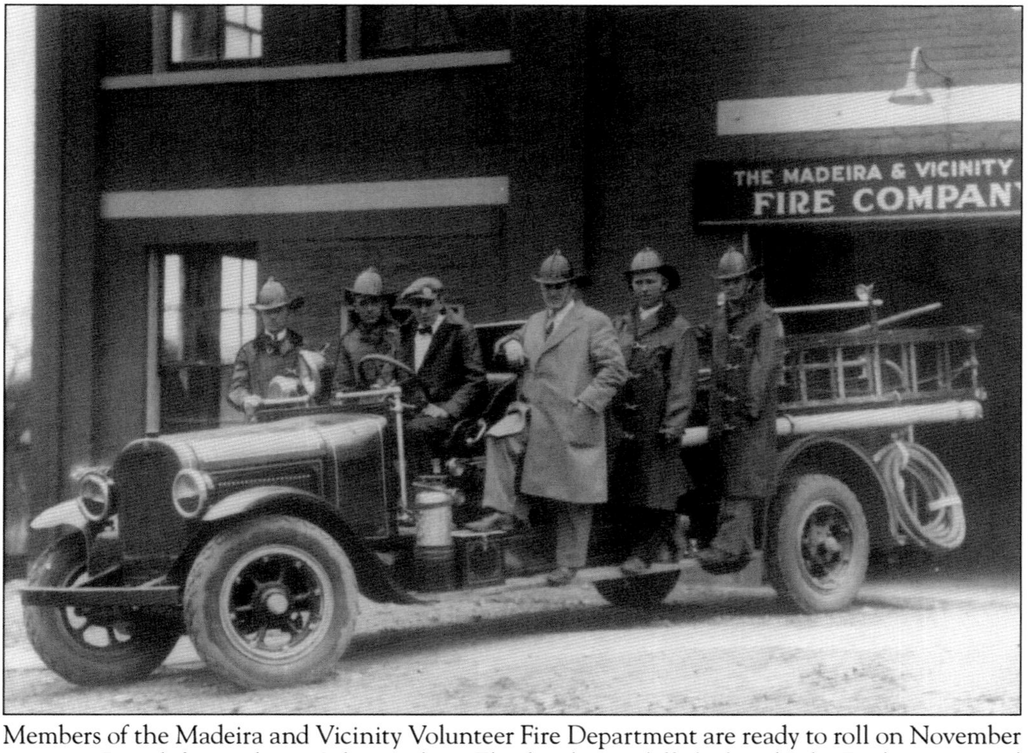

Members of the Madeira and Vicinity Volunteer Fire Department are ready to roll on November 18, 1929. From left to right are Julian Nelson, Floyd Nelson, Cliff Slagle, Charles Dodson, Howard Dodson, and Auldin Nelson. Efforts to form a volunteer department quickened in the early 1920s as the community outgrew bucket brigades. Volunteers trained with the Cincinnati Fire Department and held parties and minstrel shows to raise money for uniforms, according to a 1931 *Cincinnati Enquirer* article. Rudimentary volunteer fire service existed by 1924. When Cincinnati began providing city water service to Madeira in 1925, efforts were renewed to create a larger, more trained volunteer department. (Courtesy Madeira and Indian Hill Fire Company.)

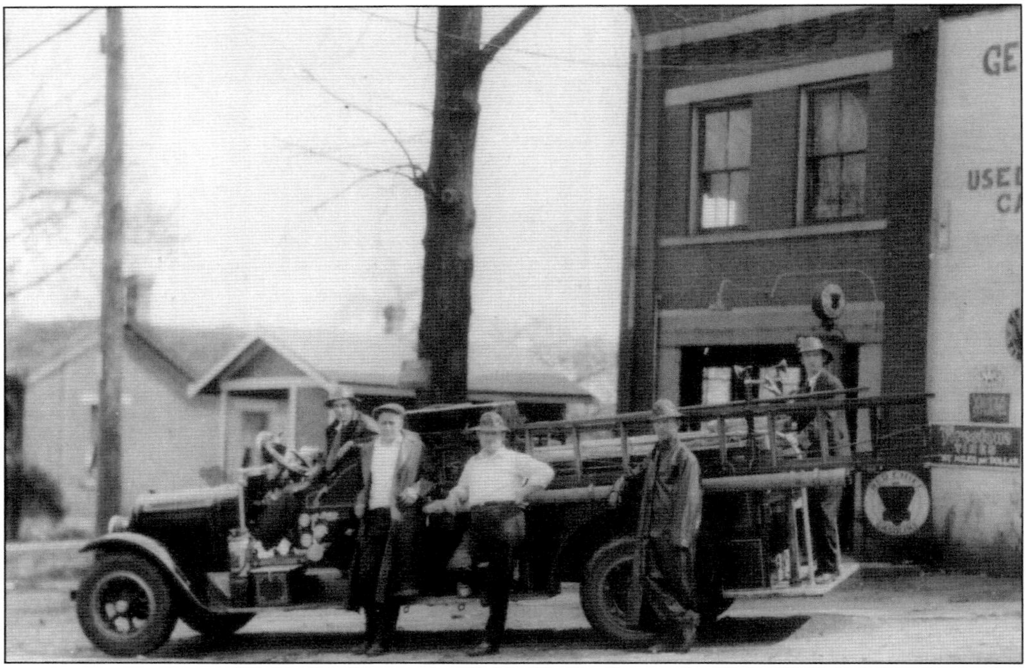

The Madeira and Vicinity Volunteer Fire Department's 1927 Graham Dodge pumper promised more efficient service for Madeira area residents. Nelson Maham, an early organizer of the department, became the first fire chief in 1927, according to current firefighter Larry A. Van Pelt. From left to right are Cliff Slagle, Warren W. Finch, Charles Dodson, Howard Dodson, and John Addison. (Courtesy Madeira and Indian Hill Fire Company.)

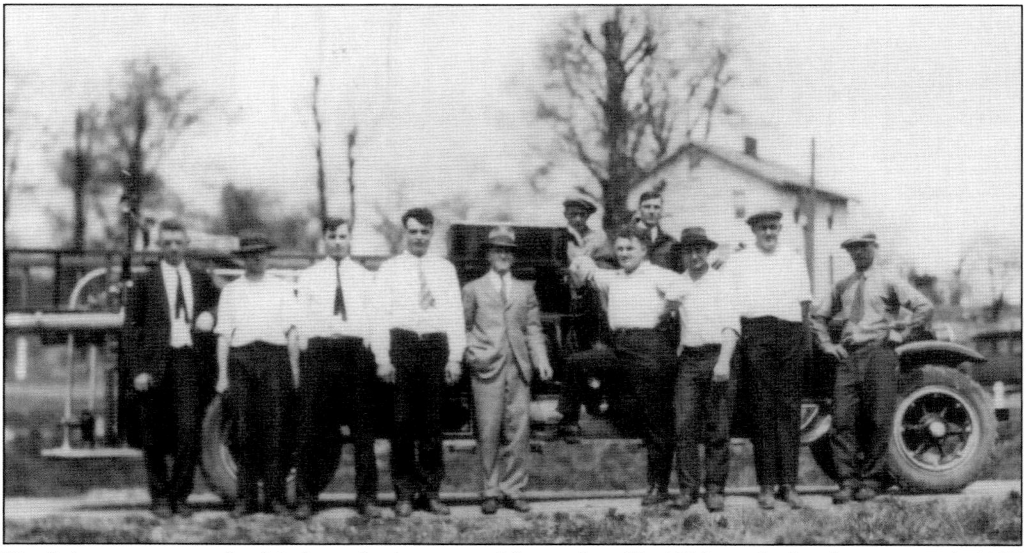

Firefighters pose at the Madeira firehouse on November 18, 1929, with the department's 1927 Graham Dodge pumper. The pumper cost $4,970 and was capable of pumping 300 gallons of water per minute. From left to right are (first row) John Addison, Julian Nelson, Sylvan Helfrich, Leroy Buck, William Goodall, Charles Dodson, Auldin Nelson, Warren W. Finch, and Howard Dodson; (second row) Floyd Nelson and Cliff Slagle. (Courtesy Madeira and Indian Hill Fire Company.)

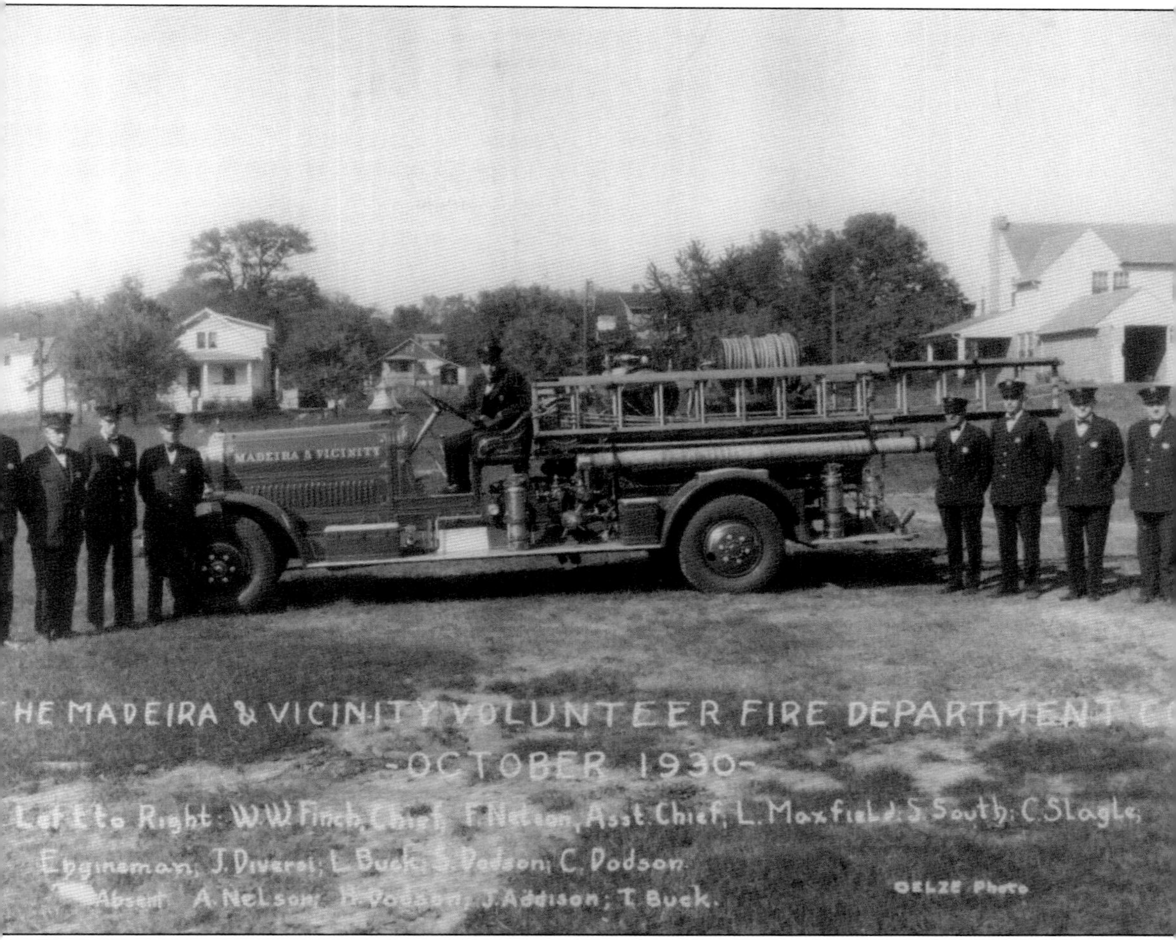

Firefighters show off a new Ahrens Fox 750 GPM pumper in October 1930. To lessen demands on the small department's budget, the department became a non-profit organization in 1931, exempting it from paying property taxes. The photograph is taken near Miami Avenue and Dawson Road, looking west to Maple Avenue. From left to right are Warren W. Finch, Floyd Nelson, assistant chief L. Maxfield, S. South, Cliff Slagle (engineman), Jack Diversi, L. Buck, S. Dodson, and Charles Dodson. While working his regular job with Crew Construction Company in 1933, Finch was killed in an accident, resulting in Floyd Nelson being named fire chief. The department's only on-duty fatality occurred on February 7, 1944, wrote Larry A. Van Pelt in a department history. Firefighters were responding to a residential fire on Camargo Road when fireman Elmer C. Schroer was accidentally electrocuted. (Courtesy Madeira and Indian Hill Fire Company.)

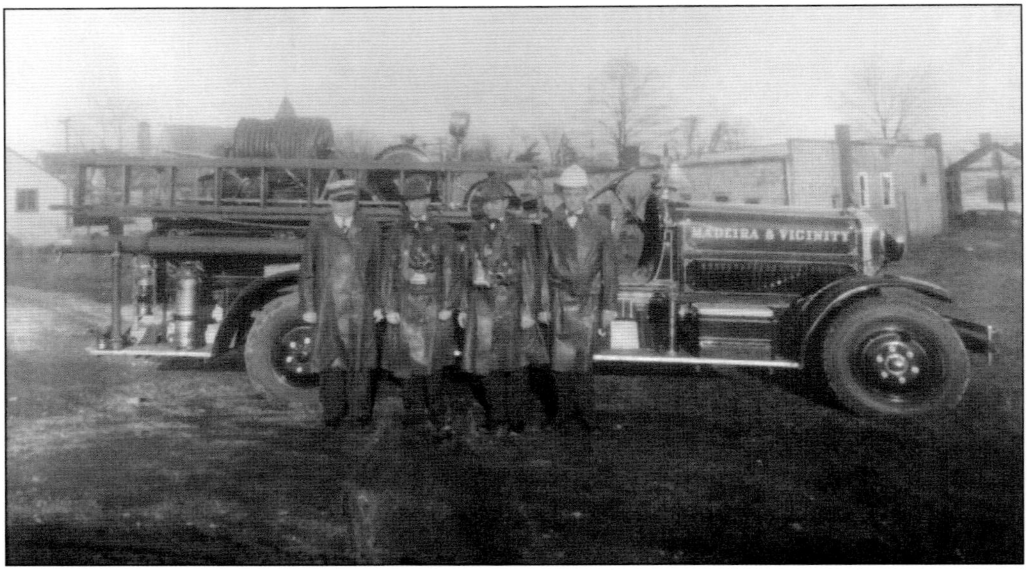

From left to right are Chief Warren W. Finch, Julian Nelson, Jack Diversi, and assistant chief Floyd Nelson as they line up in front of the 1930 Ahrens Fox pumper. The photograph was taken near Dawson Road and Maple Avenue looking northeast toward Miami and Laurel Avenues. (Courtesy Madeira and Indian Hill Fire Company.)

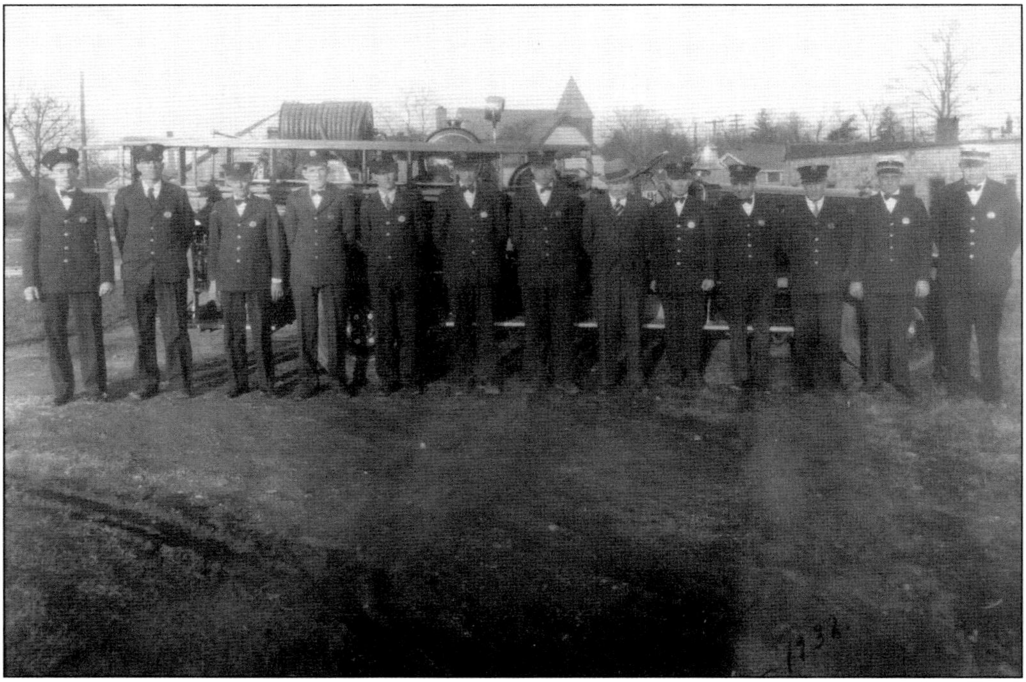

Officials pose at the Madeira and Indian Hill Fire Station on Shawnee Run Road. A two-bay fire station was built there in 1940 to keep pace with Indian Hill's growing population, wrote Larry A. Van Pelt in a department history. Chief Floyd Nelson moved into a house adjoining the station, and assistant chief Jack Diversi occupied the residence at the Madeira station. (Courtesy Madeira Historical Society.)

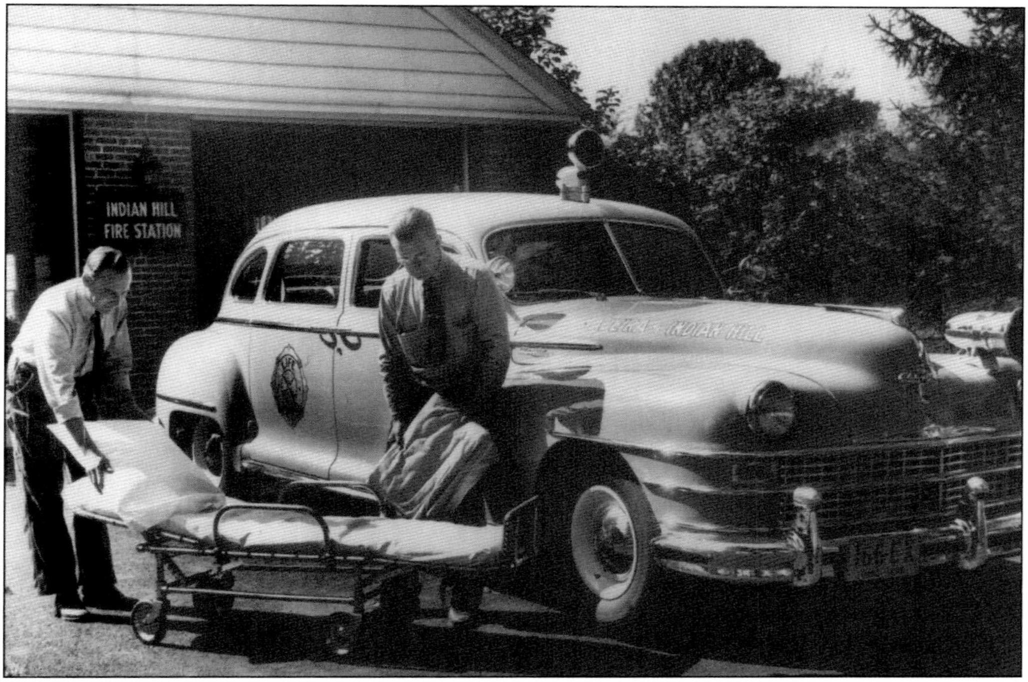

Men at the Indian Hill station look over the gurney for the department's new 1948 Chrysler ambulance. Ambulance service began that year thanks to $3,500 in contributions from the community, according to Larry A. Van Pelt. (Courtesy Madeira and Indian Hill Fire Company.)

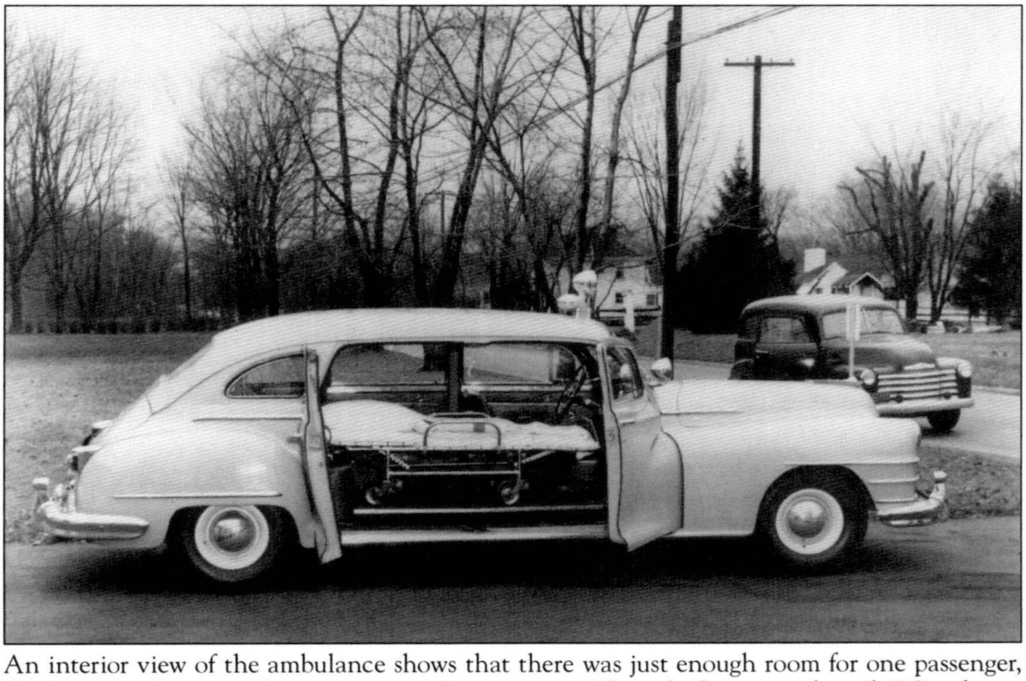

An interior view of the ambulance shows that there was just enough room for one passenger, the driver, and an attendant to monitor the passenger. The vehicle was used until 1951, when a traditional ambulance was purchased. (Courtesy Madeira and Indian Hill Fire Company.)

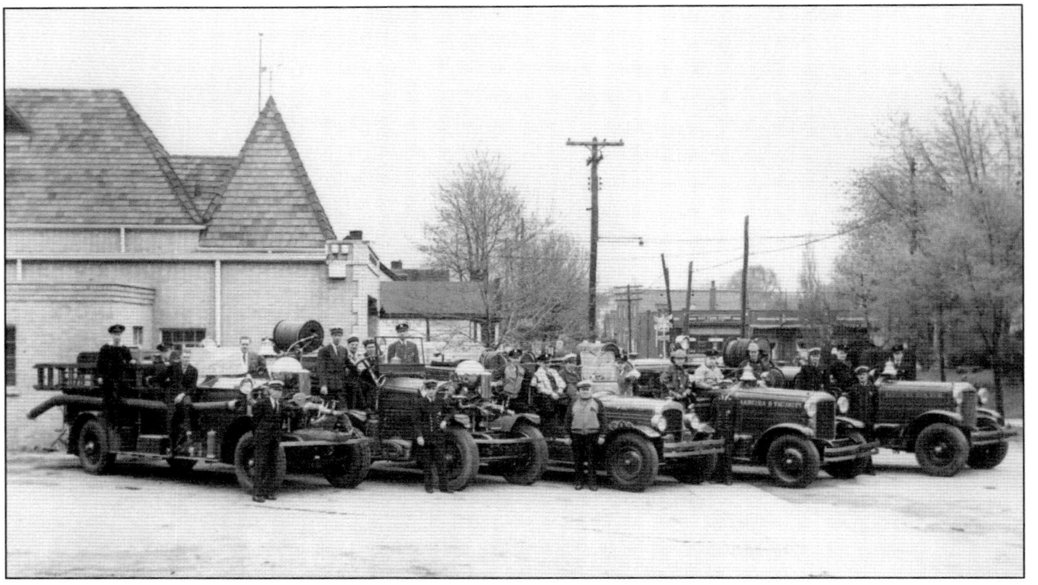

A Madeira pumper joins the lineup of the Five Points Mutual Aid Association in 1947 in Deer Park. Madeira, Montgomery, Rossmoyne, Silverton, and Deer Park assisted each other in emergencies when additional firefighters and equipment were needed. Standing with Madeira's fire truck are, from left to right, Sylvan "Hap" Helfrich, Junior Hambly, Floyd Nelson, and Waldron Julian. (Courtesy Madeira and Indian Hill Fire Company.)

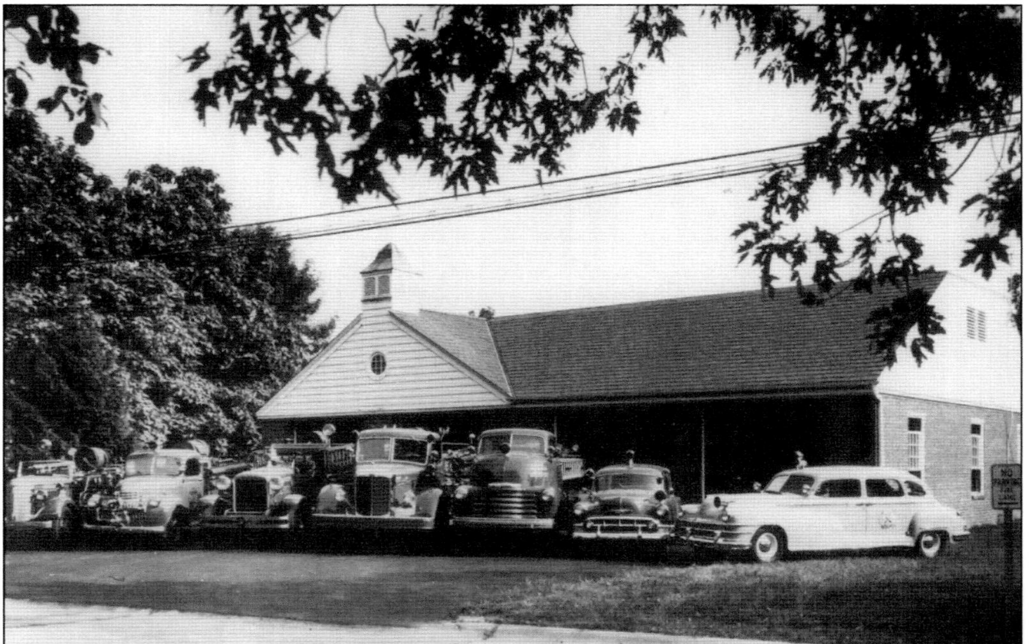

A full squad of fire trucks and emergency vehicles are shown at the Shawnee Road station around 1951. The department was officially renamed the Madeira and Indian Hill Fire Company in 1944 as its primary focus had become those two growing communities. (Courtesy Madeira Historical Society.)

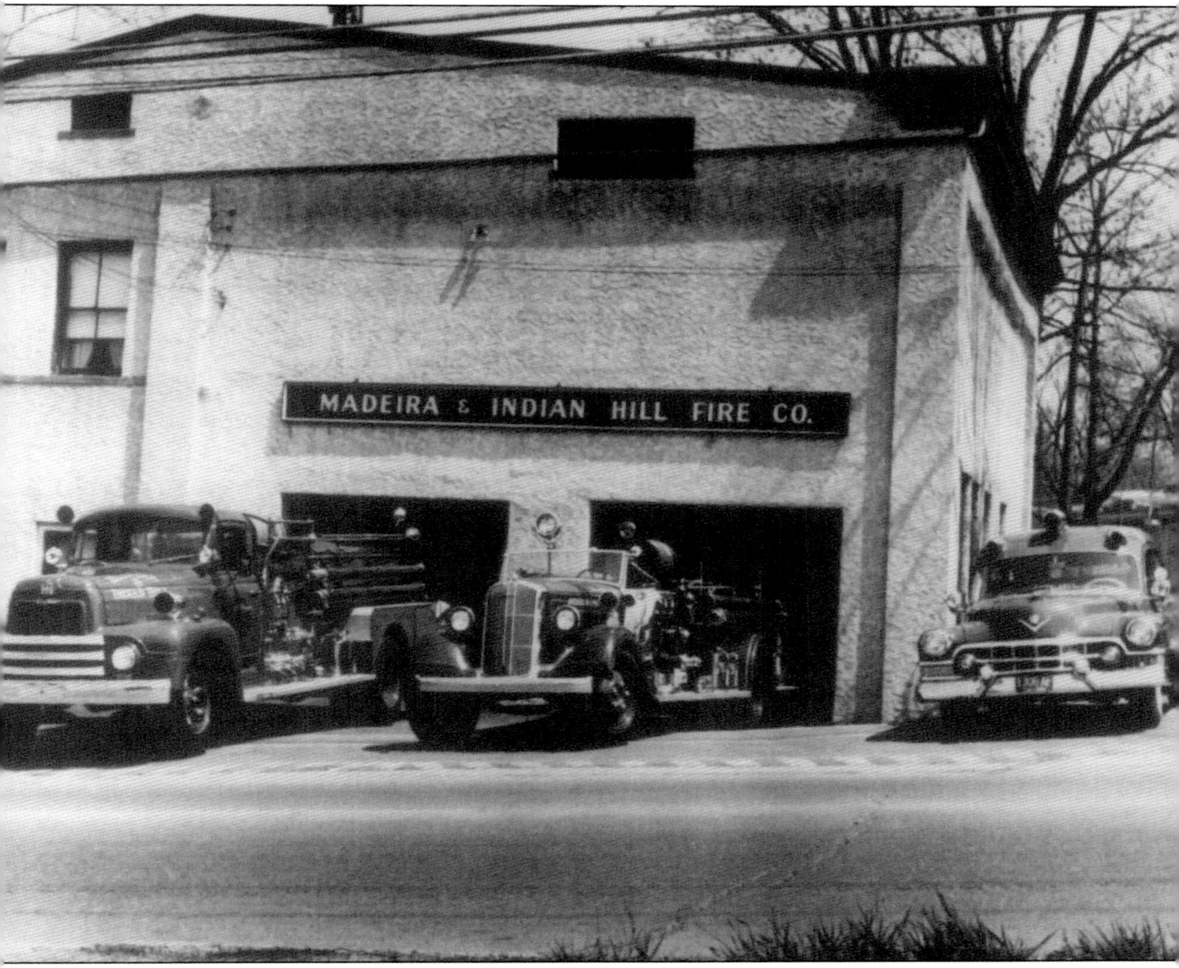

The Madeira fire station, shown in this photograph from around 1950, operated out of the former traction car substation on Miami Avenue for many years. (Courtesy Madeira and Indian Hill Fire Company.)

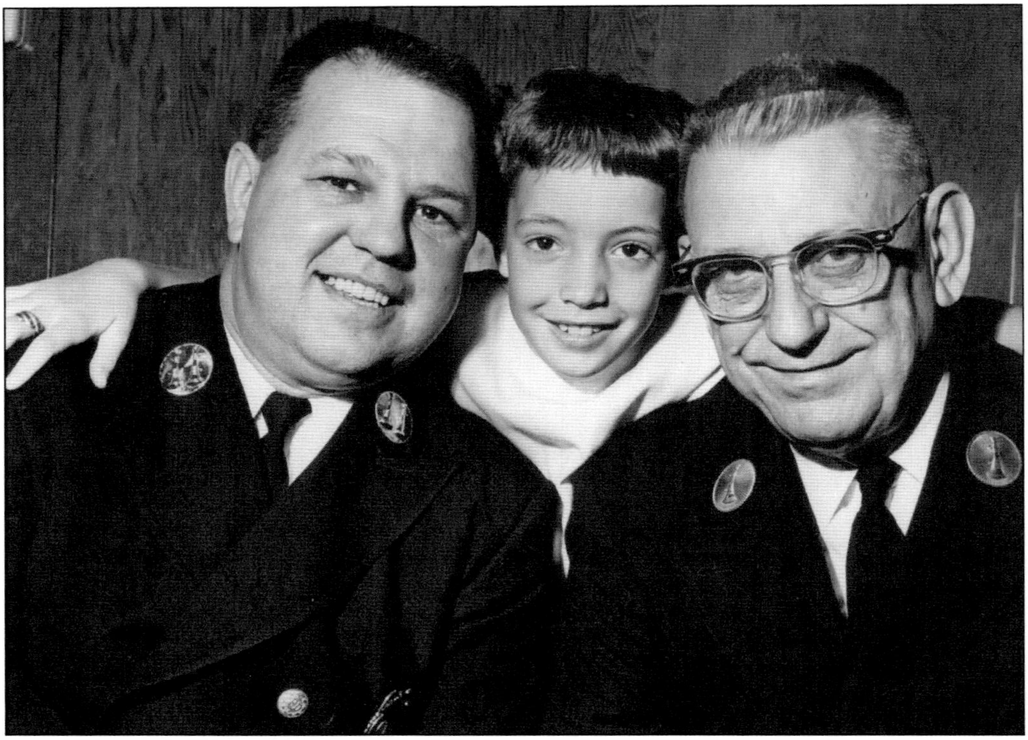

Janice Feller celebrated a special birthday on January 27, 1968, with her family and Lt. Sylvan Helfrich (left) and Capt. Ed Lewis. Mrs. A. C. Feller Jr. of Iuka Avenue had been in the department's ambulance en route to Christ Hospital's maternity department 10 years earlier when the ambulance collided with a panel truck at the intersection of William Howard Taft and Reading Roads. "The shock of the crash sped up the stork, and within a minute I had a little girl on my hands," recalled Helfrich. Mother and daughter both did well despite Janice's chaotic birth and soon returned home to Madeira with their family. The department held a special place in their memories after that. (Both courtesy Madeira and Indian Hill Fire Company.)

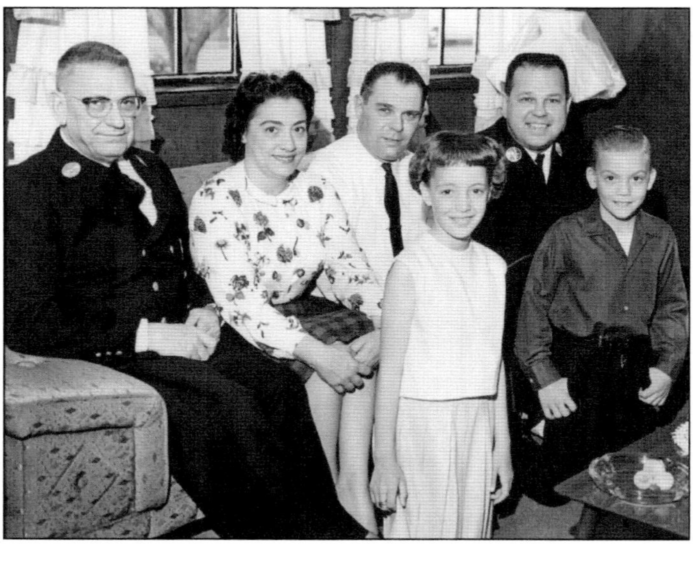

Chief Clifford Behrmann inspects equipment in this *c.* 1965 photograph. A longtime firefighter, he was named chief in 1960 and served until 1977. (Courtesy Madeira and Indian Hill Fire Company.)

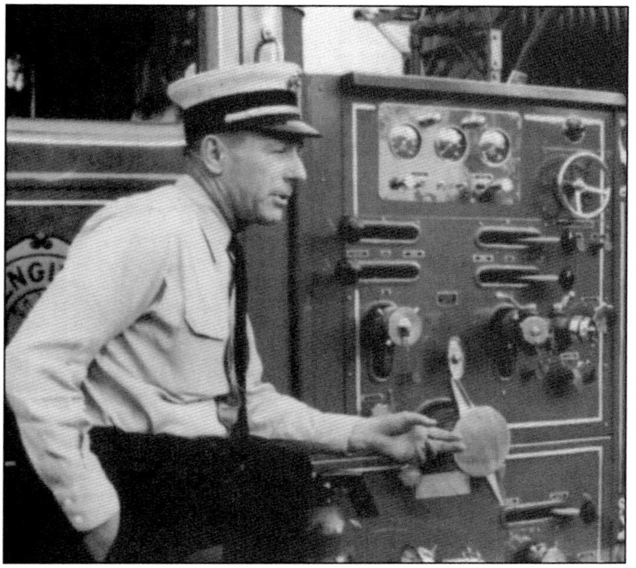

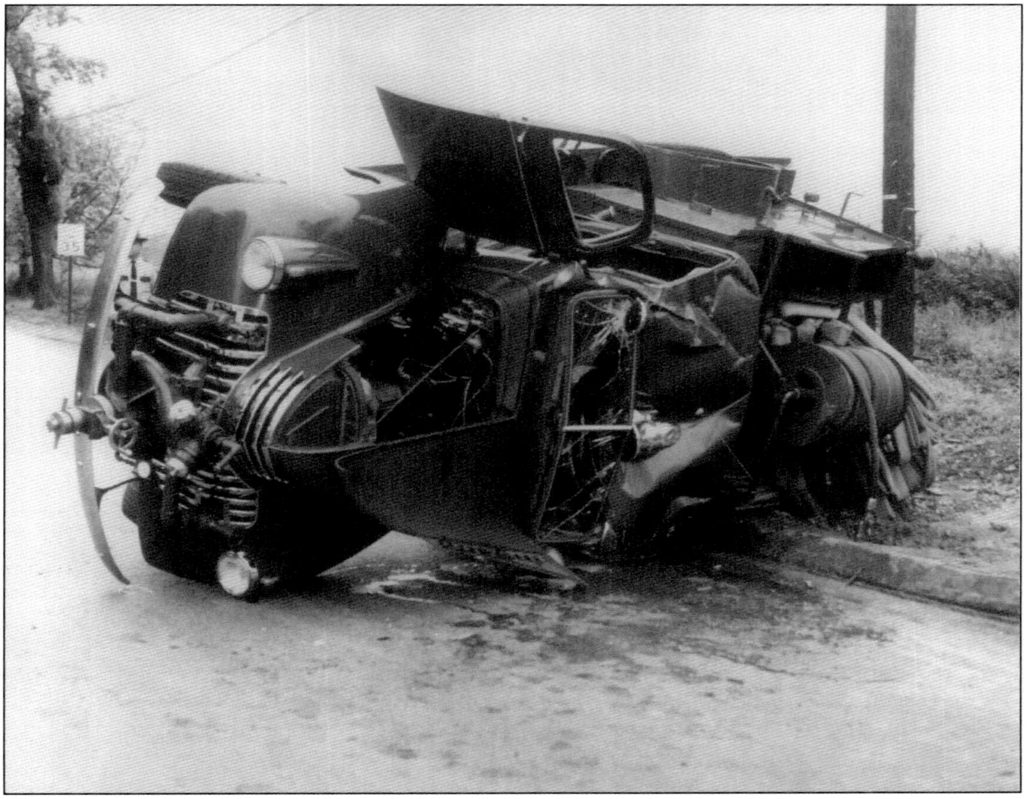

A twisted frame was all that remained of this fire department vehicle after a collision at Galbraith Road and Miami Avenue in 1957. Miraculously no one was killed in the accident. The vehicle was a 1941 dump truck that had been donated by a volunteer and converted to a fire truck during World War II when equipment was in short supply. (Courtesy Madeira and Indian Hill Fire Company.)

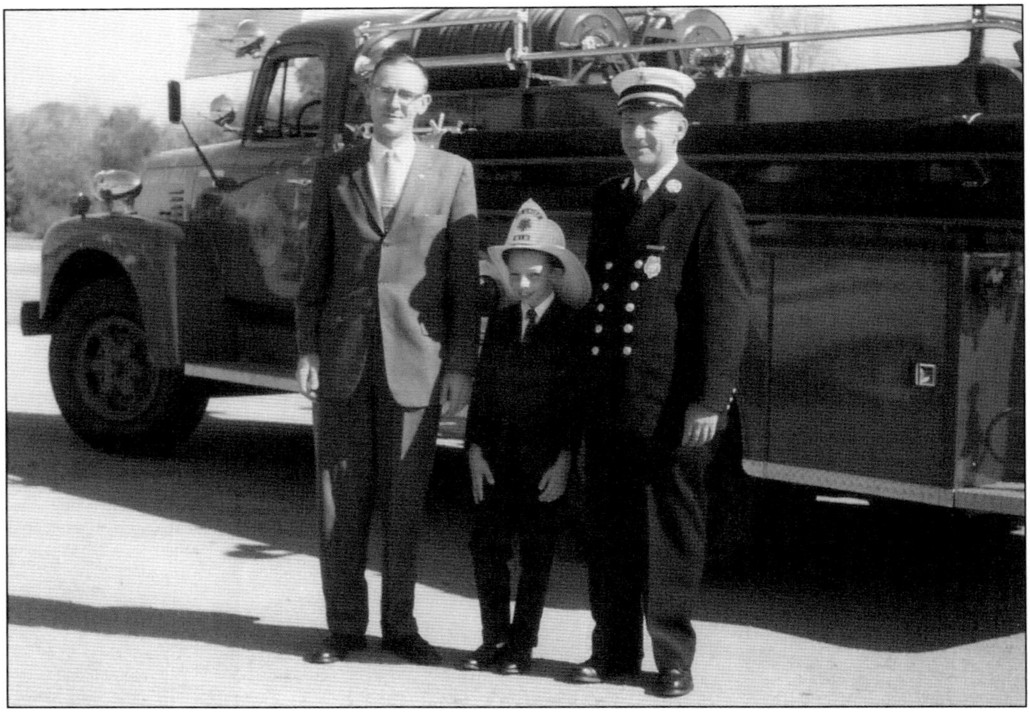

Chief Clifford Behrmann (left) and Miami Hills Elementary Principal John F. Dumont congratulate student David Shivers, winner of a junior fire chief competition in 1963. Shivers won by writing a short essay on why he wanted to be junior fire chief. He received a firefighter's helmet, model searchlight truck, presentation by city council, and lunch with firefighters. Vickie Ellis was runner-up. (Courtesy Madeira Historical Society.)

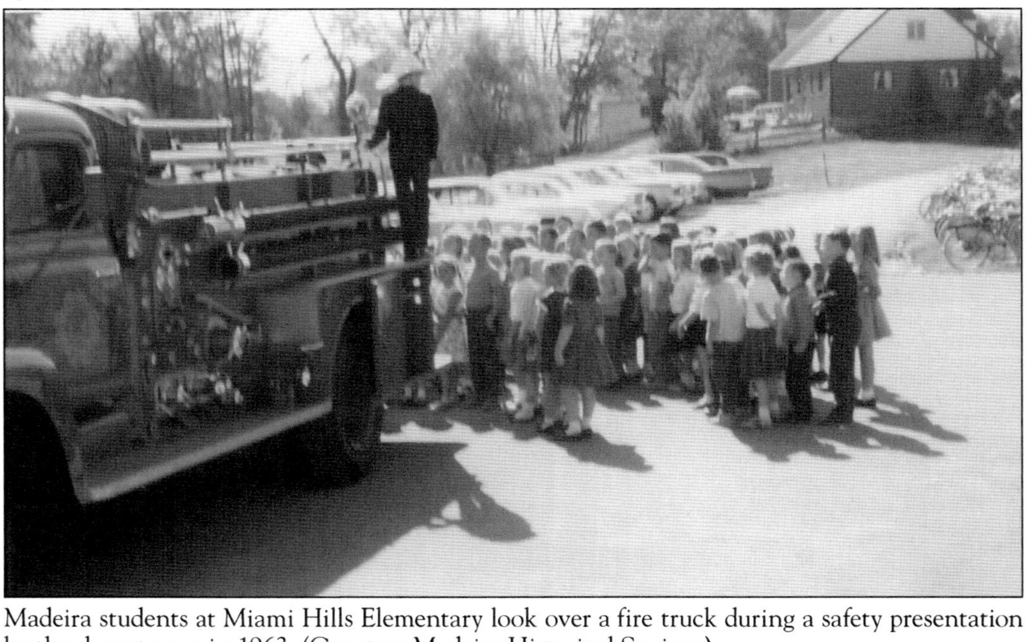

Madeira students at Miami Hills Elementary look over a fire truck during a safety presentation by the department in 1963. (Courtesy Madeira Historical Society.)

Seven

War Years and Warriors

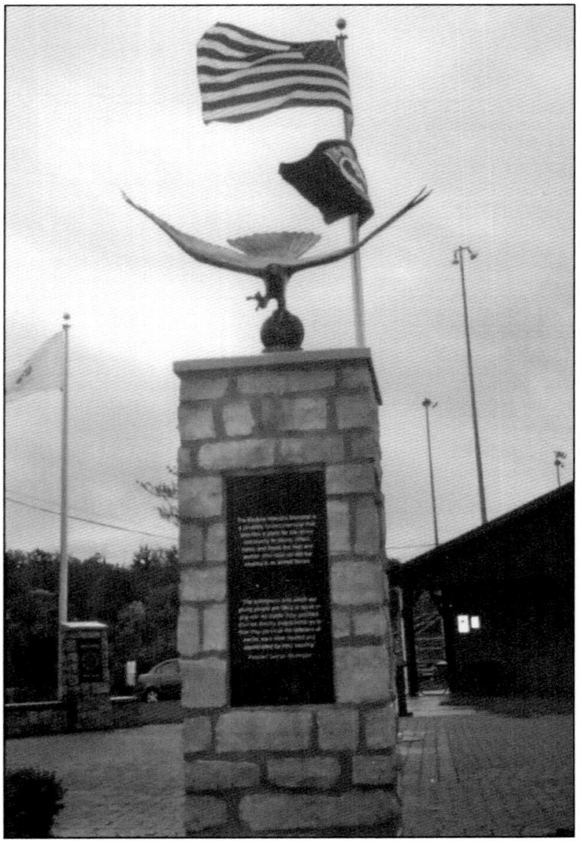

Revolutionary War veterans helped to found Madeira, and its citizens have served in all branches of the military since then. The monument at McDonald Commons honors service people who have sacrificed over the generations to preserve freedom. The following pages represent a cross-section of Madeira residents' wartime experiences, whether they were helping on the home front, fighting overseas, serving in support positions stateside, or being detained in relocation camps. (Photograph by Randy McNutt.)

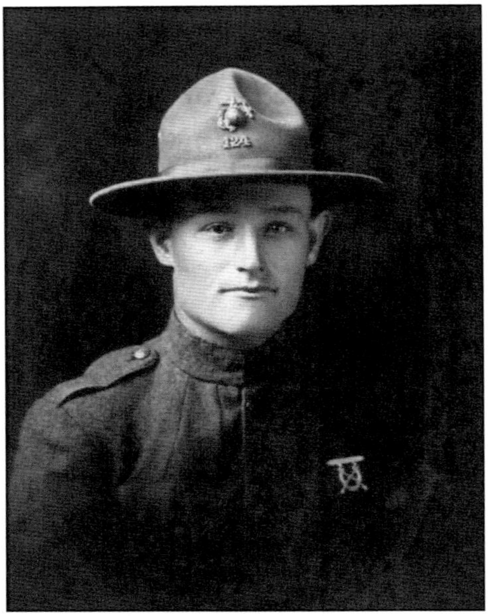

Allen E. Teal left his family's gas station in Clermont County to serve as a U.S. Marine private in Europe during World War I. In this photograph, he is wearing an expert rifleman badge. Back at home, Madeira men who were not in the service formed a home guard to protect the community. (Courtesy Holly Perin Richard.)

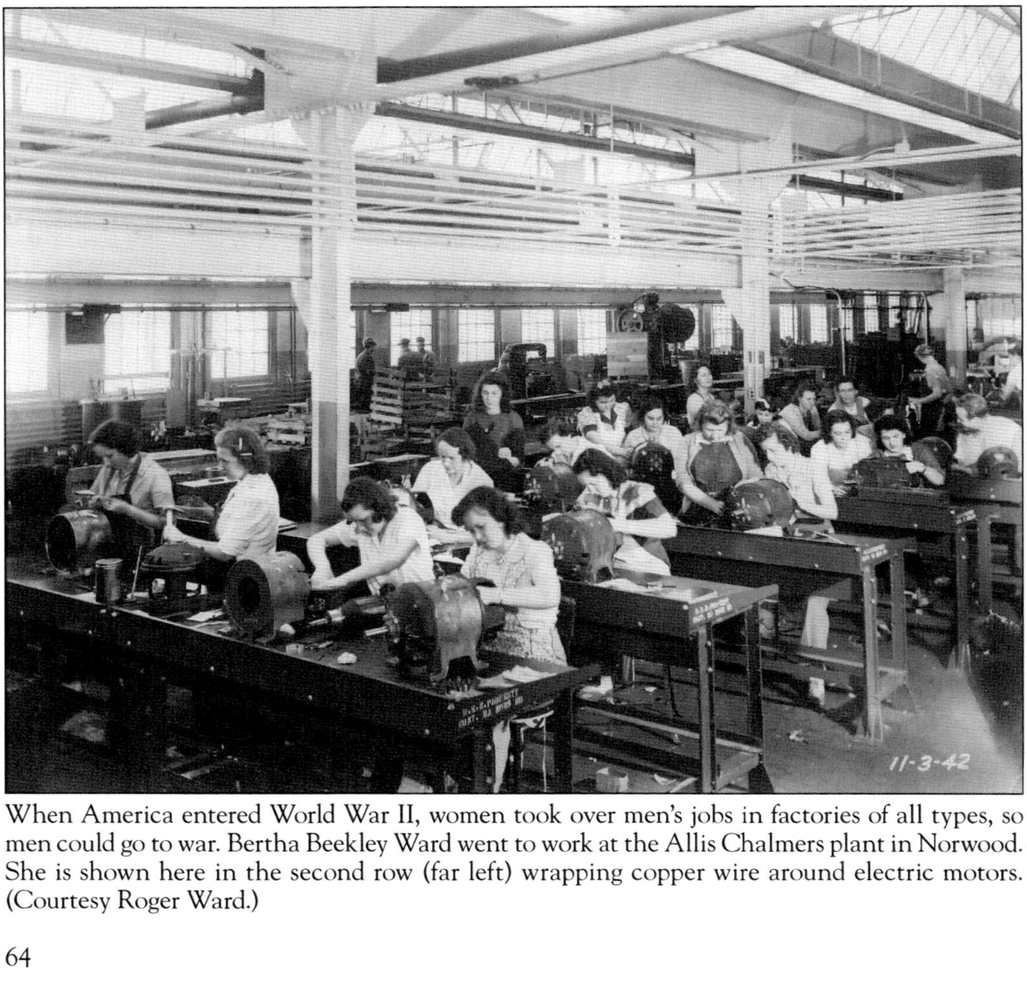

When America entered World War II, women took over men's jobs in factories of all types, so men could go to war. Bertha Beekley Ward went to work at the Allis Chalmers plant in Norwood. She is shown here in the second row (far left) wrapping copper wire around electric motors. (Courtesy Roger Ward.)

George A. Storch (at right and below left) was drafted by the U.S. Army in May 1943. As a private with Company F, 120th Regiment, 30th Infantry Division, he saw action in five major campaigns and was awarded two Purple Hearts and a Bronze Star. On July 25, 1944, he was wounded near Normandy, France, while under attack by a German Tiger tank. That December his company was north of Bastogne near the Ardennes where the German breakthrough that came to be called the Battle of the Bulge occurred. Storch was wounded by an artillery round on Christmas Day. He was discharged in October 1945 as private 1st class. In the 1920s, his maternal grandparents, Mr. and Mrs. August W. Blesh, lived on Miami Avenue at the intersection of Laurel Avenue where Fifth Third Bank is today. (Both courtesy George and Ted Storch.)

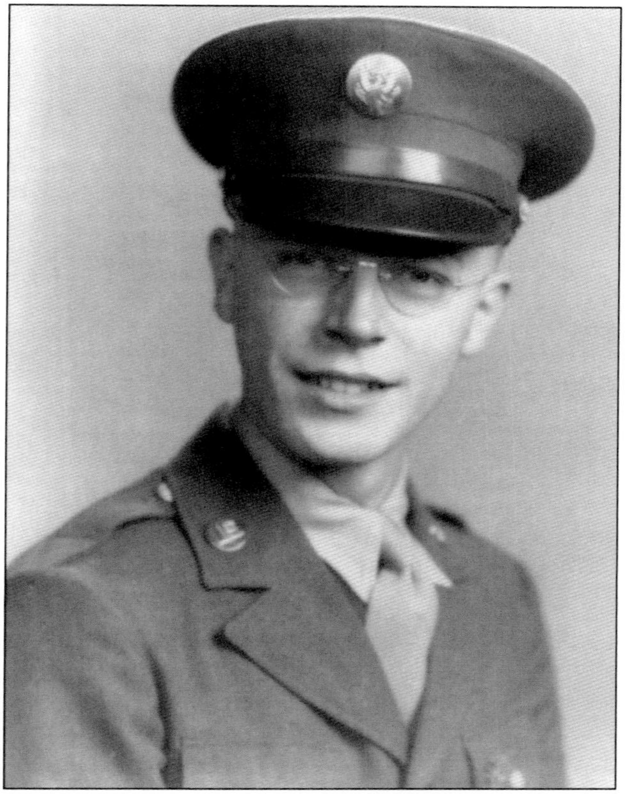

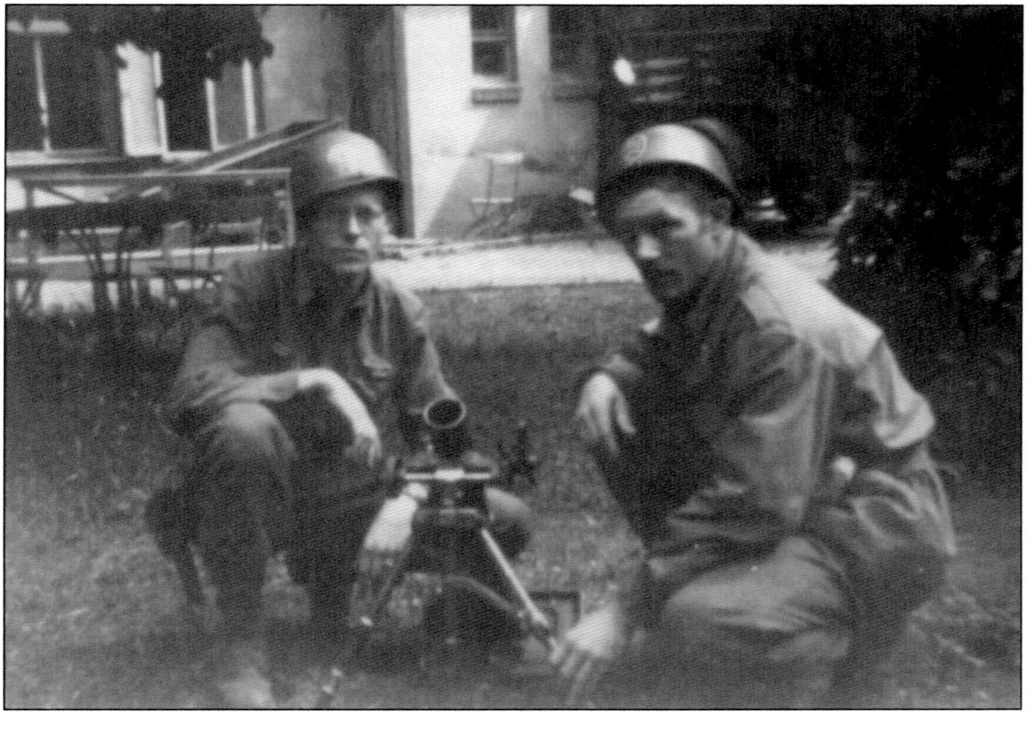

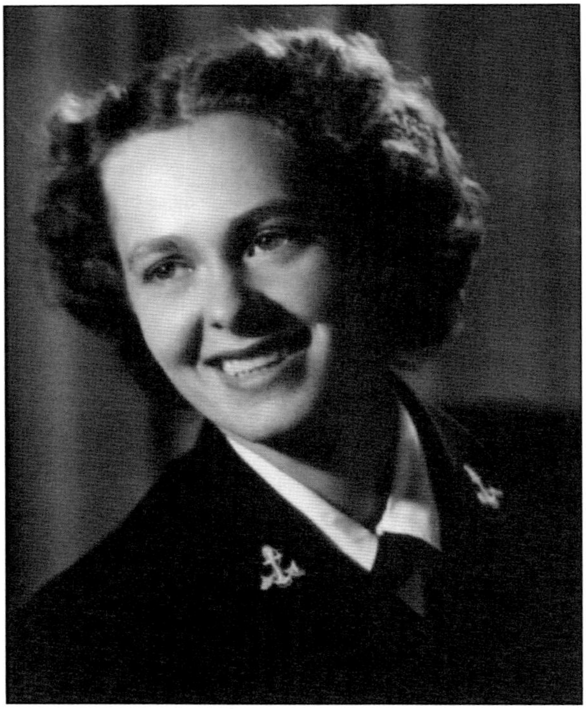

Helen L. Bartush Bachman was among the first generation of women in the military, serving with the WAVES (Women Accepted for Voluntary Emergency Service) as an Aviation Machinist Mate 2nd class in the U.S. Navy. As an aircraft mechanic, she worked on SNJ trainers and Stearman biplanes that navy cadets first learned to fly at the Naval Training Center at Ottumwa, Iowa. (Courtesy Helen Bachman.)

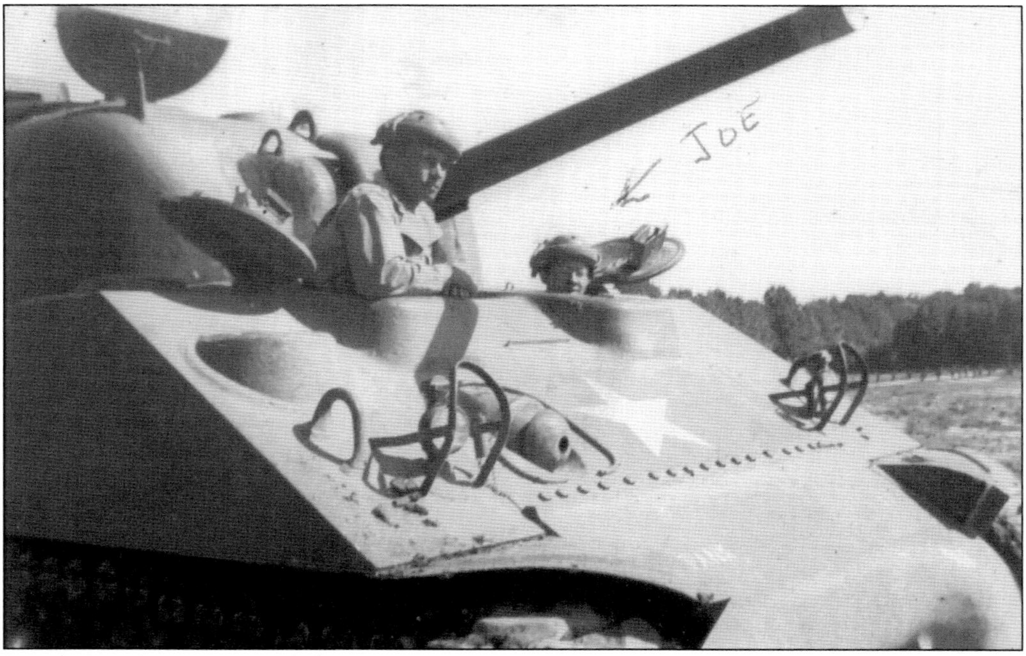

Joseph E. Schirmer entered the U.S. Army Air Force in 1943. A sergeant, he taught soldiers at the 40th Ordinance Company at the Aberdeen Proving Grounds in Maryland how to repair tracked and wheeled vehicles under fighting conditions. This is where he drove the Sherman tank shown here. Transferred to the 2118th Air Service Unit, 6th Air Force, Island of Baltra, Galapagos Islands, he performed the same duties. (Courtesy Joseph E. Schirmer.)

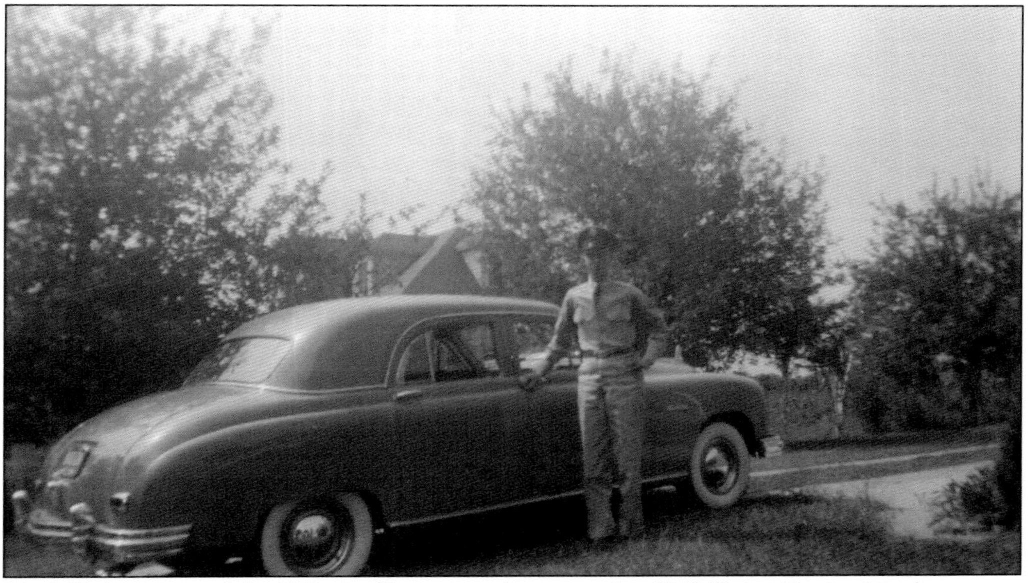

Clark F. Anstaett, of the U.S. Air Force, stands next to his 1949 Kaiser-Frazier Manhattan on the Fleishman estate in Indian Hill in 1951. After basic training at Lackland Air Force Base, San Antonio, Texas, he attended Radio Operator School in Biloxi, Mississippi. Anstaett was next sent to the 3525th Pilot Training Wing at Williams Air Force Base in Chandler, Arizona, where there were no openings for the job he was trained for. He became a personnel records clerk and was a staff sergeant when he was discharged in 1955. (Courtesy Clark F. Anstaett.)

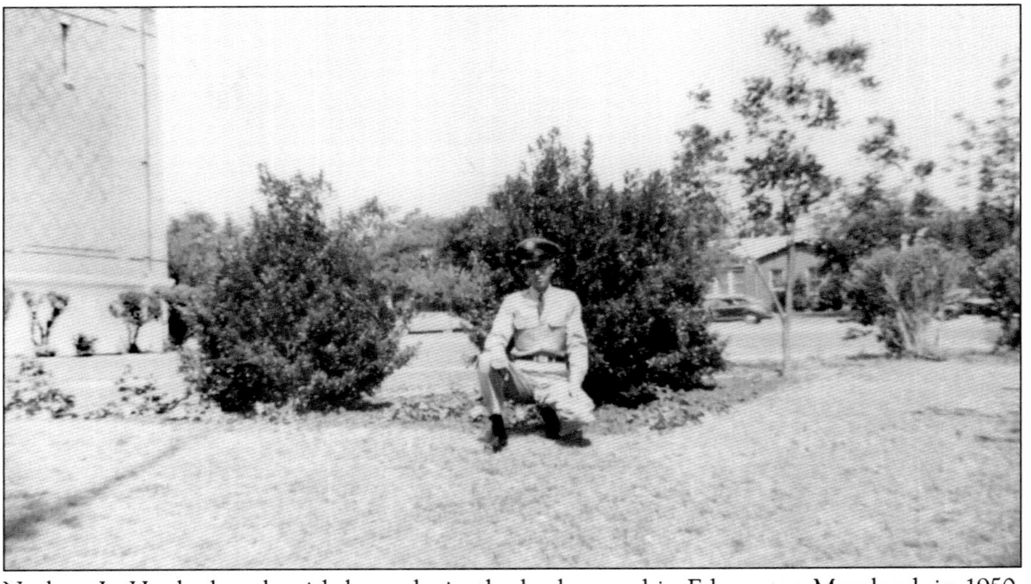

Norbert L. Henke kneels with barracks in the background in Edgewater, Maryland, in 1950. He spent most of his service as a clerk at the Engine School at Fort Belvoir, Virginia, where his primary duties were personnel work and the handling of classified material. He was a corporal when he was discharged from the U.S. Army Corps of Engineers in 1952. (Courtesy Doris and Norbert L. Henke.)

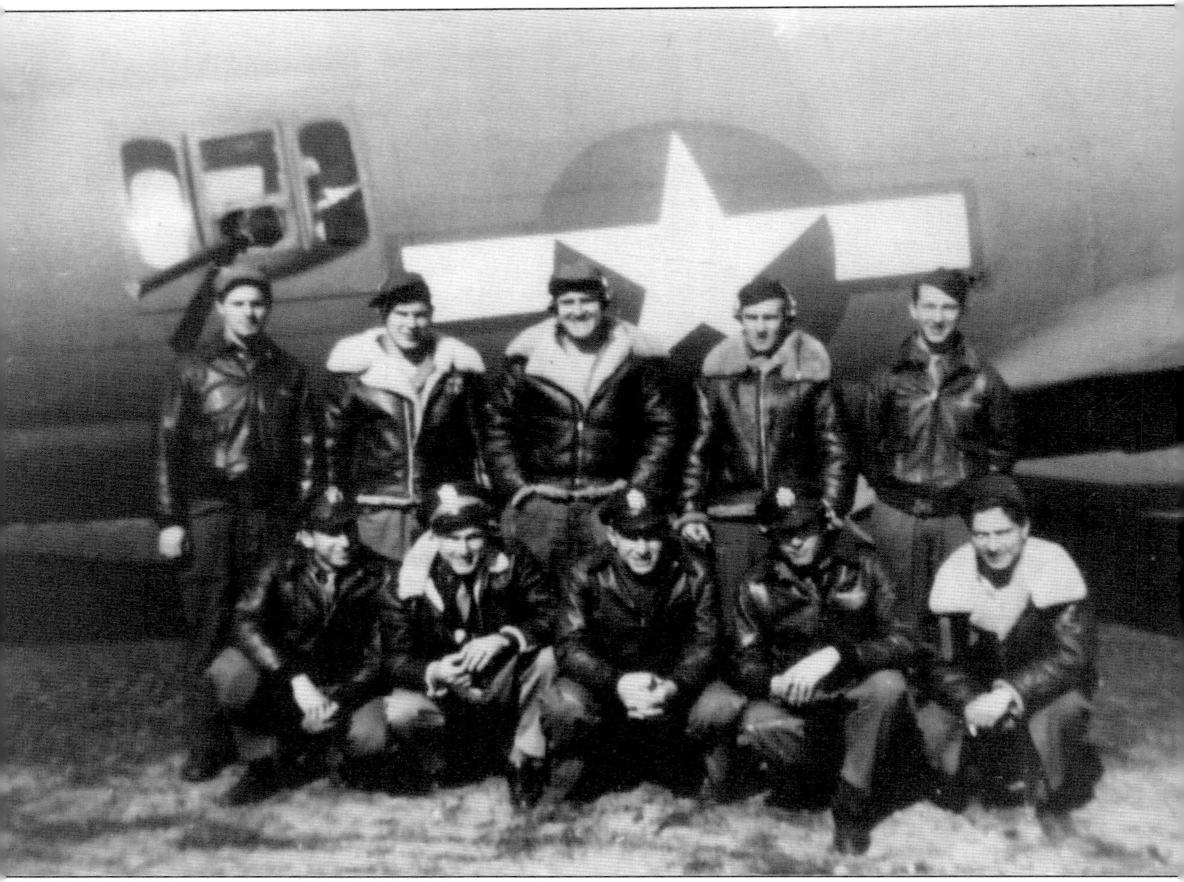

First Lt. Thomas E. Howard, a bombardier on a B-17, kneels in the middle with his original crew. They were assigned to the 15th Air Force, 97th Bomb Group in Amendola, Italy. His plane was shot down in March 1944 by German fighters, and he was forced to bail out. He landed in enemy-held Austria, breaking his leg. Captured by civilians, he eventually escaped and was helped into Yugoslavia by partisans—and sometimes children—before being picked up by a rescue plane. Howard had been listed as "missing in action." His mother received a telegram on Mother's Day 1944 notifying her that her son was alive. He was promoted to captain and discharged in 1946 with an Air Medal, Purple Heart, and Presidential Unit Citation (PUC). (Courtesy Thomas E. Howard.)

Theodore A. "Ted" Scherpenberg entered the U.S. Army Air Force in March 1943. He was trained in high-speed Morse code and network procedures. In May 1944, he was assigned to U.S. Army Airways Communications Systems with the 14th Air Force in Yunanyi, China. His primary job was to locate lost or downed aircraft by using a direction finder. He is pictured here (right) in China with his buddy in a slit trench. Such trenches were used in the event of a Japanese air raid. (Courtesy Theodore A. Scherpenberg.)

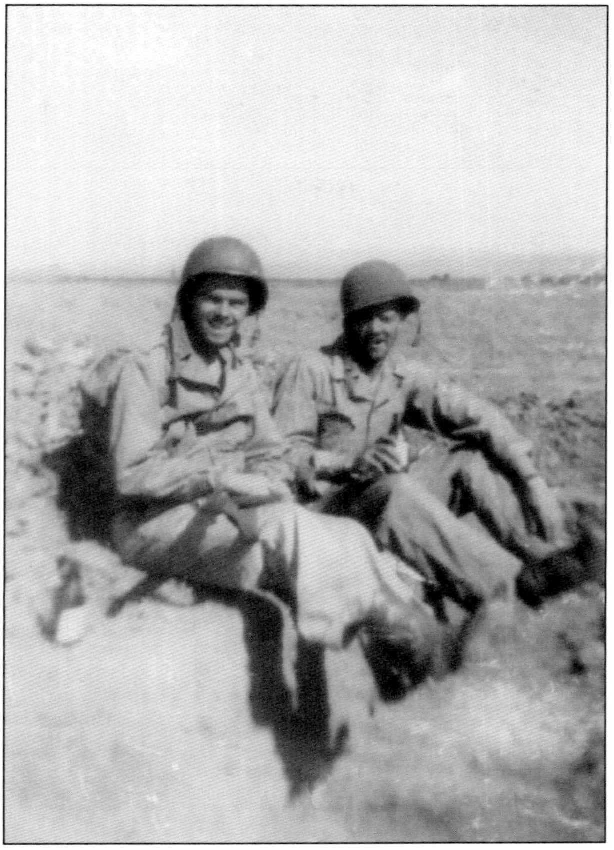

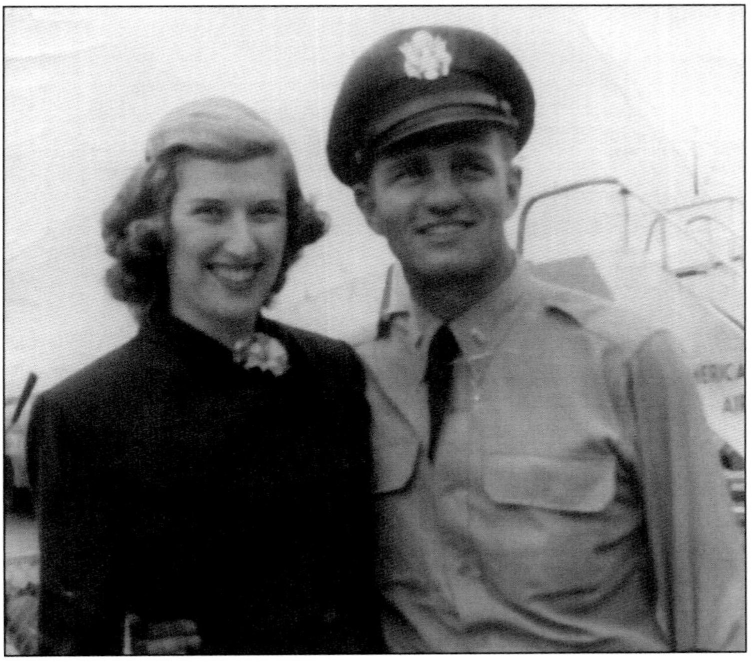

Discharged a staff sergeant in early 1946, Scherpenberg attended engineering ROTC at the University of Cincinnati, where he was commissioned a second lieutenant in the new U.S. Air Force. He was called up in 1951, spent six weeks evaluating intelligence tests in San Antonio, Texas, and was discharged. His wife, Marian, met him at the Nashville airport. (Courtesy Theodore A. Scherpenberg.)

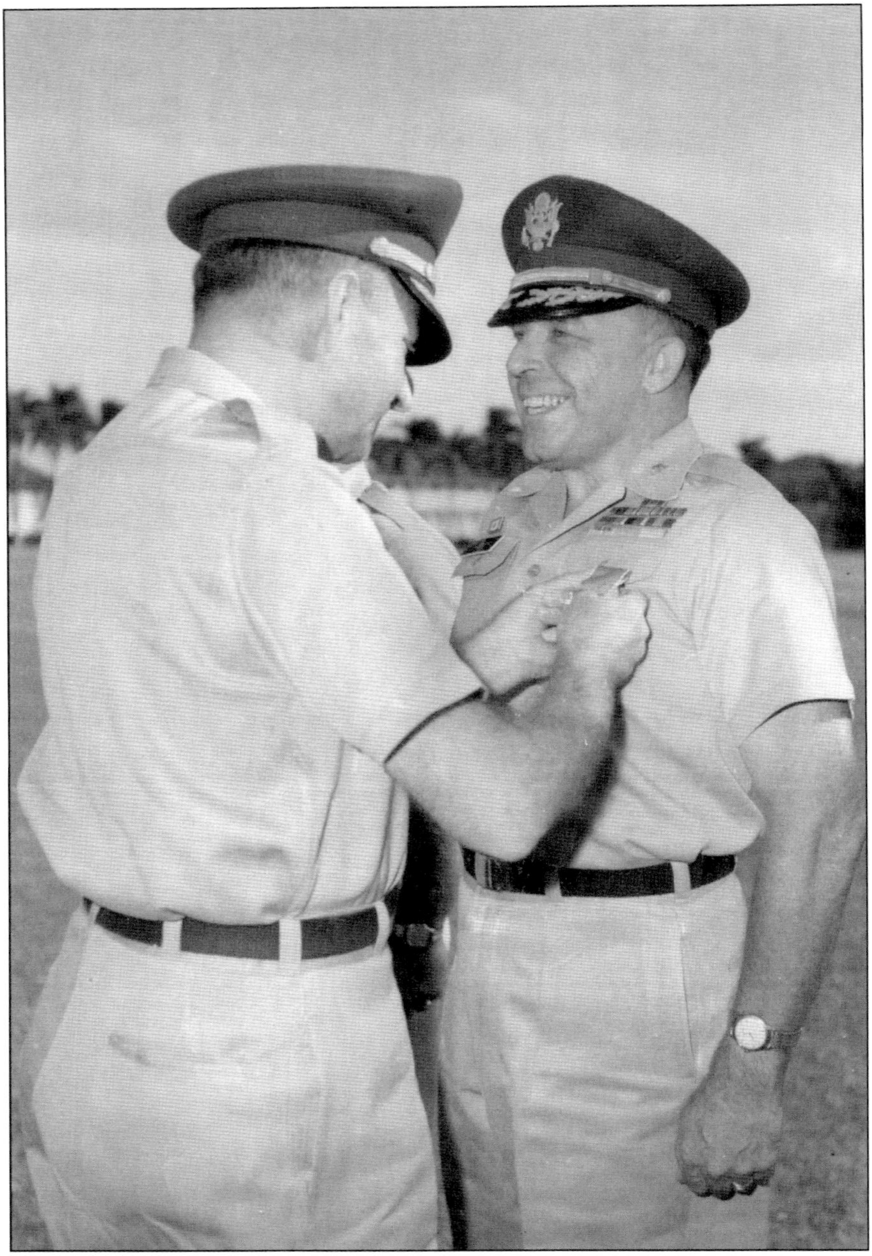

Lt. Col. Donald L. Wagner receives the Legion of Merit from Brig. Gen. William E. Potts at Fort Shafter, Hawaii, in June 1968 shortly before he retired. Wagner entered the army as a private in 1942, was commissioned a second lieutenant before the war was over, and decided to stay in. His duties included processing German prisoners in World War II, working in medical services in a MASH unit of the 8th Army Surgeon's Office in Korea in 1950, and being an instructor in intelligence schools in 1954—the job that he enjoyed the most. Following other assignments, he went back to intelligence school as chief of the training division. Besides the Legion of Merit, he was awarded two Army Commendation Medals and the Republic of Korea PUC. (Courtesy Donald L. Wagner.)

Doris Eileen Hull Johnson was sworn into the U.S. Navy on D-Day (June 6, 1944). Prior to that she worked as a secretary for the U.S. Army Corps of Engineers at Wright Field in Dayton, Ohio. She attended Yeoman School in Stillwater, Oklahoma, and spent two years as a WAVE. (Courtesy Doris Johnson.)

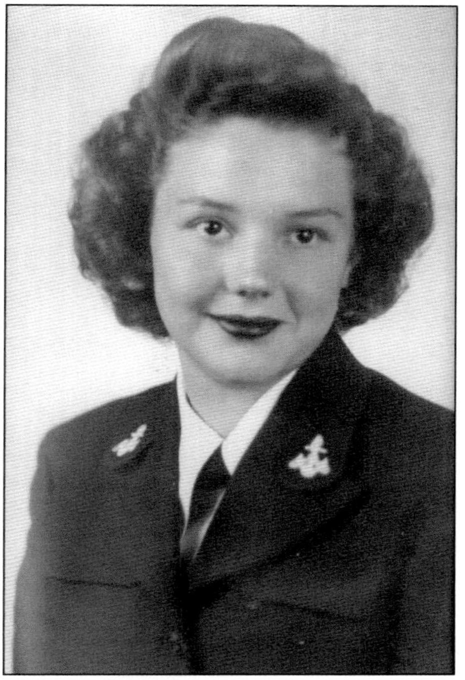

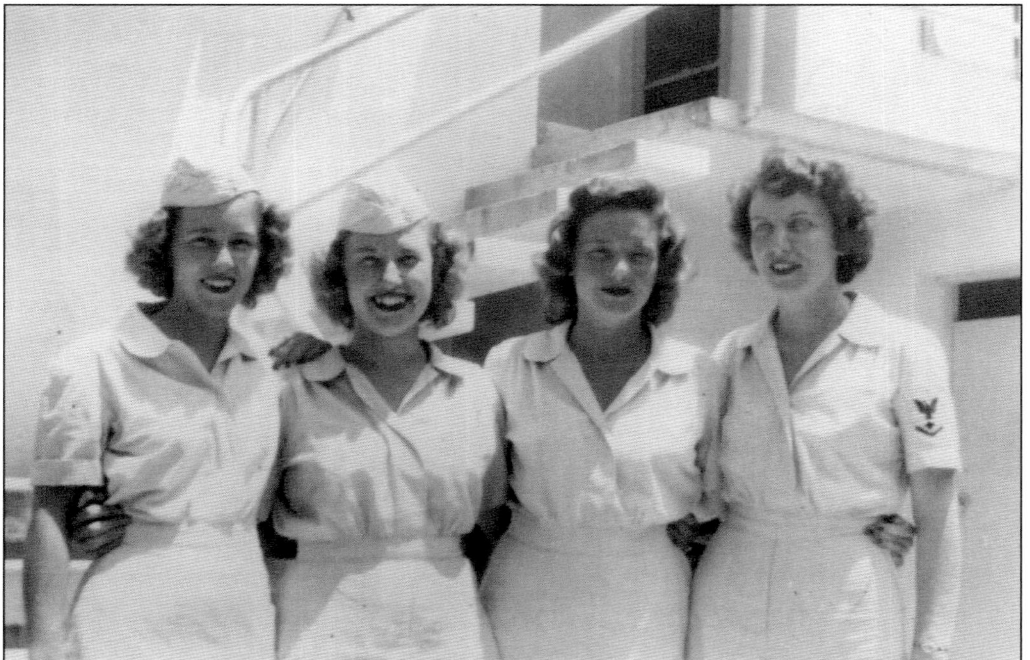

Yeoman 2nd Class Hull worked at the Naval Training School in Fort Lauderdale, Florida. Pictured here with her roommates are, from left to right, storekeeper 3rd Class Beatrice Garber, yeoman 3rd Class Frances Clouser, Hull, and pharmacist's mate 3rd Class Ruth Whidby. (Courtesy Doris Johnson.)

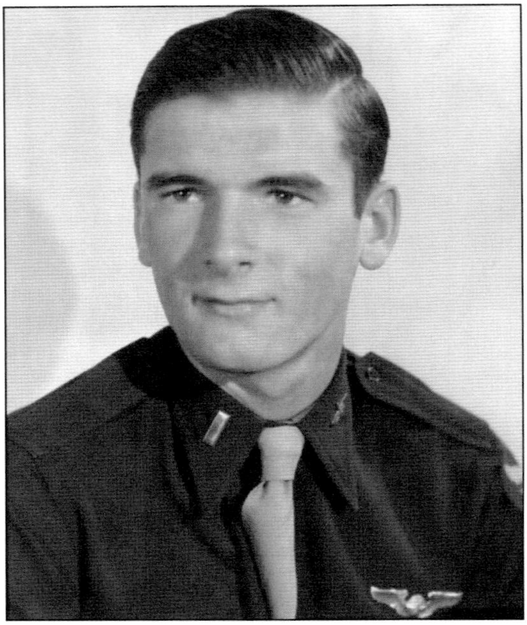

Robert D. Johnson was commissioned a second lieutenant following graduation from the Army Air Forces Navigation School at Hondo Army Air Field in Texas. He went to Bombardier School in New Mexico and Radar Bombardment School at Williams Field in Arizona. He had received orders to report to a B29 group bound for the Pacific when World War II ended. He was discharged in 1946. (Courtesy Robert D. Johnson.)

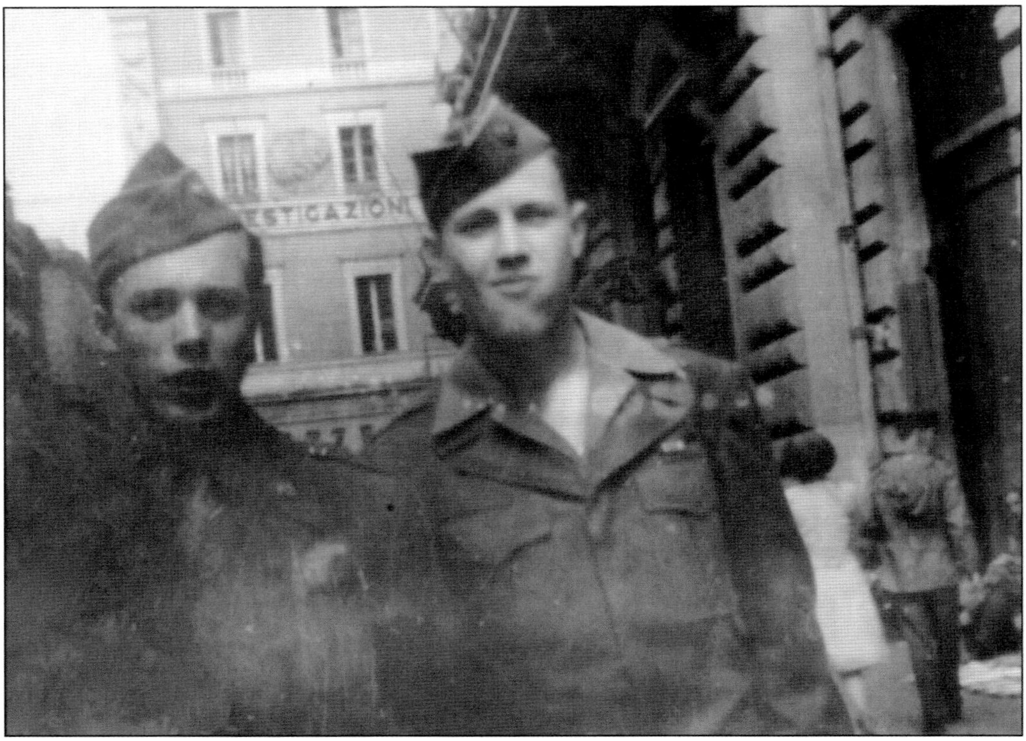

U.S. Army Cpl. James H. Giles (right), who was a radio operator, was hitchhiking with friends in Italy when this photograph was taken. In 1945, while serving at Allied Force Headquarters in Salzburg, Austria, Giles witnessed an incident involving General Eisenhower. While Ike was riding his favorite white horse, an unknown GI shouted "Hi Ho Silver!" That untimely comment cost his company their leave and liberty for one week. (Courtesy James H. Giles.)

Paul Wilson poses (right) in his U.S. Navy uniform in 1944. In 1943, when he received his draft notice, he requested the U.S. Navy, and once there he requested submarine duty. He trained to be a motor machinist's mate in Chicago and then attended submarine school in New London, Connecticut. Wilson was assigned to a new construction sub, the USS *Cobia*, but he was injured and transferred to Midway, one of the biggest submarine bases in the Pacific. He refitted and refurbished submarines returning from patrol, usually working 18- to 20-hour days. He spent a year on Midway and then received orders to another submarine in Pearl Harbor, Hawaii, the USS *Trepang*. The submarine (below) nears Stockton, California, after departing Pearl Harbor when World War II ended. Wilson was discharged in 1946 as a motor machinist's mate 2nd class. (Both courtesy Paul Wilson.)

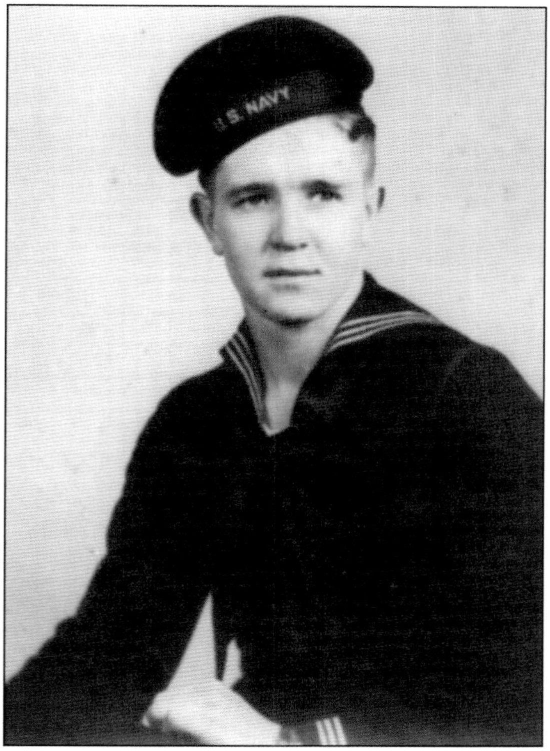

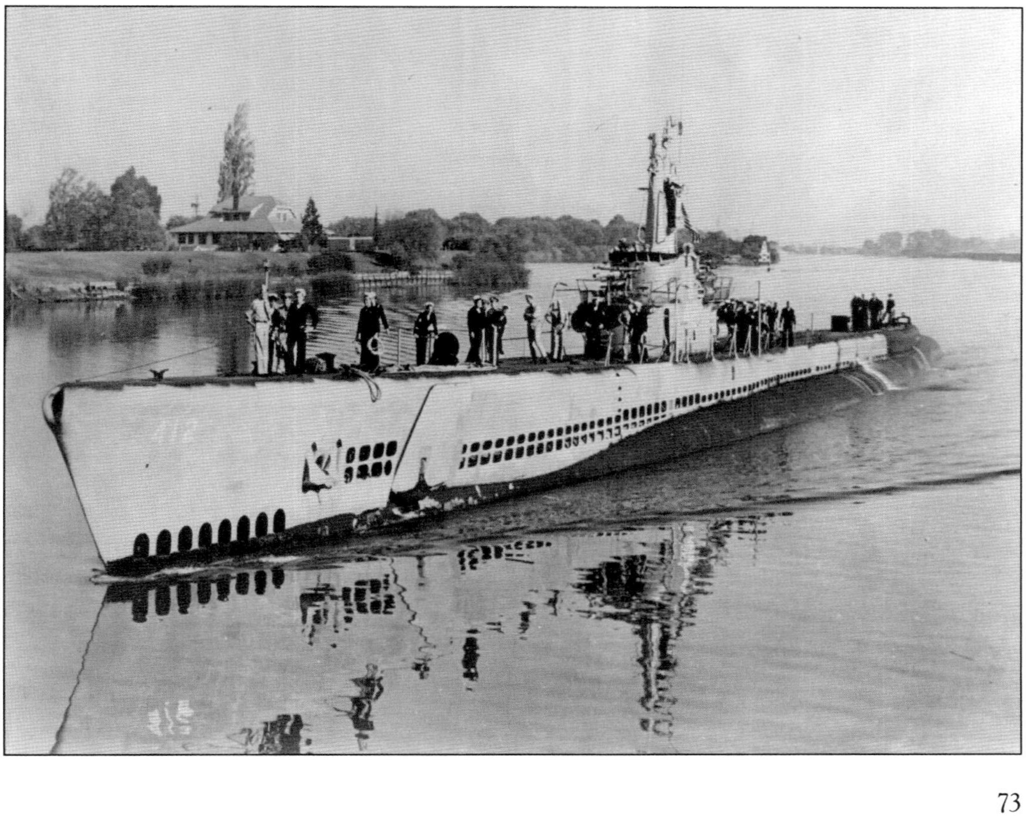

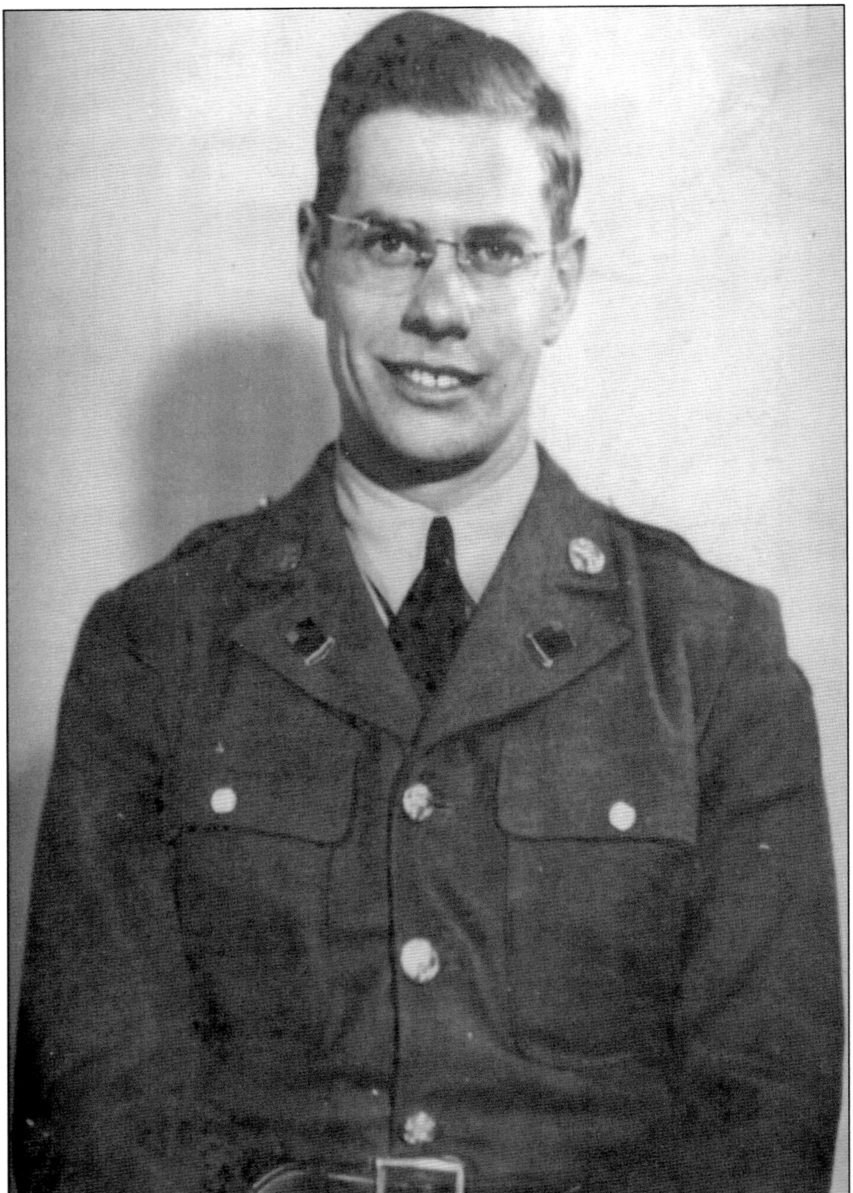

First Lt. Benjamin F. Klein Jr. enlisted in the U.S. Army in 1941 as a private, rose to staff sergeant, and was commissioned a 2nd lieutenant in 1943 following Tank Destroyer Officer Candidate School. He joined the 805th Tank Destroyer Battalion on the Anzio beachhead as an "extra." (The practice was to send new 2nd lieutenants to outfits that had all needed officers but expected to lose some soon.) He earned a pair of Purple Hearts as a result of proximity to minefield explosions while he was an armored reconnaissance unit commander. In addition, he was awarded a Silver Star on April 28, 1945, for gallantry in action near Citadella, Italy. Klein would later write, "It was over on the Yugoslav border, above Trieste—the war was over—when I was presented my Silver Star by—guess who—General Hospital. No dignity to my life." (Courtesy Benjamin F. Klein and Edward Klein.)

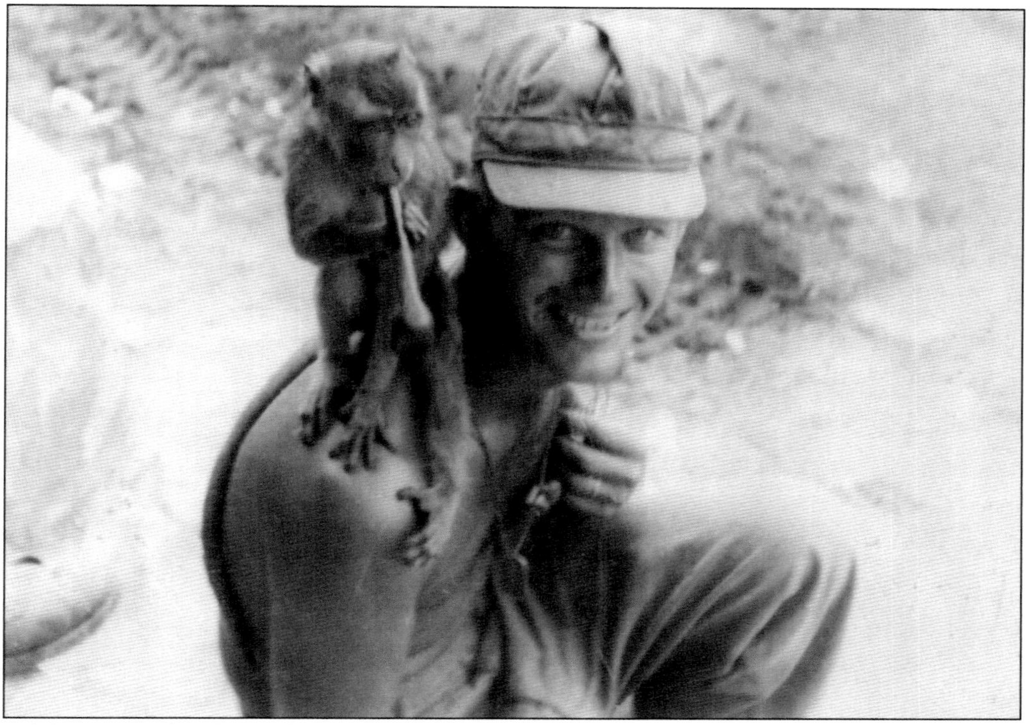

While stationed in the Philippines as an U.S. Army medic, Bronze Star winner Sgt. Russell Ward and his fellow soldiers befriended a monkey they named Jabo. "Jabo was extremely important to the soldiers," said Ward's son Roger. "I think Jabo took care of the soldiers as much as they took care of him." Whenever the company was being shelled, Jabo would hide in an ammunition box. (Courtesy Roger Ward.)

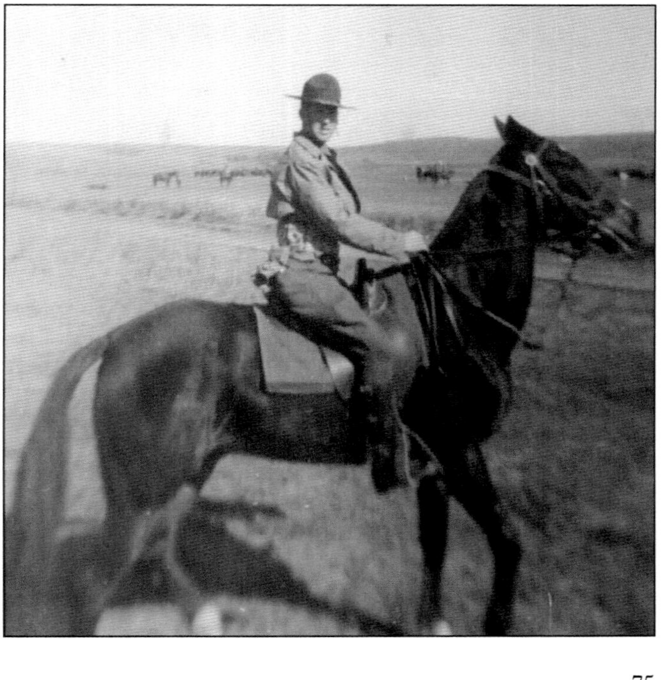

After training with the U.S. Army Cavalry, Emery M. Gardner was reassigned as a cook for the 9th Armored Division's medical corps. As a sergeant, he landed with his division from a PT boat at Normandy on D-Day after the initial bloody landings. His division was surrounded for five days during the Battle of the Bulge in 1944. In 1945, they helped take the strategic Ludendorff Bridge at Remagen, Germany. (Courtesy Emery M. Gardner.)

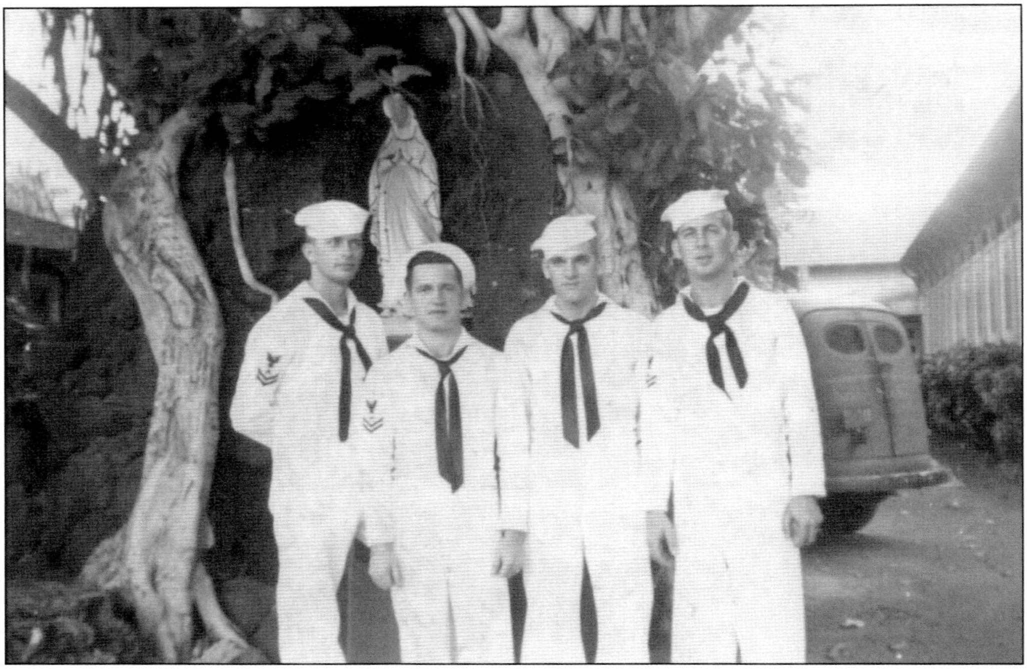

Charles B. Shea, seen on the far left as a gunner's mate 2nd class with three navy shipmates in Hawaii, was assigned to the USS *Aaron Ward* (below), a destroyer-minelayer. On May 3, 1945, the *Ward* was on picket patrol about 70 miles off the Okinawa coast, tasked with preventing Japanese aircraft from reaching American ships and soldiers fighting to gain a foothold on Okinawa. Japanese aircraft attacked the ship at dusk and six kamikazes scored successive direct hits, setting the ship afire, and killing or wounding 42 men. Shea was blown overboard with his dungarees on fire. He was rescued after three hours in the South China Sea and later awarded a Purple Heart and PUC. Damage-control parties worked tirelessly to keep the *Ward* afloat until she was towed back to port. (Both courtesy Phyllis Shea.)

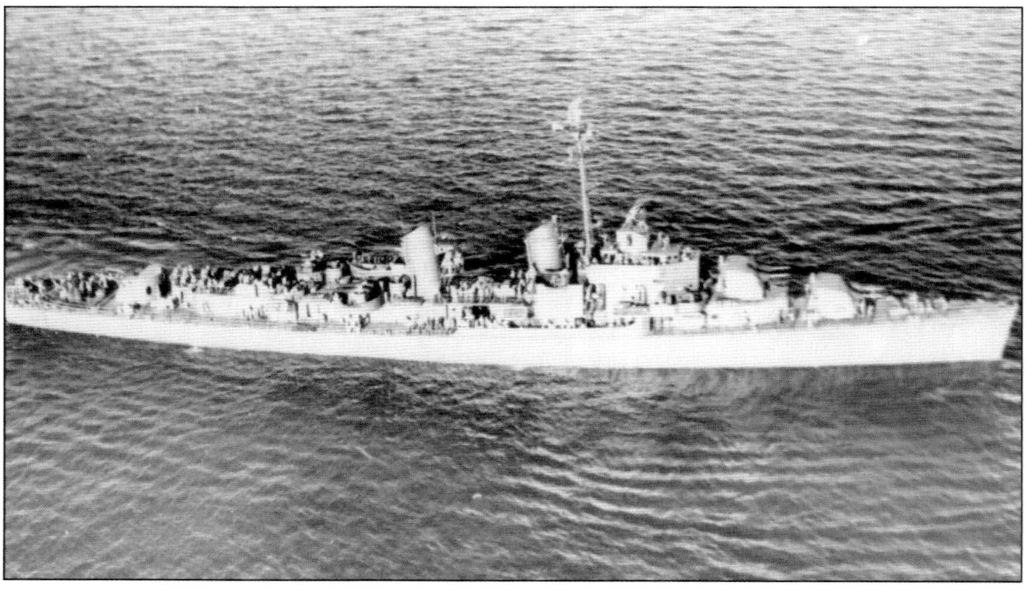

Alvin E. Stotler is shown at right as an U.S. Army staff sergeant at Fort Riley, Kansas, in 1952 after returning from Korea. In Korea, he served with Company K, 31st Infantry Regiment, 7th Infantry Division, earning his first Purple Heart at Panmunjon in late November 1950. When Stotler's friend Jimmy Bowman was killed that same month, Stotler took over his machine-gun squad. Stotler received his second Purple Heart—and more serious wound—on December 1 at the Chosin Reservoir. Only 12 of his company made it out of the reservoir. Stotler was hospitalized for five months for gunshot wounds and frostbite. He received an Army PUC (twice), a Navy and Marine Corps PUC, and a Republic of Korea PUC. Below, Stotler (far right) poses with Bowman (left) and Ray Adkins before they went to Korea. (Both courtesy Alvin E. Stotler.)

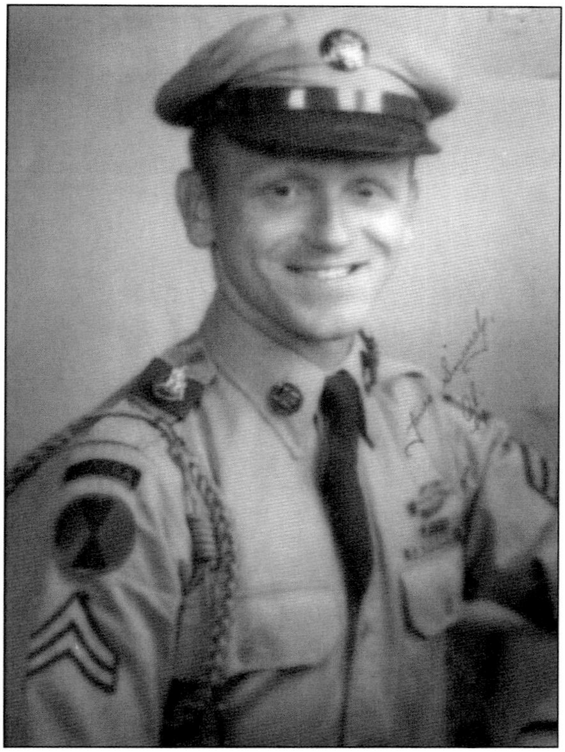

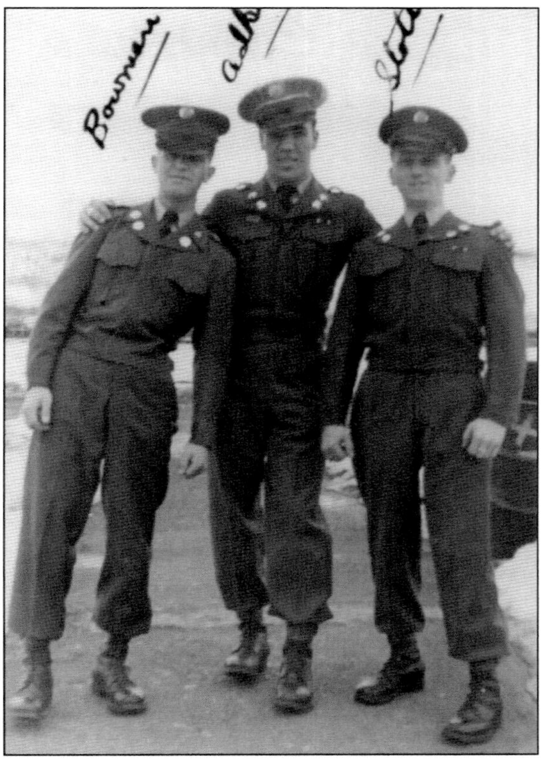

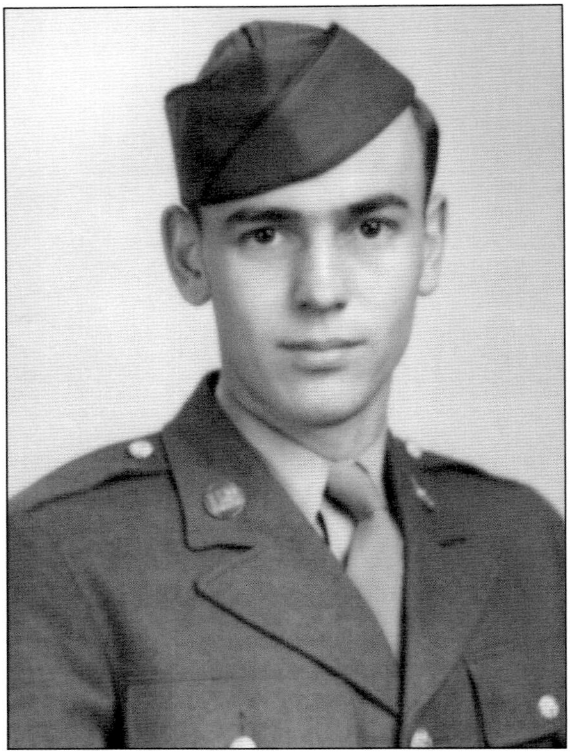

William P. Kincaid Jr., a technical sergeant, served as a U.S. Army radio operator with Company B, 94th Signal Battalion. He received the Bronze Star for service during the Battle of the Bulge. In March 1945, Kincaid participated in the Allies' successful defense of the Ludendorff Bridge over the Rhine River at Remagen, Germany. (Courtesy Mildred Kincaid.)

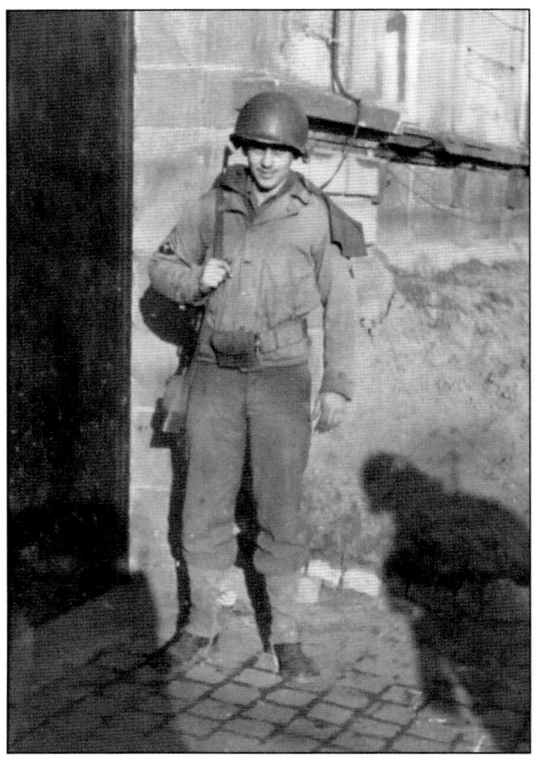

Kincaid is shown here in December 1944 in Arlon, Belgium. After being discharged in 1946, Kincaid raised his family in Madeira and became a respected English teacher and varsity golf coach at Indian Hill High School. He was named coach of the year by the *Cincinnati Enquirer* in 1976. Kincaid also founded the Indian Hill High School Alumni Association. (Courtesy Mildred Kincaid.)

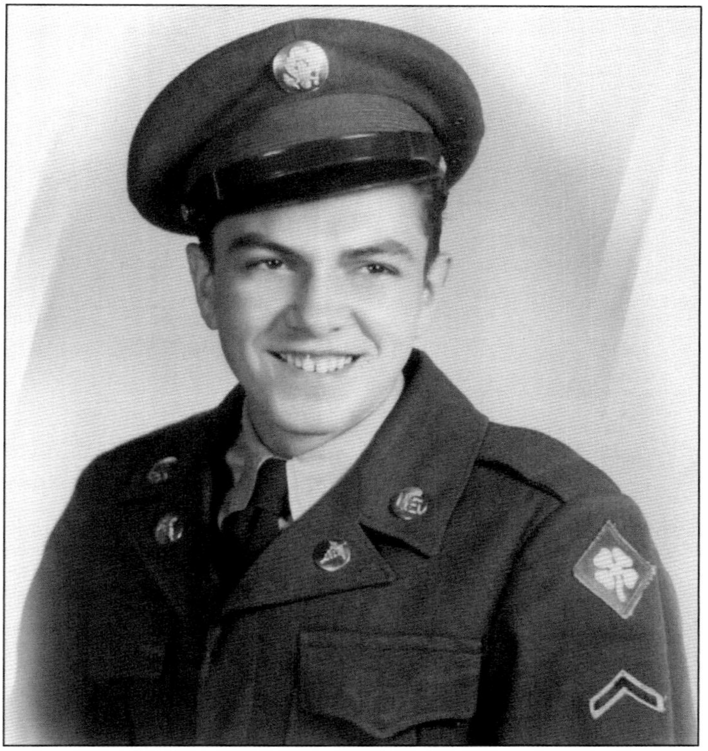

Trained as a medic, William J. Brown (pictured) spent Memorial Day 1949 with his friend Matty Williams on Guam at the 222nd General Army Hospital. In January 1950, both men were reassigned alphabetically by surname. Corporal Brown went to the 526th AAA Gun Battalion, remaining stateside. Williams went to South Korea with another unit. When North Korea invaded South Korea, Williams, 20 years old, was killed in action. (Courtesy William J. Brown.)

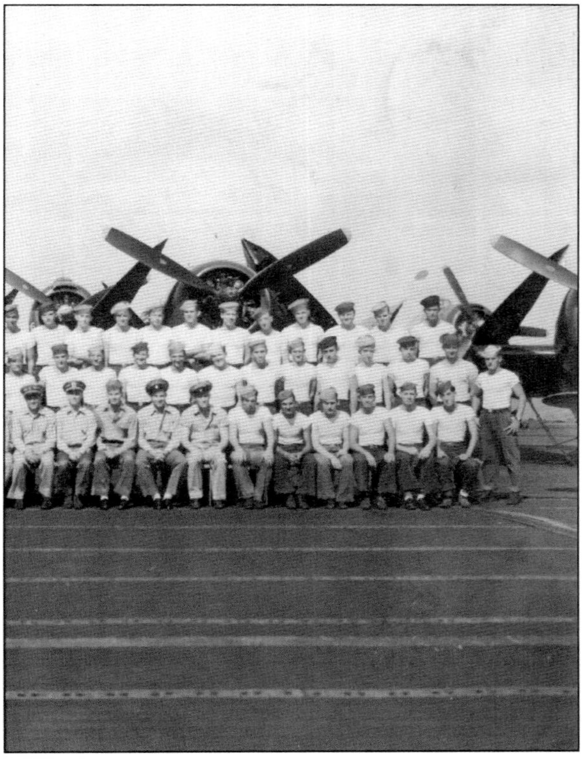

Aviation machinist's mate 3rd Class Joseph P. Villari, seated fifth from right with V2F Fighter Plane captains and engineering crew, served as a Hellcat fighter mechanic on the aircraft carrier USS *Wasp*. On August 9, 1945, off Honshu, Japan, the *Wasp* was attacked by what is believed to be the last kamikaze of the war. Villari had to jump into a starboard safety net to escape the kamikaze. (Courtesy Joseph P. Villari.)

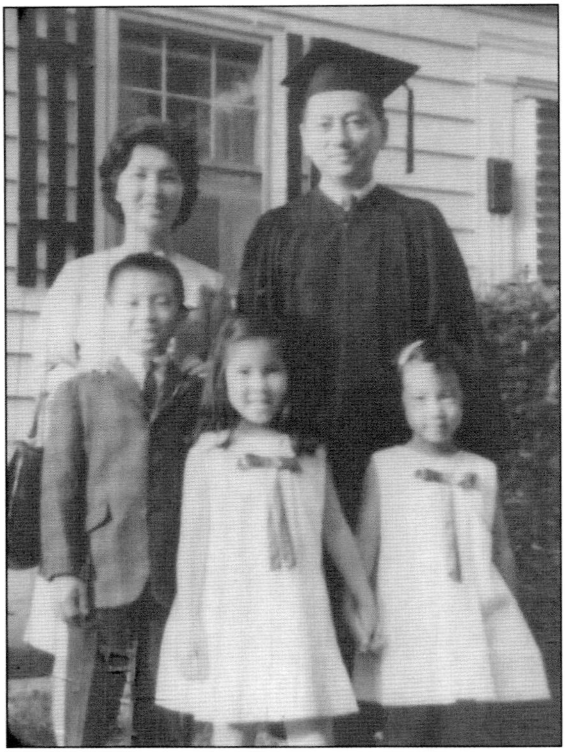

Masaji S. Toki, with his wife, Taeko, and children (left to right) Jon, Jeri, and Carole, moved to Madeira after graduating from the University of Cincinnati in 1965. After Pearl Harbor, Toki, a second-generation Japanese American (nisei), along with 120,000 others, was sent to what were euphemistically called Temporary Assembly Centers in California. While he was detained behind barbed wire and guarded by machine guns, his older brother, James Toki, became a member of the highly decorated Nisei 442nd Regimental Combat Team. Masaji, who had been classified 4F, was released in 1944 and came to Cincinnati where the War Relocation Authority helped him find a job at a machine shop making parts for submarines and PT boats. He was inducted into the Madeira High School Athletic Hall of Fame in 1993 for his contributions to the Boosters Club. He speaks to school groups about his World War II experiences. (Both courtesy Masaji S. Toki.)

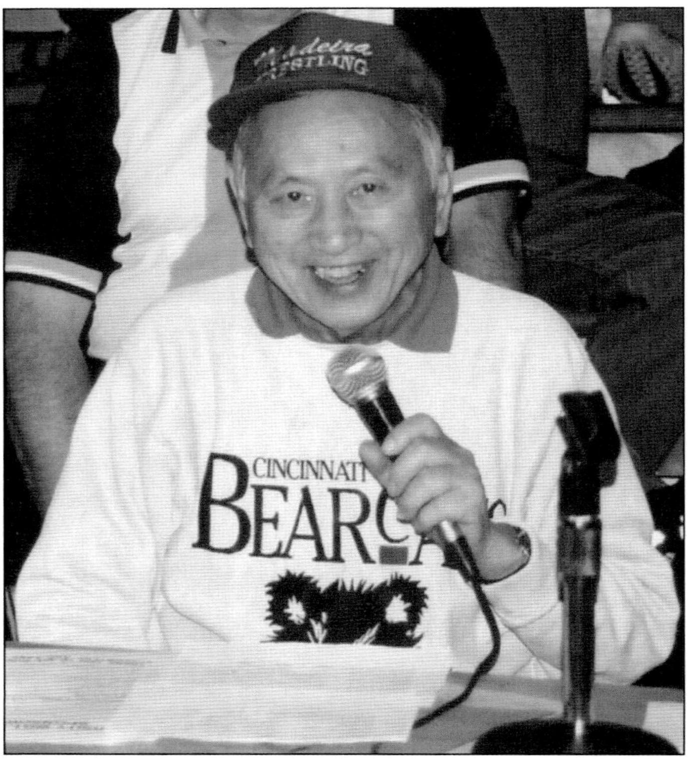

Eight

Wind, Fire, and Rain

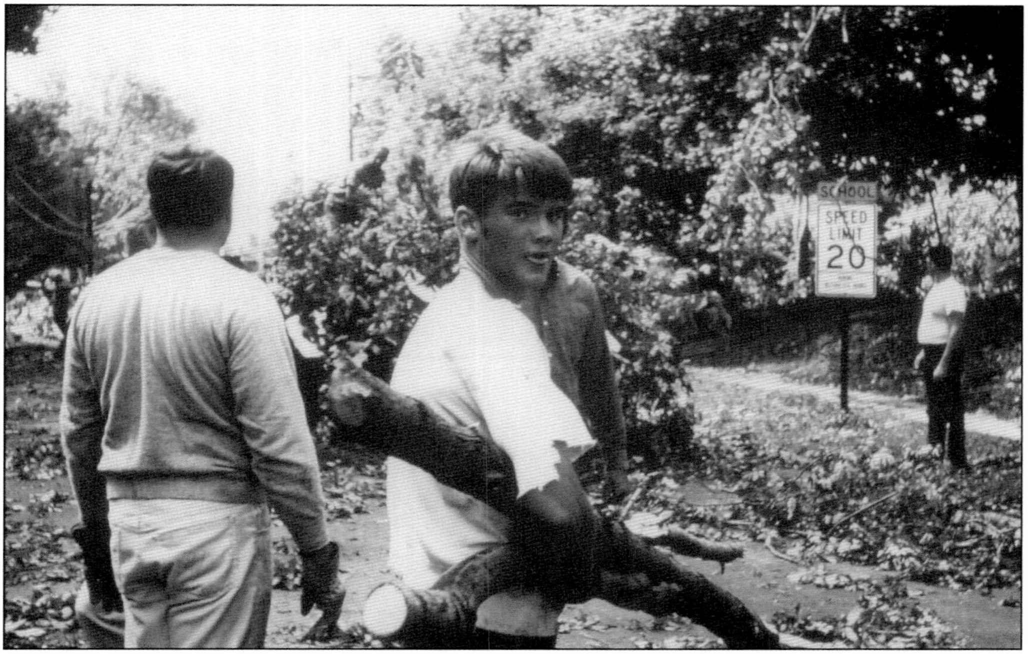

Seventeen-year-old Stephan Johnson and other volunteers clear debris left by the August 9, 1969, tornado that caused an estimated $3 million worth of damage in the city. Several people were injured, but fortunately no one died. After the tornado passed through on Saturday, Mayor Daniel D. McDonald and councilman Carl Schneider rode through town using a bullhorn to encourage residents to help clean up the aftermath. Hundreds of people turned out to help their neighbors. This photograph was taken on August 10, 1969, on Miami Avenue near W. M. Sellman Junior High School. The photograph was originally one slide picked up randomly by the coauthor in a box of slides marked only "tornado, August 9, 1969." (Courtesy Madeira Historical Society.)

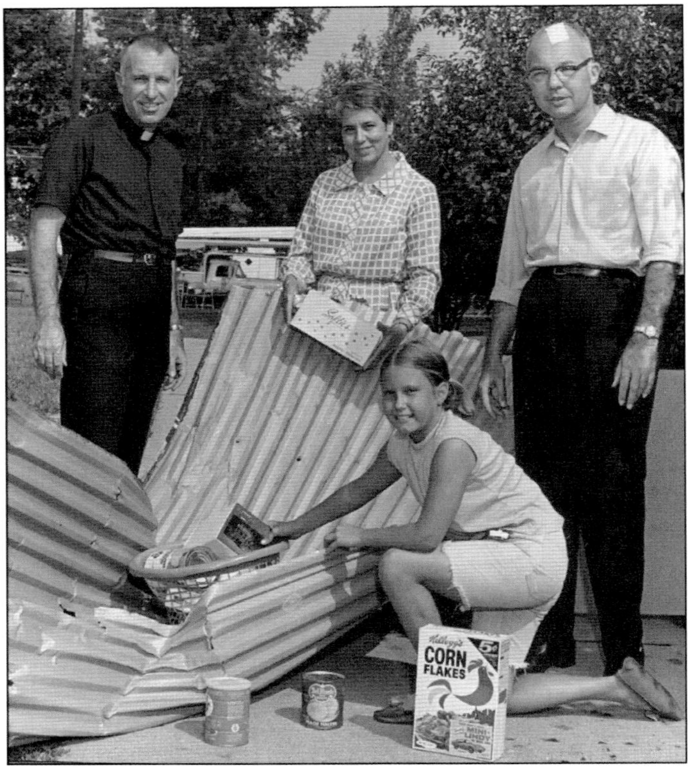

St. Gertrude's annual festival was disrupted by the tornado, and several people at the festival were injured when a tent collapsed. Volunteers, including the people in this photograph, pitched in to hold another church festival on August 24. From left to right are Fr. Thomas V. DiFede, O. P., Mrs. Thomas J. McClorey, Paula Muenchen, and Fr. Jerome Conroy, O. P., who was among the injured. (Courtesy St. Gertrude Church.)

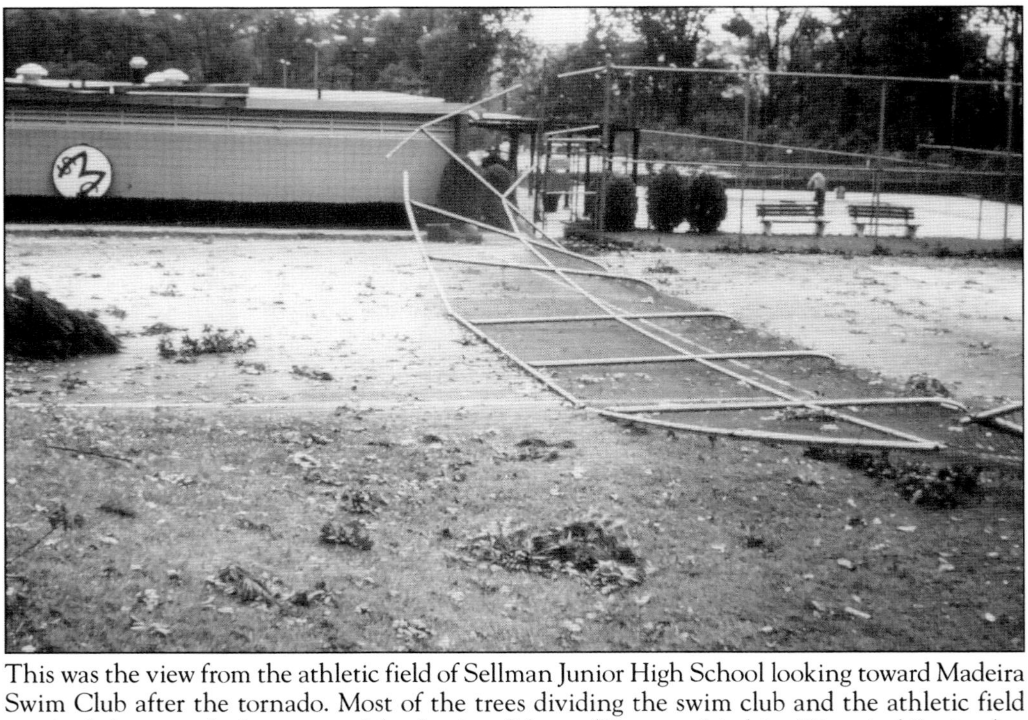

This was the view from the athletic field of Sellman Junior High School looking toward Madeira Swim Club after the tornado. Most of the trees dividing the swim club and the athletic field survived the tornado, but some of the fencing did not. (Courtesy Madeira Historical Society.)

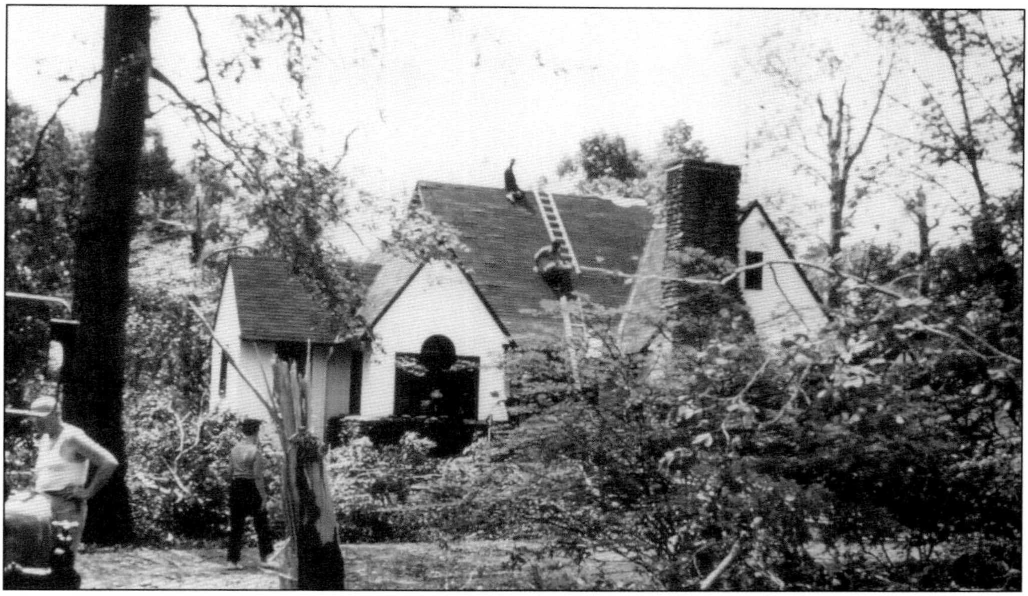

Volunteers work at one of the many Madeira area homes that suffered minor damage with mostly shingles blown off the roofs and trees broken or missing branches. Residents awoke Sunday morning to the sound of chainsaws cutting up downed trees. (Courtesy Madeira Historical Society.)

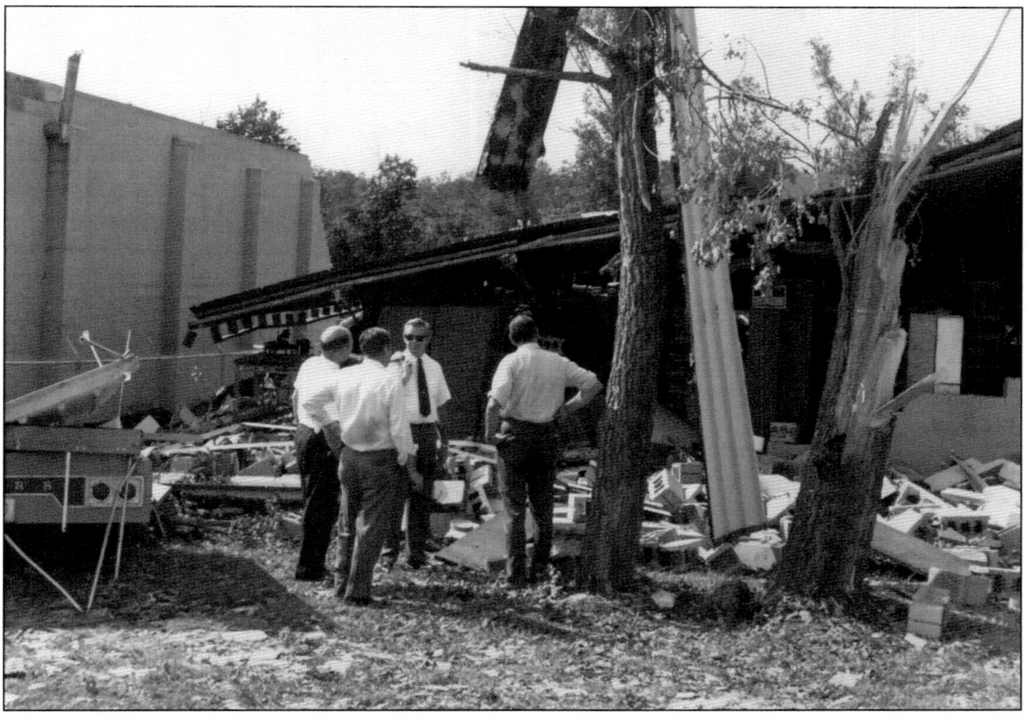

Mayor Daniel D. McDonald (third from left) and other officials inspect tornado damage at a leather factory on Morrison Avenue. Gov. James Rhodes also visited the area. Police, firemen, rescue squads, and service departments worked through Saturday night and were at times hindered by main thoroughfares being blocked by downed trees and wires. (Courtesy Daniel D. McDonald.)

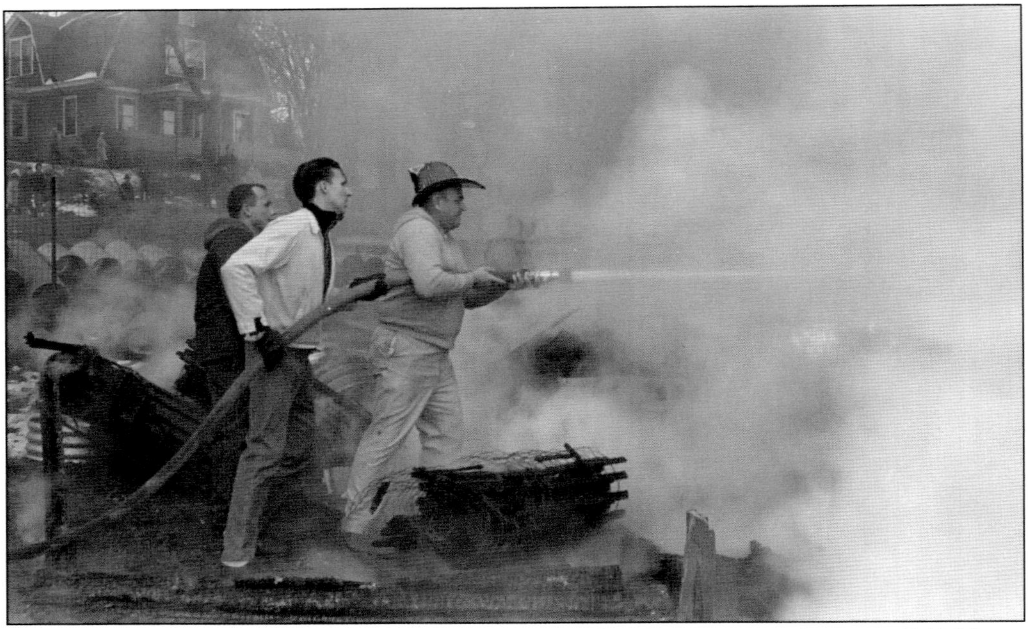

Three firemen fought a blaze at the George Meyer Lumber Company warehouse at 6940 Miami Avenue on Sunday, January 29, 1967. Three hundred to five hundred gallons of paint and lacquer stored in the building exploded, shooting flames through the roof almost immediately and endangering firefighters, according to the *Cincinnati Enquirer's* January 31 article. The *Cincinnati Post* reported that the blaze was so intense that the asphalt beneath the firemen's feet melted. Water had to be sprayed on the men to cool them. Above, note the fireman with his helmet reversed to protect himself from the heat as he leans towards the fire. Next to the unidentified man are Jim Lydon (far left) and Capt. Ed Lewis, then acting chief of the department. Below, firefighters from Madeira and Indian Hill, Silverton, Fairfax, and Newtown monitor the fire. (Both courtesy Larry A. Van Pelt.)

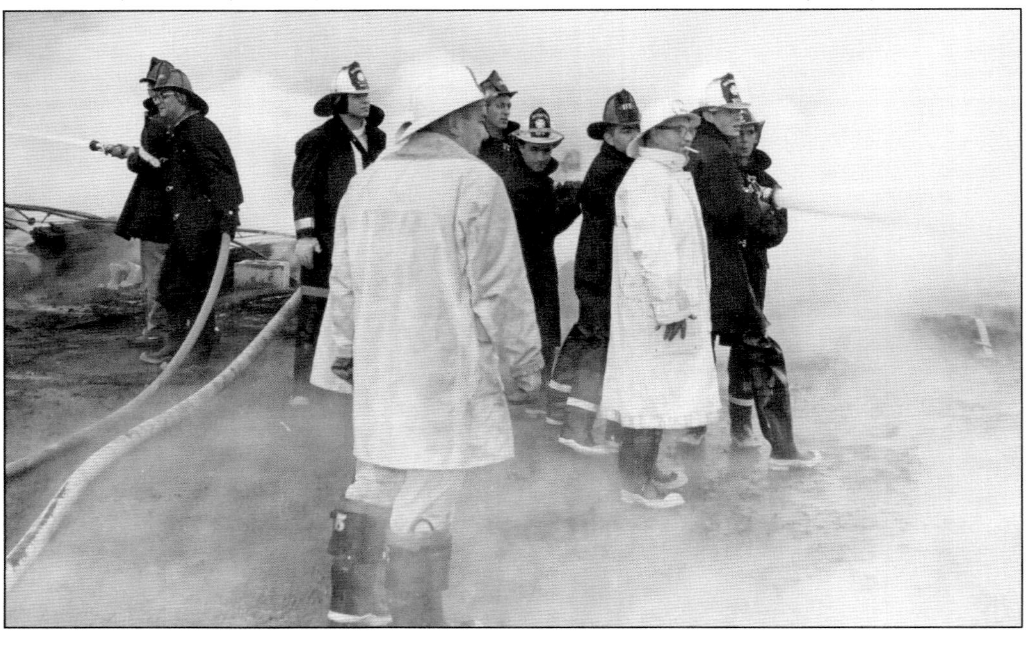

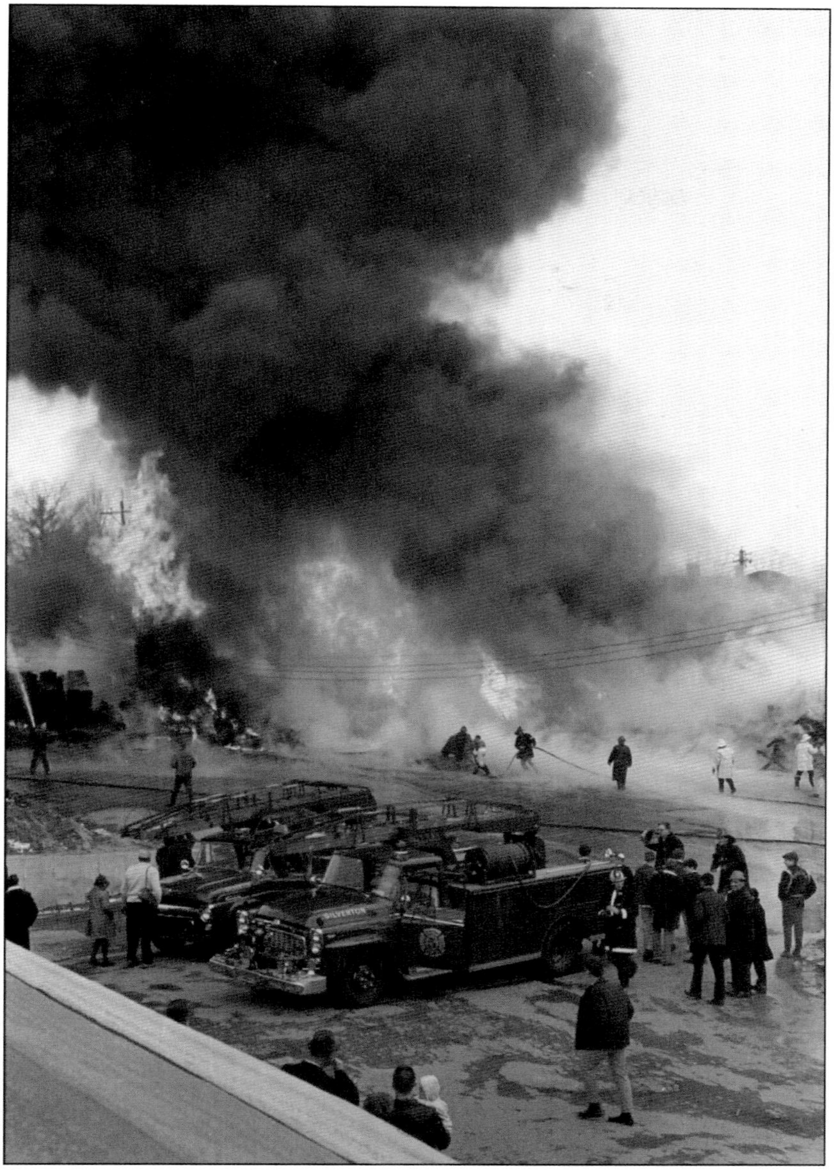

The warehouse fire was reported at 1:13 p.m. on January 29, 1967, by a caller from the Madeira Food Shop on Camargo Road. Although the fire station was just minutes away, the building full of flammables was engulfed by flames when firefighters arrived. The flames "must have been out of control by the time we got the alarm," Capt. Ed Lewis told the *Enquirer.* Firefighters concentrated on keeping the fire from spreading to adjacent properties, some of them within 10 feet of the burning building. They set up water curtains to keep flames away from the Boerger Dairy store and the 5¢ to $5 Store on Miami Avenue. At one point, they had to stretch fire hose beneath the tracks of the B and O Railroad at its Miami crossing to fight the flames. The fire was reported out at 5:30 p.m. Damage was estimated by company owner Henry Hilberg at $100,000. Hilberg told the media that he had to chase juveniles away from the warehouse on previous Sundays, but the official cause of the fire remained undetermined. No one was injured in the blaze. (Courtesy Larry A. Van Pelt.).

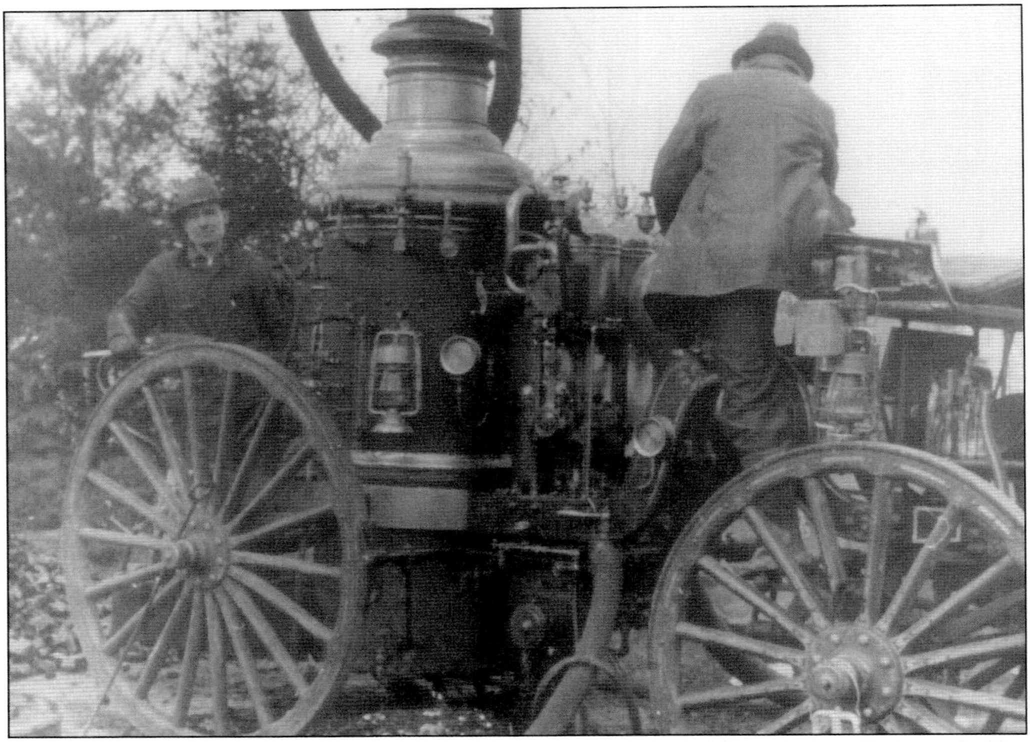

During the January 1937 flood that affected greater Cincinnati, public water supplies—including Madeira's—were contaminated. To supply clean drinking water and water for fire protection, the Madeira and Indian Hill Fire Company's 1930 Ahrens Fox pumper was used to convey clean water from the Milford water mains to the Madeira and Indian Hill mains. One fire line was laid from Glendale-Milford and Shawnee Run Roads up the hill to Shawnee Run and Park Roads, according to Larry A. Van Pelt in his 1982 history *The Madeira and Indian Hill Fire Company.* A second line from Milford ran from near Terrace Park to the top of the hill on Old Indian Hill Road. A 1906 Ahrens Fox steam pumper from Loveland (shown in these two photographs) was placed at the top of the hill to help transfer water continuously to Madeira and Indian Hill for 11 days until the Cincinnati water system was restored. (Both courtesy Larry A. Van Pelt.)

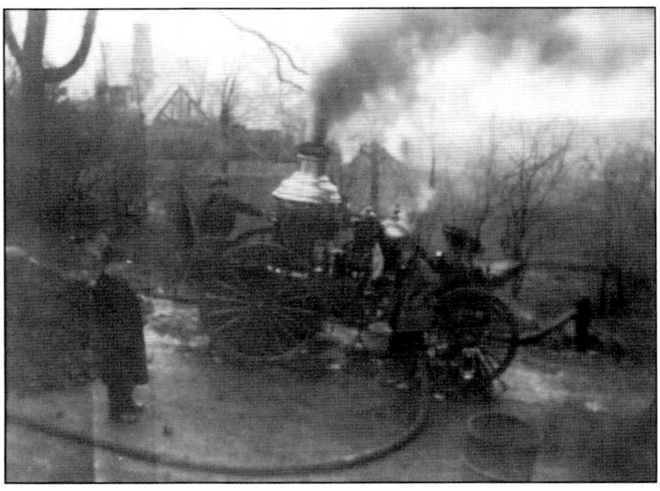

Nine

MADE IN MADEIRA

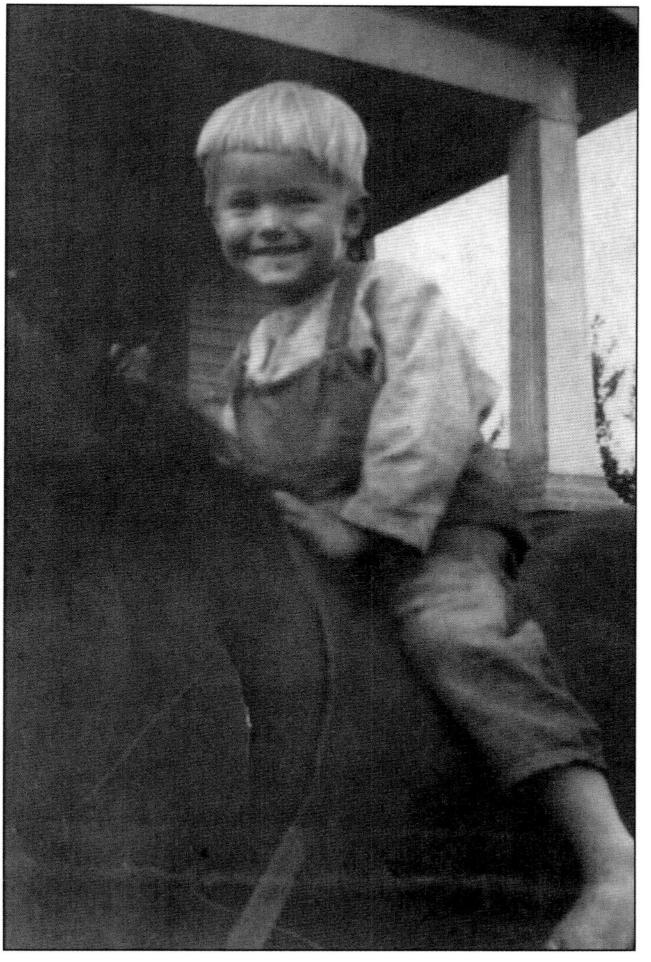

A towheaded Russell Ward Jr. grins atop a horse in front of his family's home in rural Madeira around 1924. His father, who was a builder by profession, constructed the home in 1917. Ward Sr. built many homes in Madeira, Indian Hill, and Madisonville; Ward Street in Madisonville is named for him because he built most of the homes on it. Russell Jr. followed in his father's footsteps, starting a subcontracting business after being discharged from the U.S. Army following World War II. He eventually sold that business and joined the Madeira Police Department, where he was a respected officer for decades. He and his wife, Betty, raised their four children in Madeira. He passed away in 2009. (Courtesy Roger Ward.)

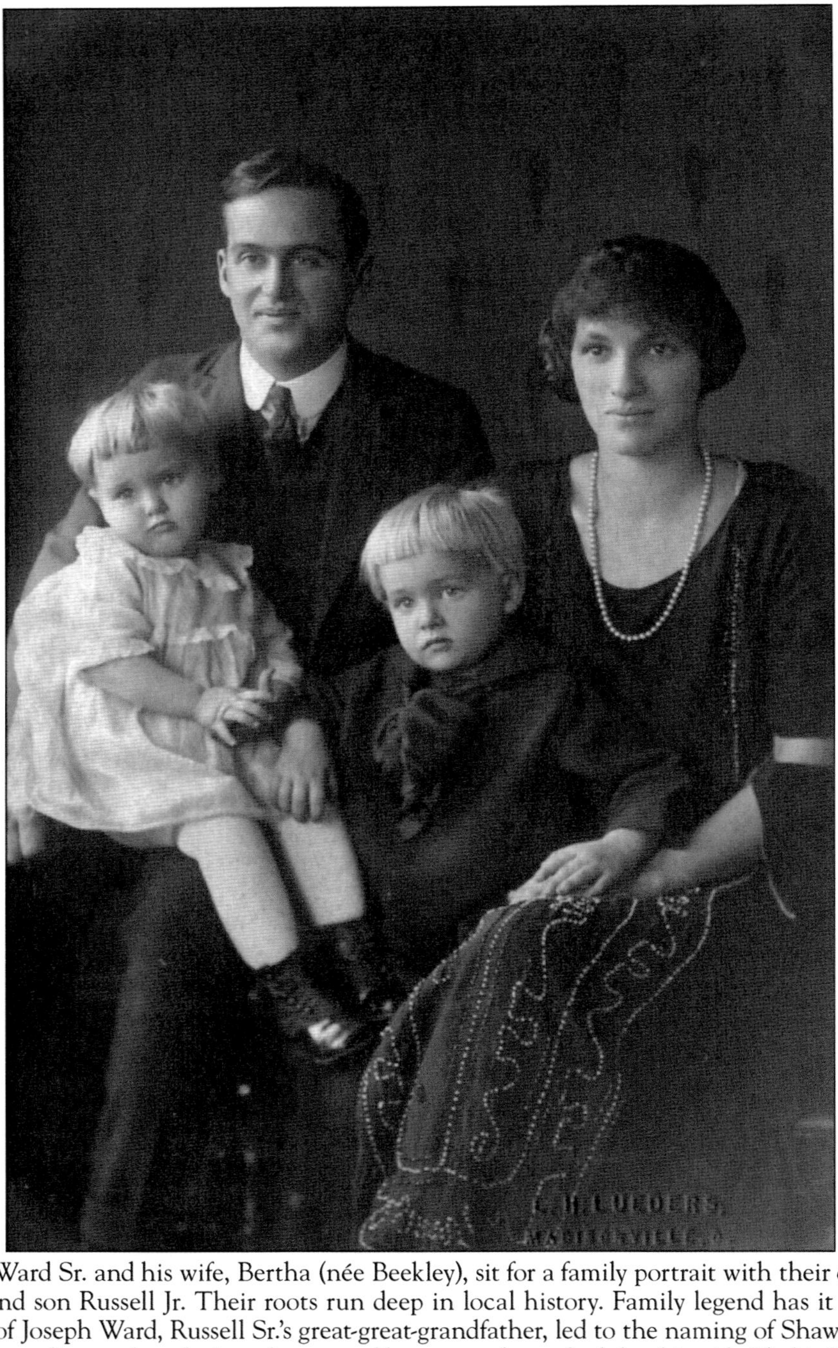

Russell Ward Sr. and his wife, Bertha (née Beekley), sit for a family portrait with their daughter Helen and son Russell Jr. Their roots run deep in local history. Family legend has it that the actions of Joseph Ward, Russell Sr.'s great-great-grandfather, led to the naming of Shawnee Run Road. According to the tale, Joseph returned home one day to find that his wife, Phebia Parkhurst Ward, had just been killed by Native Americans. Joseph pursued them along a nearby trail and caught up with one of the men—believed to be a Shawnee—and took his revenge. The trail was later named McCullum Road for a family who lived there and then renamed Shawnee Run Road. Joseph later married Rachel Muchmore. Russell Sr.'s life was also touched by tragedy when Helen died of scarlet fever at age seven. (Courtesy Roger Ward.)

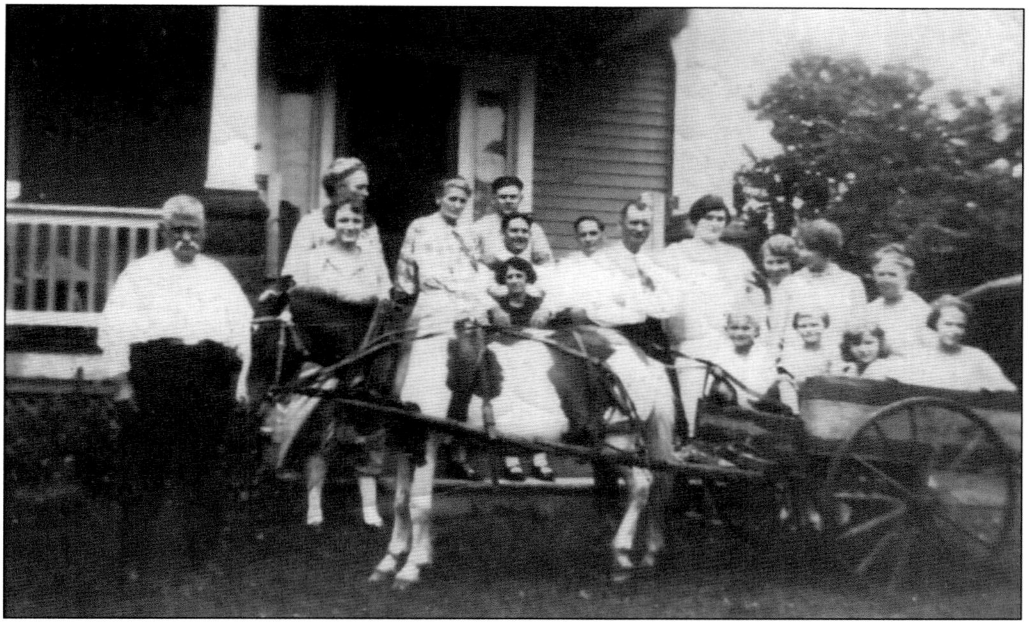

A pony cart and a yard full of relatives at the home of Bertha and Russell Ward Sr. promise an eventful Sunday afternoon around 1927. Bertha (first woman on the left) often cooked Sunday dinners for up to 25 people, recalls grandson Roger Ward. Russell Sr. is the second man to the left in the photograph; Russell Jr. holds the pony's reins, with Helen beside him. (Courtesy Roger Ward.)

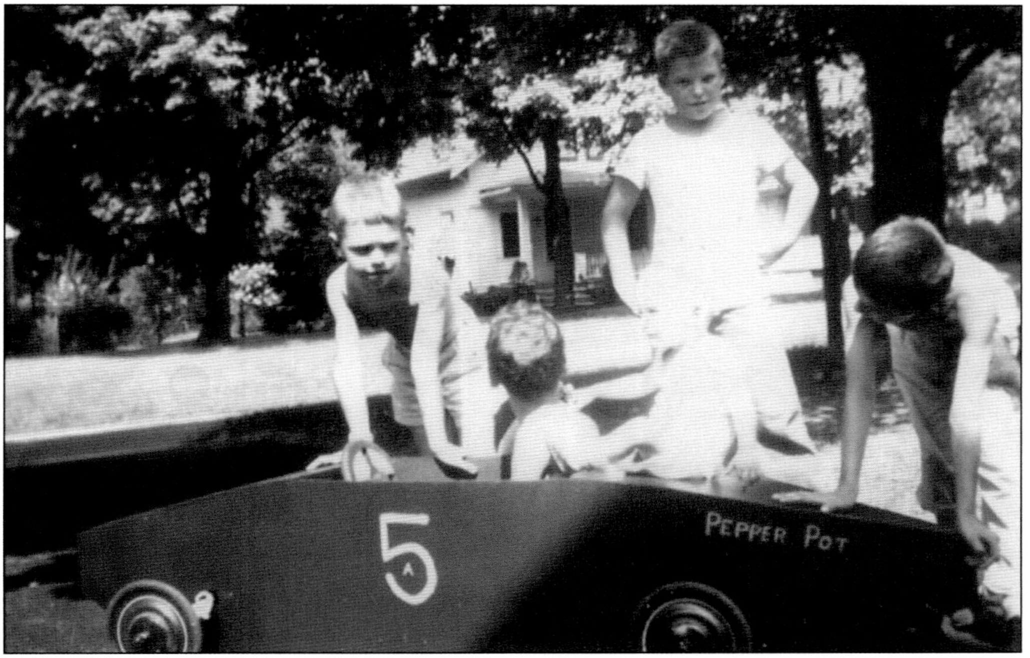

From left to right, Cub Scouts Don Scherer, Jack Akester, David Akester, Bill Williamson, and Larry Bobb prepare their jitney for a race. In the late 1940s, the scouts participated in soapbox races down Euclid Hill. They were led by James C. Perin and Martin Strifler. (Courtesy Madeira Historical Society.)

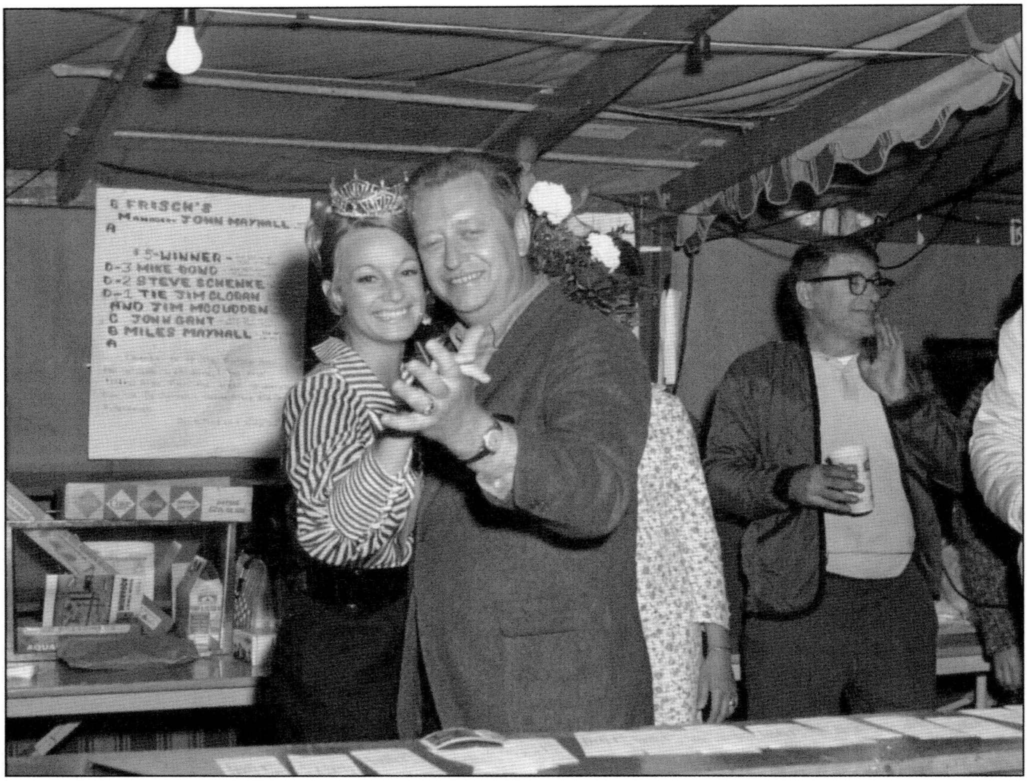

Mayor Daniel D. McDonald and Patty Perin dance at the 1969 Madeira Recreation Association Festival, which was held annually to raise funds for parks and recreation. Perin, daughter of James C. and Virginia Perin, was named Miss Madeira for the day; she had been chosen Miss Cincinnati for 1968. Another Madeira girl, Karen Stewart, was Miss Cincinnati in 1967. (Courtesy Daniel D. McDonald.)

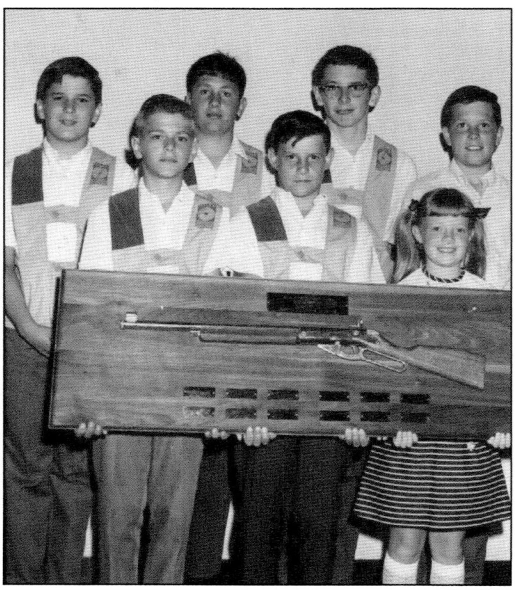

Members of the Madeira-Kenwood Jaycees Air Rifle Team won the Ohio air-rifle competition and placed 17th internationally in the spring of 1968. The shooters are, from left to right, (first row) James Arthur, Jerry Johnson, and Susan Floer; (second row) Robert Uecher, Randall Marts, William Powell, and Kent Ernsting. Floer shot 366 out of 400 points, with Powell close behind with 363. Floer, 8 years old, was the daughter of coach Richard Floer. (Courtesy Daniel D. McDonald.)

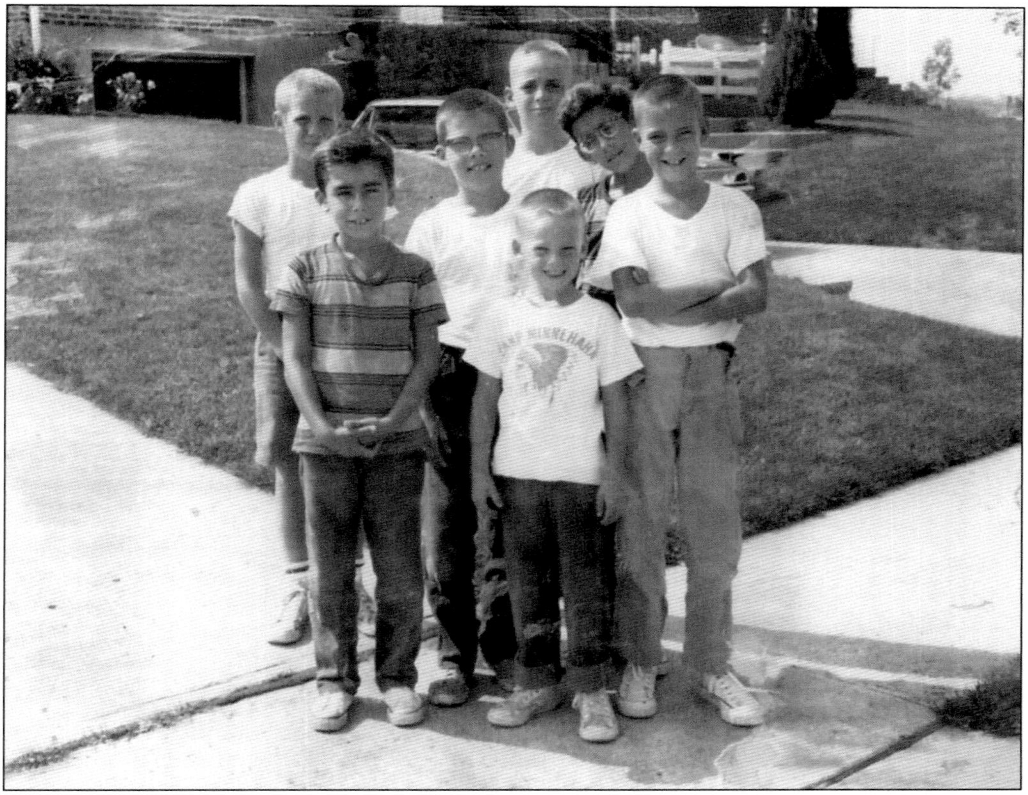

The Buckeye Crescent gang takes a break from play in the summer of 1960. From left to right (first row) are Richie Basile, Scott Kincaid, and Steve Kincaid; (second row) Steve Pieczonka, Billy Grundemann, Jeff Kincaid, and Tommy Basile. The gang was named for a street in their neighborhood. (Courtesy Mildred Kincaid.)

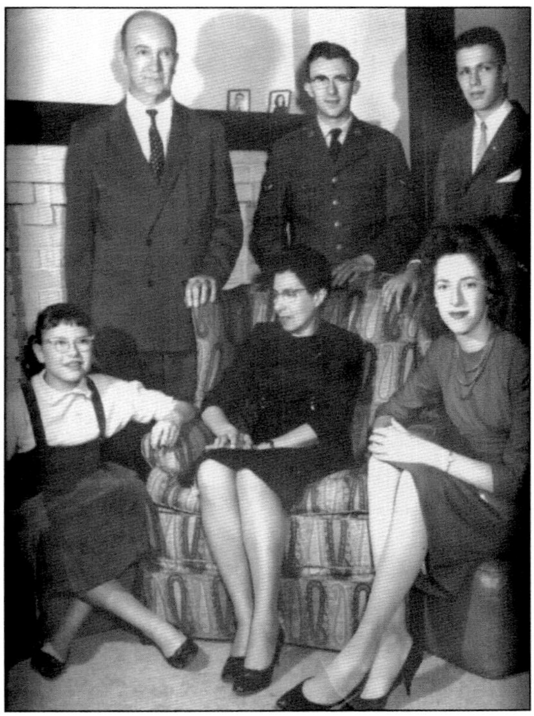

Bruce and Elizabeth Miller's family was the fourth to live in the 1922 Sears and Roebuck catalog house at 7226 Miami Avenue. The home's large lot was enhanced by a pond (which was home to a pet alligator), fruit trees, and gardens over the years. In 1999, Elizabeth Miller donated the property to the Madeira Historical Society, which uses it as a headquarters and museum. (Courtesy Madeira Historical Society.)

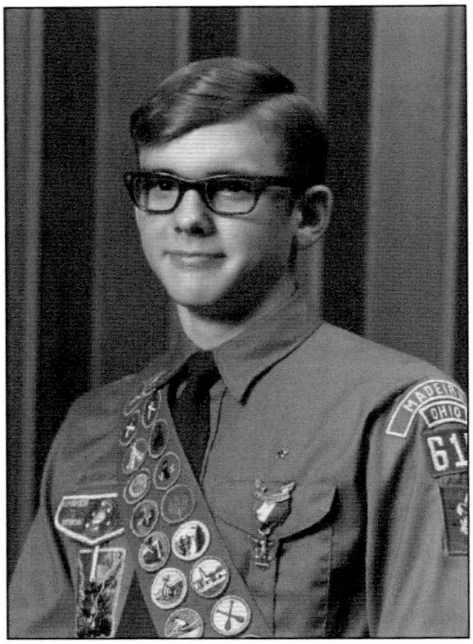

Fifteen-year-old Scott D. Johnson, a sophomore at Madeira High School, shows off an awarded Eagle Scout badge at a court of honor on Sunday evening, March 1, 1970, at St. Paul United Methodist Church. He was a senior patrol leader for Troop 616 at this time and active in Scouting since 1966. He served as a crew leader at Dan Beard Council Aquatic Camp and earned the Scout lifeguard award in 1969. (Courtesy Scott Johnson.)

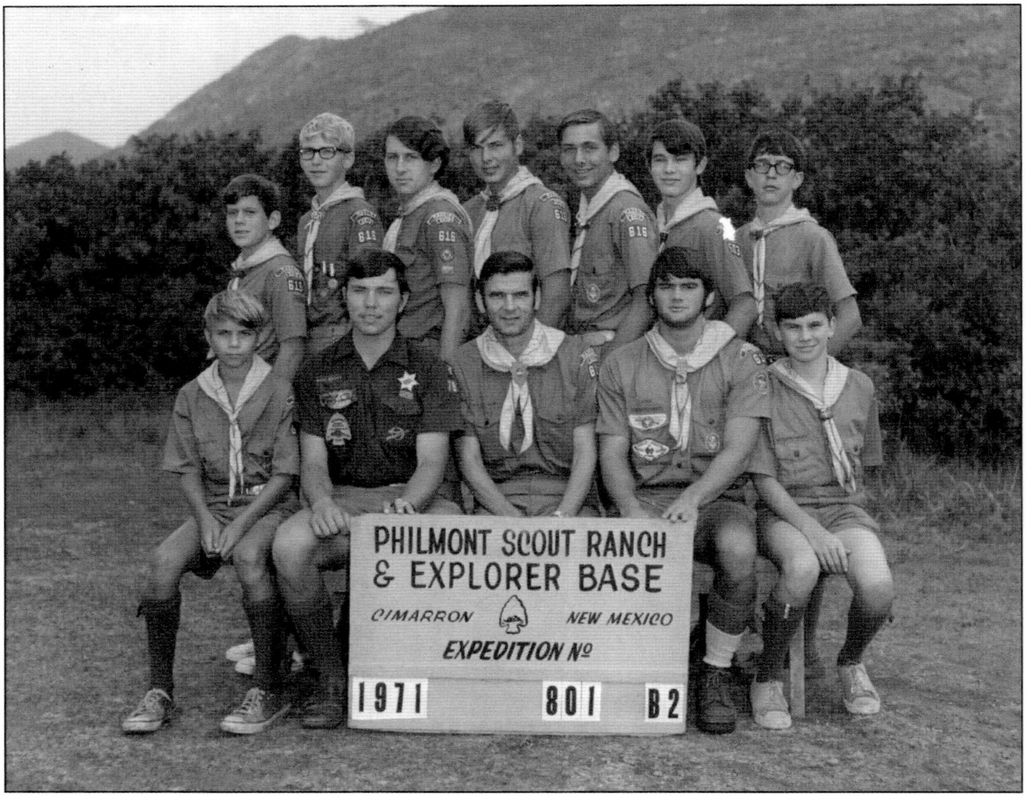

Scouts from Troop 616 pose for a picture at Philmont Scout Ranch in Cimarron, New Mexico, where they hiked, camped, and rappelled in 1971. From left to right are (first row) William Toth, guide Mark Brixey, scoutmaster Robert D. Johnson, assistant scoutmaster Stephan Johnson, and Steve MacWilliams; (second row) Bruce Spitler, James Rindin, Thomas Storch, Steve Hanor, Mark Axelson, Dan Quinn, and Steve Wilson. (Courtesy Stephan Johnson.)

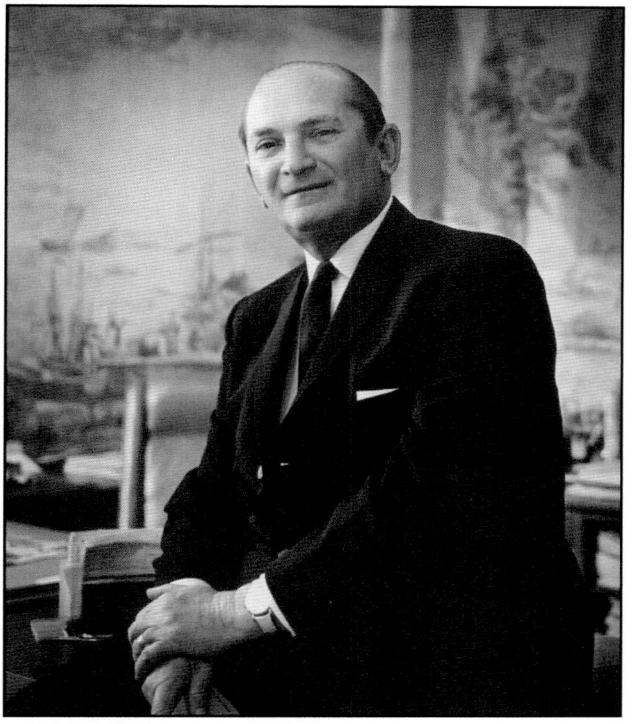

Arguably the best-known Madeira resident, David Frisch opened the first year-round drive-in restaurant, the Mainliner, in Fairfax in 1939. In 1946, Frisch introduced the Big Boy sandwich based on Californian Bob Wian's idea. Frisch and his wife, Annette, lived in Madeira in the 1950s and 1960s, as did their daughters and their families. "It was a great place to grow up," said granddaughter Karen Maier. (Courtesy Karen Maier.)

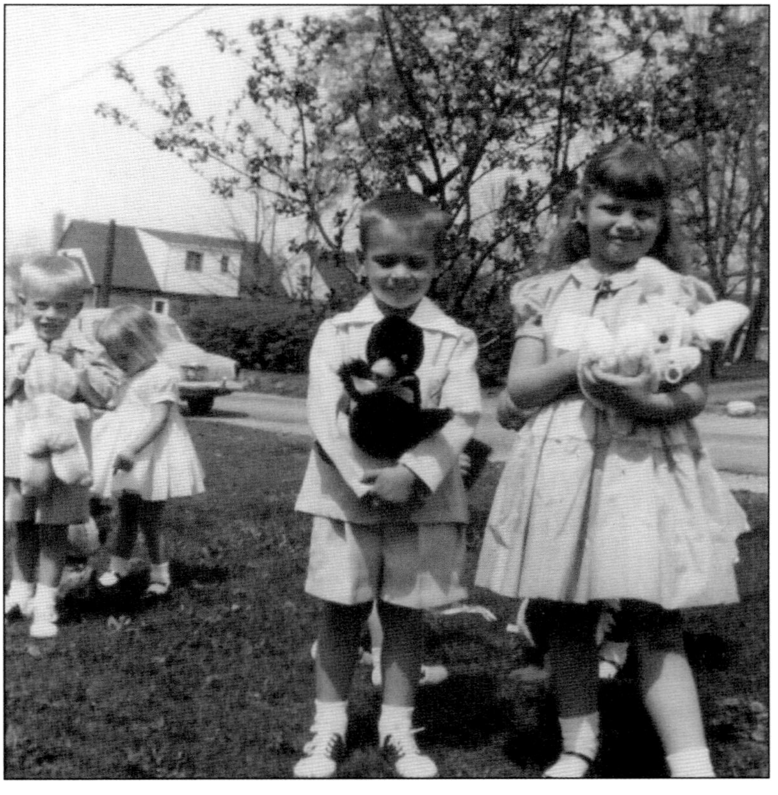

From left to right, Michael Maier, Karen Maier, Craig Maier, and Pam Heinechen enjoy Easter activities around 1954 at the Cherokee Lane home of their grandparents David and Annette Frisch. The Cherokee house was the site of many sleepovers, and on Monday nights (when Frisch's restaurants were closed), the men of the family cooked for the large clan. The Frischs also participated in the Madeira Recreation Association's annual festival. (Courtesy Karen Maier.)

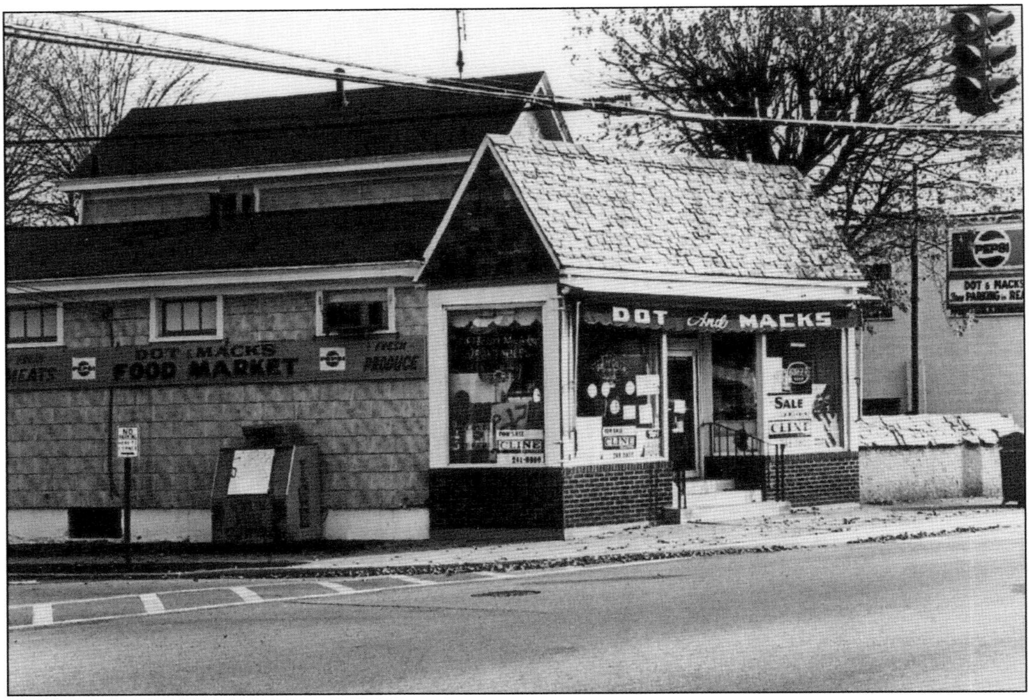

Dot and Mack's grocery was a popular destination for shoppers for many years at the intersection of Miami and Laurel Avenues. Mack and Dot Baldridge lived in the house adjoining the store. The grocery was previously Hemsath's; the Tices operated it before that. (Courtesy Roger Ward.)

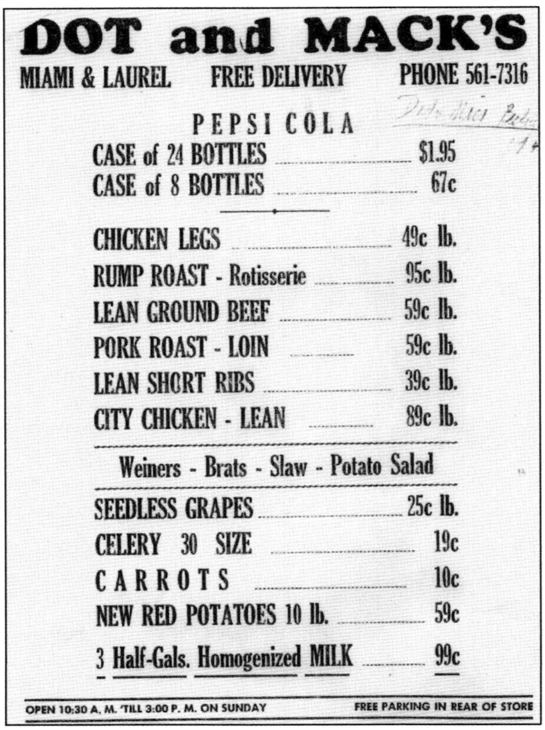

DOT and MACK'S

MIAMI & LAUREL FREE DELIVERY PHONE 561-7316

PEPSI COLA

CASE of 24 BOTTLES	$1.95
CASE of 8 BOTTLES	67c
CHICKEN LEGS	49c lb.
RUMP ROAST - Rotisserie	95c lb.
LEAN GROUND BEEF	59c lb.
PORK ROAST - LOIN	59c lb.
LEAN SHORT RIBS	39c lb.
CITY CHICKEN - LEAN	89c lb.

Weiners - Brats - Slaw - Potato Salad

SEEDLESS GRAPES	25c lb.
CELERY 30 SIZE	19c
CARROTS	10c
NEW RED POTATOES 10 lb.	59c
3 Half-Gals. Homogenized MILK	99c

OPEN 10:30 A. M. 'TILL 3:00 P. M. ON SUNDAY FREE PARKING IN REAR OF STORE

All the ingredients for a cookout were available from Dot and Mack's Market at Miami and Laurel Avenues back in the day when city chicken was 89¢ a pound, eight bottles of Pepsi cost 67¢, and Sunday hours were a novelty. (Courtesy Madeira Historical Society.)

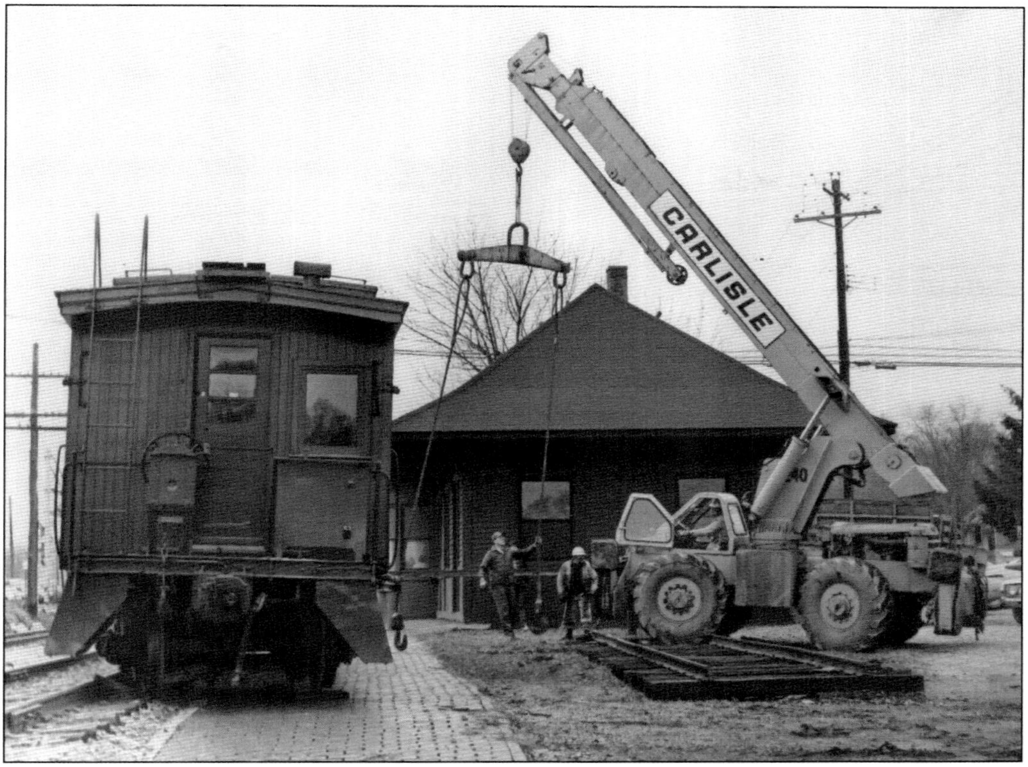

Workmen ready a caboose to be placed on the tracks at the Madeira train depot in June 1972. Nelson Stewart was railroad dispatcher at the time. (Courtesy Madeira Historical Society.)

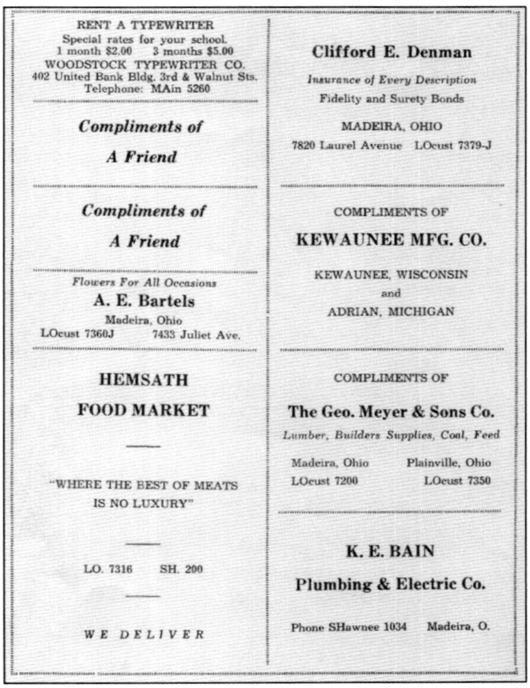

RENT A TYPEWRITER
Special rates for your school.
1 month $2.00 3 months $5.00
WOODSTOCK TYPEWRITER CO.
402 United Bank Bldg. 3rd & Walnut Sts.
Telephone: MAin 5260

Compliments of
A Friend

Compliments of
A Friend

Flowers For All Occasions
A. E. Bartels
Madeira, Ohio
LOcust 7360J 7433 Juliet Ave.

HEMSATH
FOOD MARKET

"WHERE THE BEST OF MEATS IS NO LUXURY"

LO. 7316 SH. 200

WE DELIVER

Clifford E. Denman
Insurance of Every Description
Fidelity and Surety Bonds
MADEIRA, OHIO
7820 Laurel Avenue LOcust 7379-J

COMPLIMENTS OF
KEWAUNEE MFG. CO.
KEWAUNEE, WISCONSIN
and
ADRIAN, MICHIGAN

COMPLIMENTS OF
The Geo. Meyer & Sons Co.
Lumber, Builders Supplies, Coal, Feed
Madeira, Ohio LOcust 7200
Plainville, Ohio LOcust 7350

K. E. BAIN
Plumbing & Electric Co.
Phone SHawnee 1034 Madeira, O.

Familiar Madeira names—Hemsath, Meyer, Bain—and period telephone numbers are evident on this list of businesses that helped sponsor the 1954 Madeira High Yearbook. That was when parents could rent typewriters for $2 a month to give their students an academic edge. (Madeira Board of Education.)

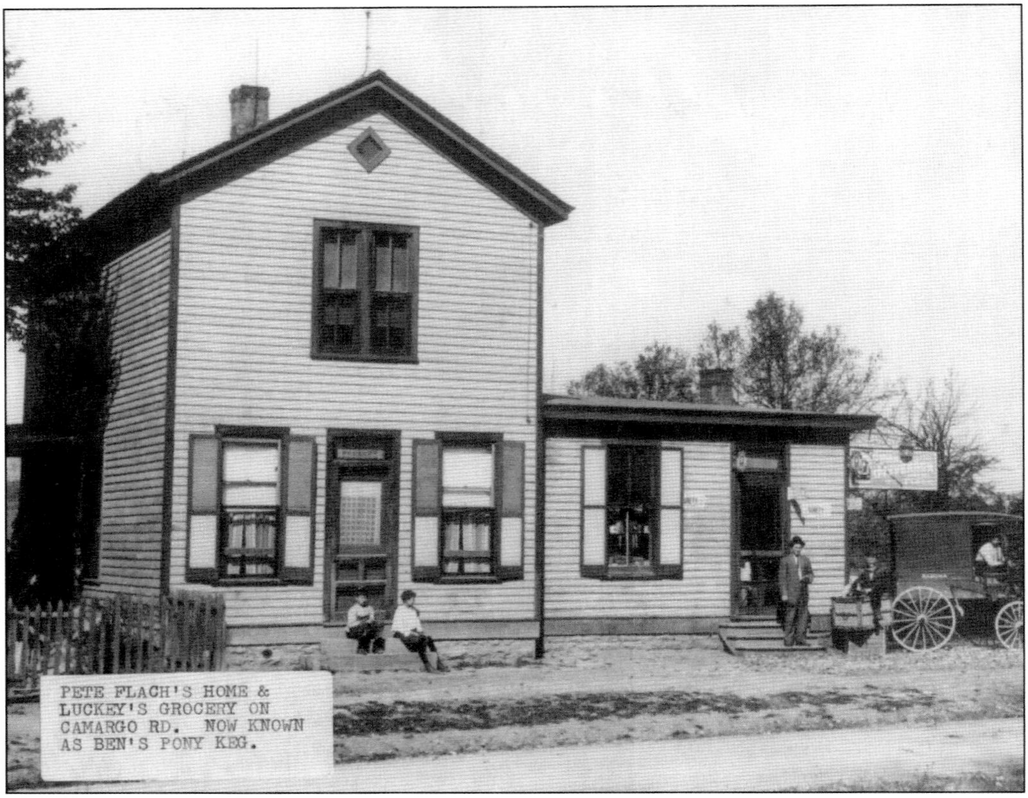

A deliveryman from Luckey's Grocery prepares to make deliveries to neighborhood homes around 1920. Every neighborhood had a corner grocery then, often attached to the owner's home. Pete Flach lived in the house shown here. The store on Camargo Road was where Ben's Pony Keg was later built. (Courtesy Madeira Historical Society.)

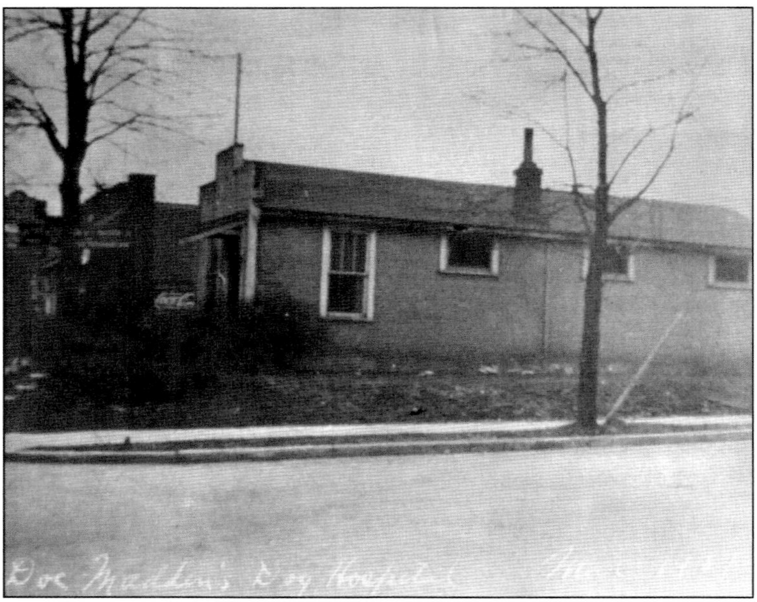

The Camargo Bank of Madeira, shown here prior to 1937, had the distinction of being written up in *Ripley's Believe It or Not* as the world's smallest bank. The building, at the corner of Miami and Laurel Avenues, later became Dr. A. G. Madden's veterinarian hospital. Adrien Pharmacy is at the location today. (Courtesy Madeira Historical Society.)

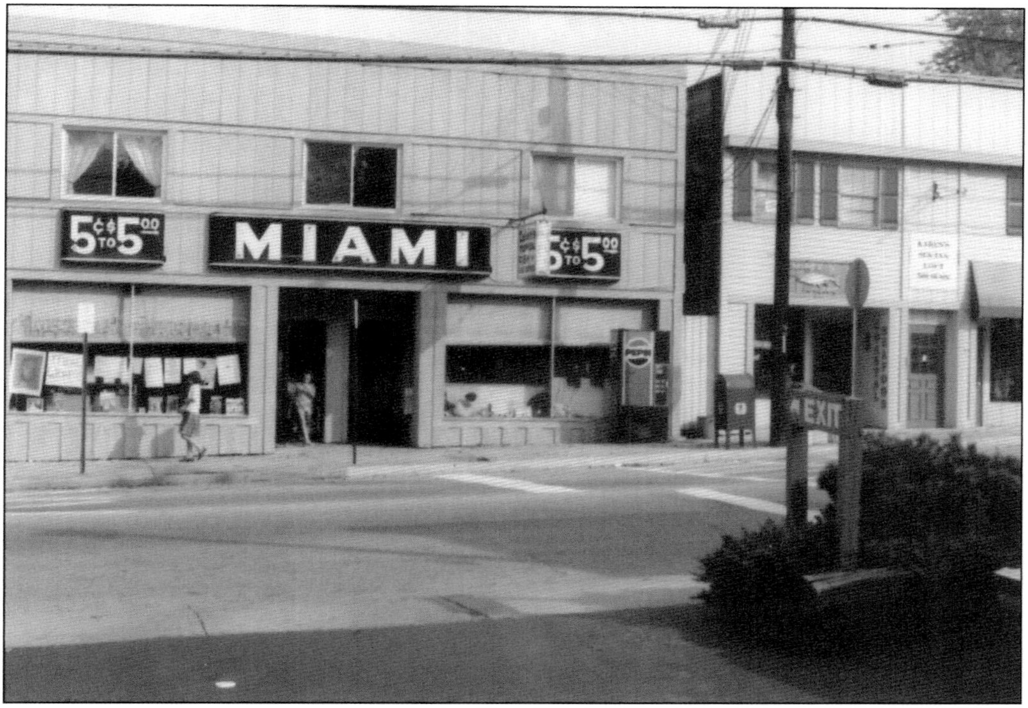

Generations of youngsters visited the Miami 5¢ to $5 Store on Miami Avenue in different reincarnations over the years to buy Aurora monster model kits, model airplanes, paper dolls, cosmetic kits, and novelty items that made their parents cringe. The whole family could buy virtually anything there, from gifts to baby supplies. (Courtesy Madeira Historical Society.)

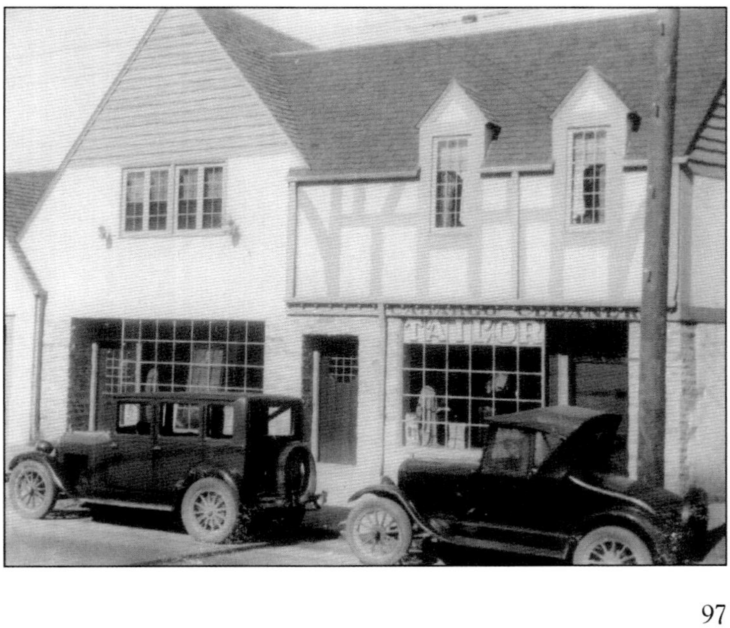

The Fleishman Building, shown here around 1936 near the northeast corner of Camargo Road near Miami Avenue, was home to many businesses over the years including a restaurant, tavern, automobile repair shop, bank, floor-covering shop, art gallery, and the Madeira Village Pharmacy. In this photograph, signs for Camargo Cleaners and a tailor shop can be seen on the right. (Courtesy Madeira Historical Society.)

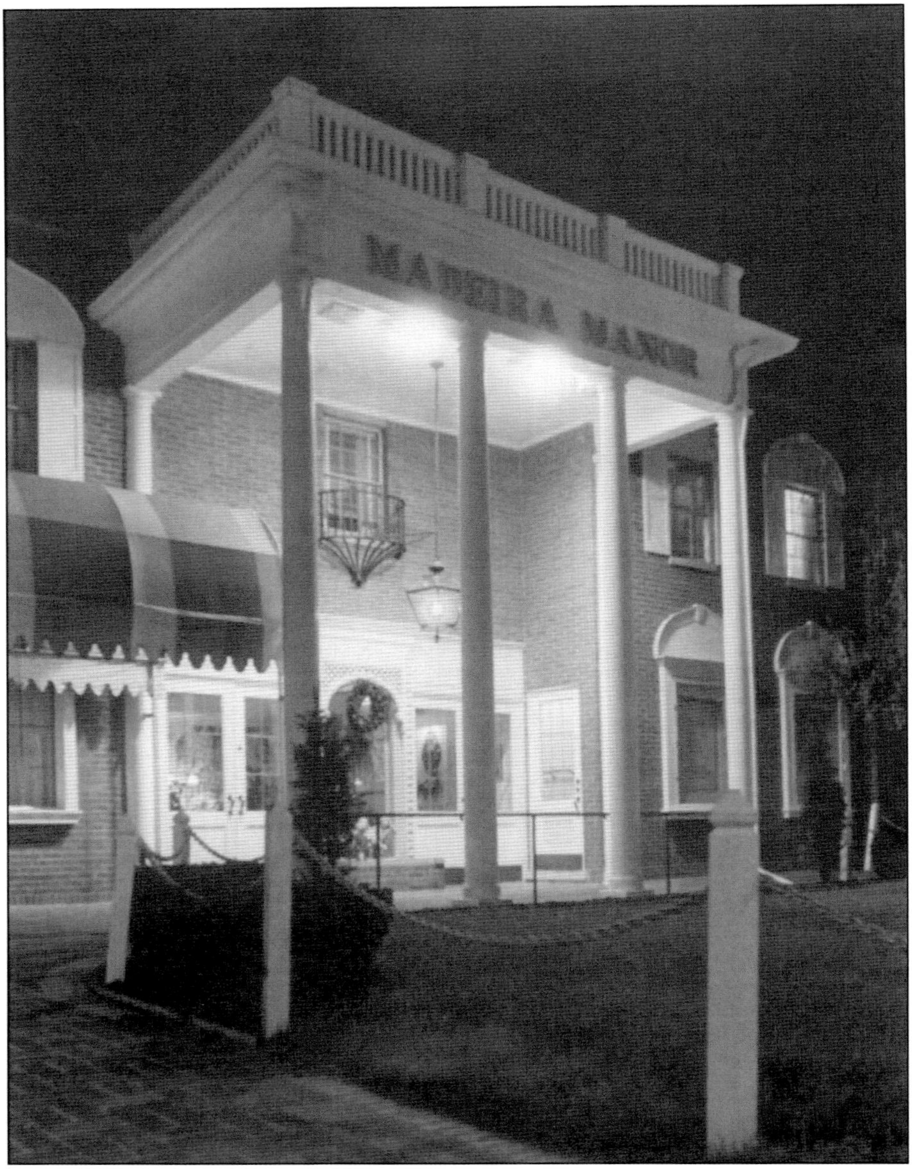

Before it was Madeira Manor, this was the Camargo Theater, built around 1946, according to resident Robert Wick. Tickets were 35¢ and popcorn was 10¢ in the 1960s, recalls Roger Ward. Owners Mr. and Mrs. Robert "Red" Strauss were strict with children. "If they made too much noise, Mr. Strauss would push a button . . . to signal Chuck Brady, the projectionist, to stop the movie. When he was done yelling, he would press it again, and Chuck would restart the film," Ward said. James Eichman, who ushered at the theater in the mid-1960s, remembers Mr. Strauss as a "grandfatherly figure" who provided a family-oriented setting where parents felt comfortable dropping the kids off for a matinee double feature. When a "racy" preview of an Elizabeth Taylor movie ran, Strauss muted the sound and had the ushers distract the youngsters. Camargo Theater closed in the late 1960s after Kenwood Theater opened. After remodeling, the Madeira Manor became the site of many banquets and special dinners. Actor Ray Bolger once lunched there after speaking to the Kenwood Women's Club. (Courtesy Daniel D. McDonald.)

Following a campaign lunch at the Madeira Manor, Sen. Robert Dole (left), Dale Schmidt (center), and Senate candidate Robert Taft step outside for a picture session on August 1, 1970. Dole was in town to support Taft. (Courtesy Daniel D. McDonald.)

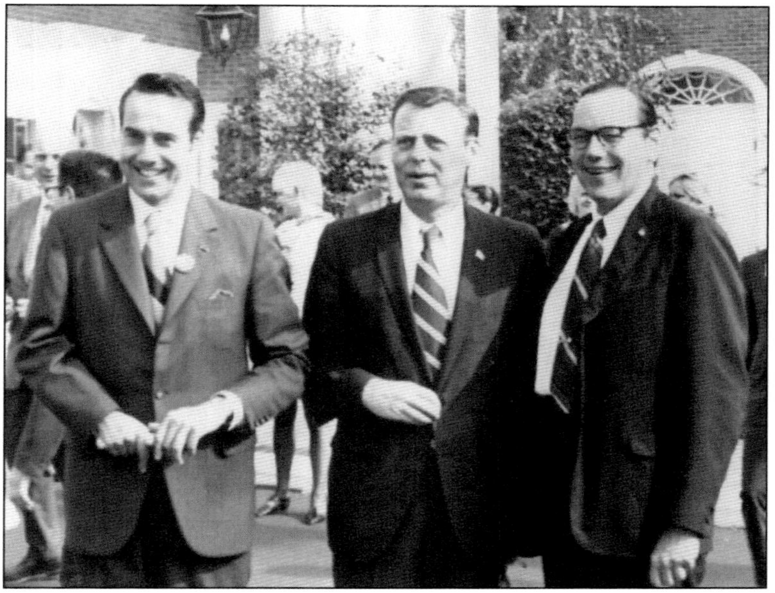

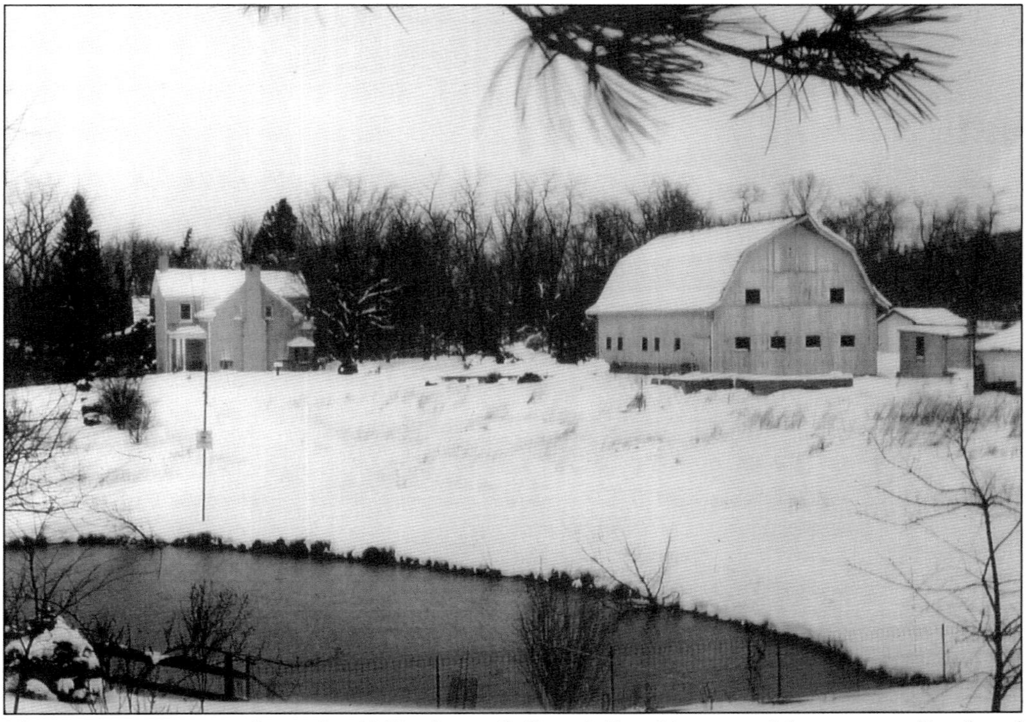

This picturesque view from the 1960s shows Galbraith Road between Montgomery Road and Miami Avenue. A spring-fed pond stocked with fish and visited by snapping turtles and muskrats harkens back to Madeira's rural past when the area was known for its apple orchards, plum and cherry trees, as well as pear trees, then a regional rarity. (Courtesy Madeira Historical Society.)

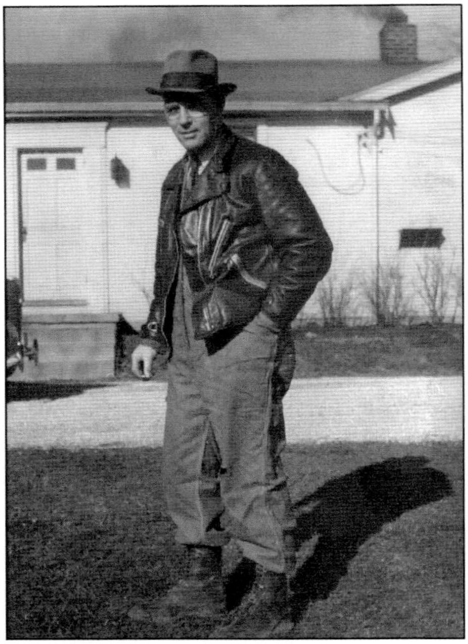

Scores of residents entrusted their pets' health to Dr. A. G. Madden (pictured), who worked as a veterinarian from the 1920s to 1979. His home and practice was at 7242 Miami Avenue on land originally owned by Christian Hetzler, son of pioneer Jacob Hetzler. Madden's daughter Phyllis fell in love with and married Bud Johnston, an Ohio State University student who came to intern with her dad. (Courtesy Madeira Historical Society.)

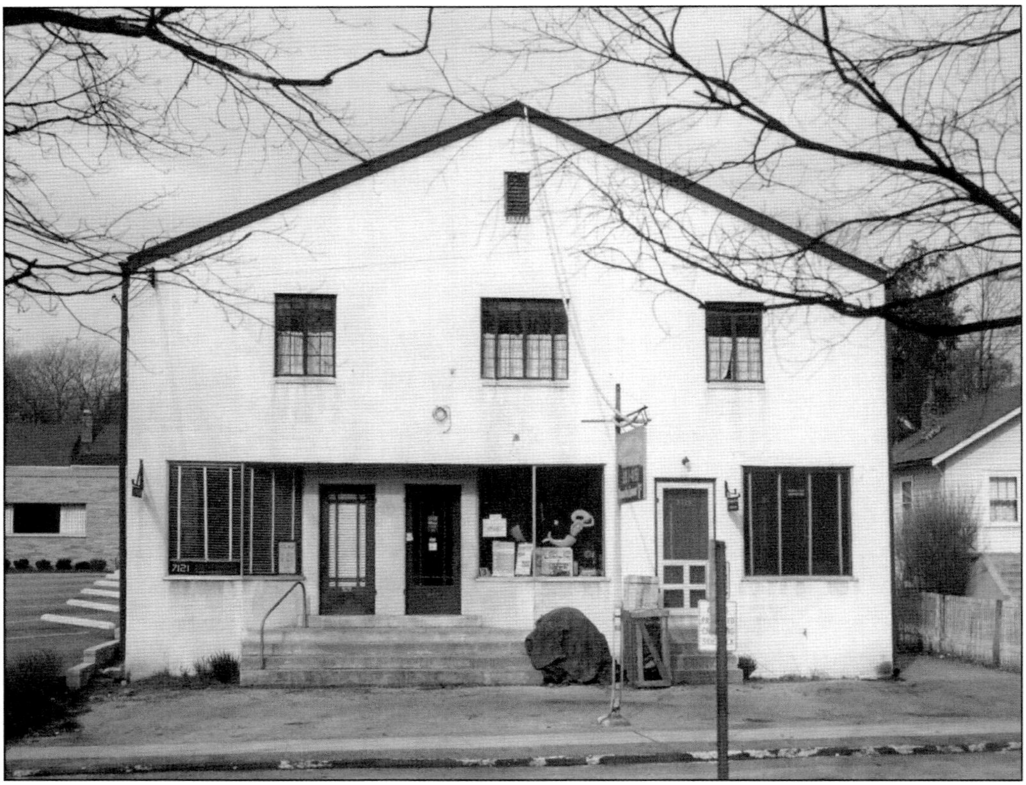

Dr. William Terwillegar hung out his shingle to practice family medicine in 1931 at 7121 Miami Avenue. He was still working in 1960 when Madeira celebrated its 50th anniversary and was very involved in the YMCA over the years. (Courtesy Madeira Historical Society.)

Charles J. Hosbrook holds his daughter, Cleo, in this *c.* 1905 photograph. She became a teacher at the Condon School for disabled children and participated in community life for many years. (Courtesy Madeira Historical Society.)

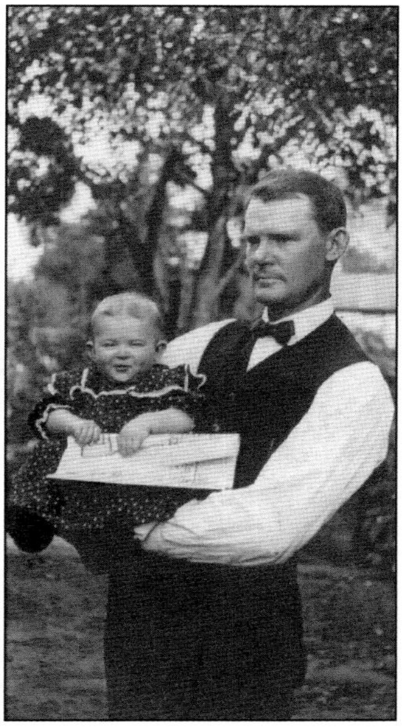

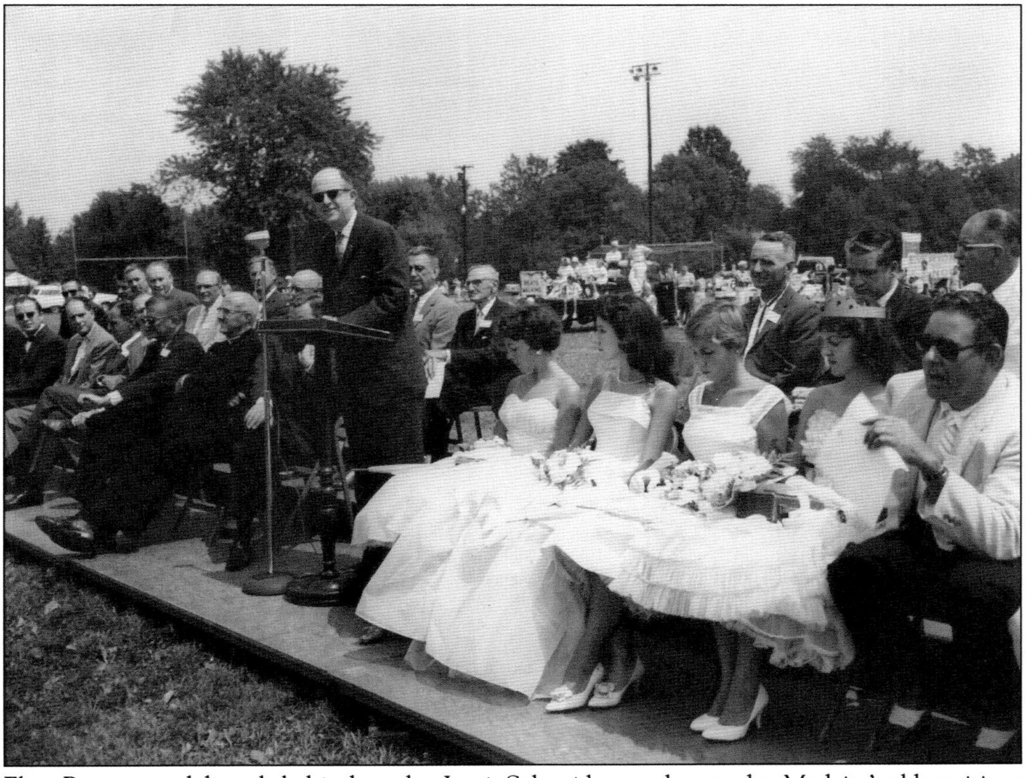

Eben Bean, seated directly behind speaker Louis Schneider, was honored as Madeira's oldest citizen at the city's 50th anniversary commemoration ceremonies at Camargo Elementary on August 13, 1960, following a welcoming speech by Mayor Daniel D. McDonald. To the right of Schneider are, from left to right, Miss Madeira candidates Sandy Perkins, unidentified, Andy Arbogast, and queen Sylvia Maxfield. (Courtesy Madeira Historical Society.)

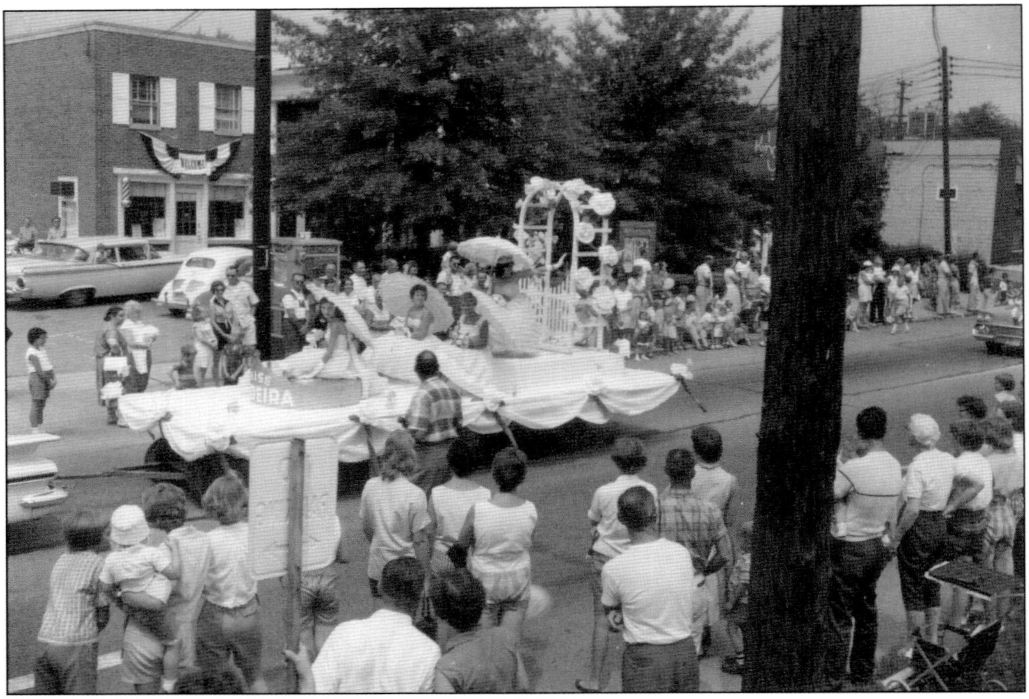

Residents watch the August 13, 1960, parade down Miami Avenue to mark the 50th anniversary of Madeira's incorporation. The American Legion sponsored the parade as part of the citywide celebration. Queen Sylvia Maxfield waves to the crowd from the queen's float. Next to the unidentified young woman to the far left on the front of the float are Sandy Perkins (left) and Andy Arbogast. (Courtesy Madeira Historical Society.)

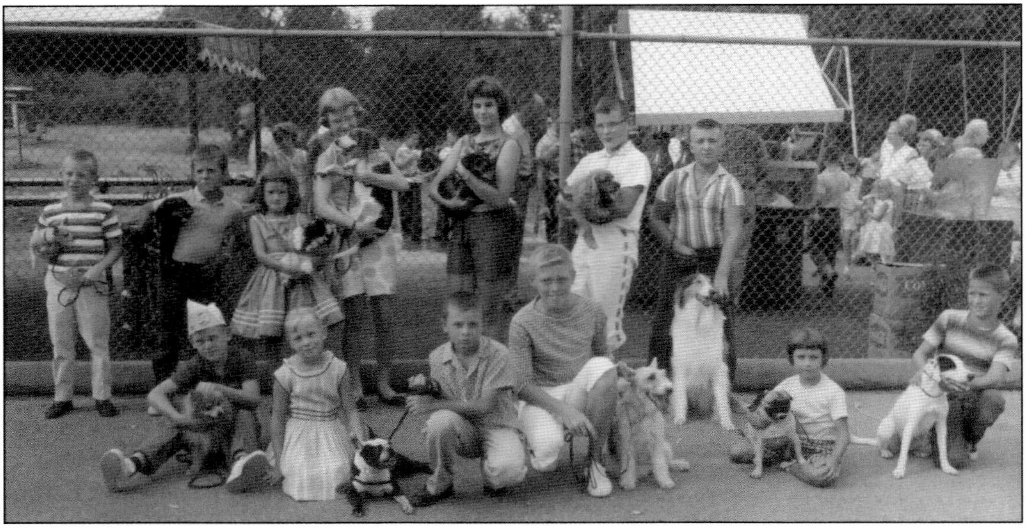

Youngsters grin with their dogs at the pet show sponsored by St. Gertrude's Boy Scout troop on August 12, 1960, in the village park as part of Madeira's 50th anniversary. The population at that time stood at 6,500 people. A baked-goods contest, baby show, refreshment stands, and dance were all part of the festivities. The 100th anniversary celebration in 2010 promises to be even bigger. (Courtesy Madeira Historical Society.)

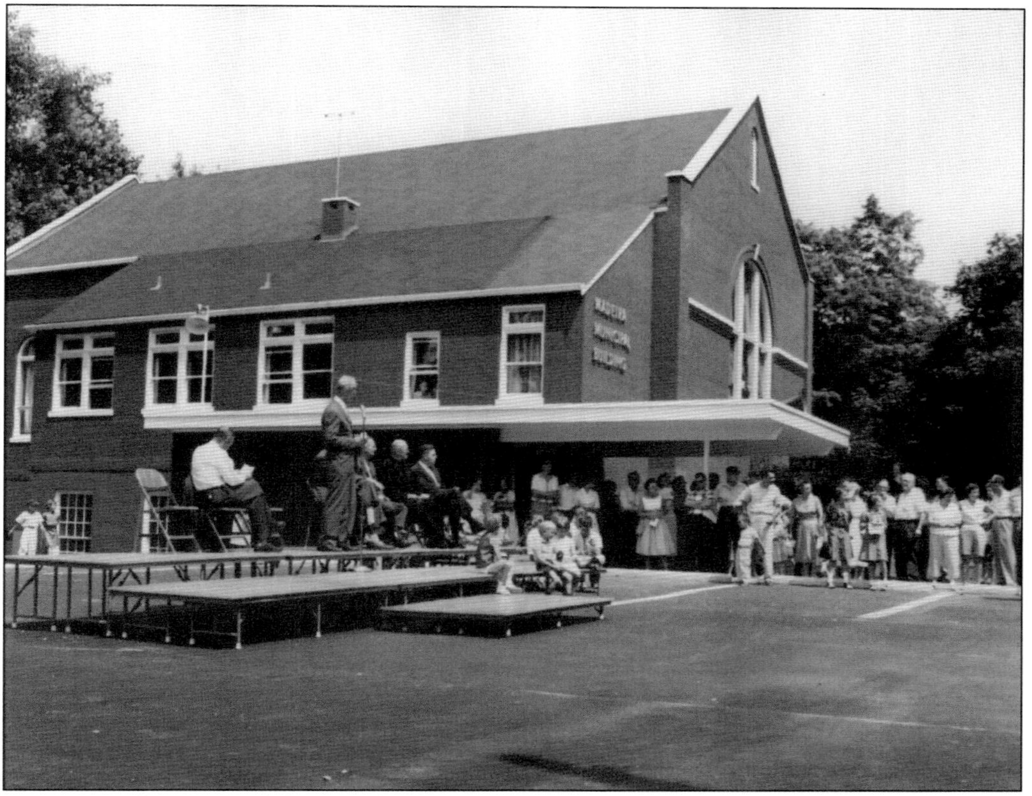

Mayor Russell Patten presides over the dedication of the new city administration building in 1958. The city purchased the former Methodist church at Miami and Euclid Avenues when the church expanded and decided to build a new sanctuary. As mayor from 1958 to 1959, Patten ushered in a charter form of government. He was succeeded by Daniel D. McDonald, who served as mayor from 1960 to 1977. (Courtesy Madeira Historical Society.)

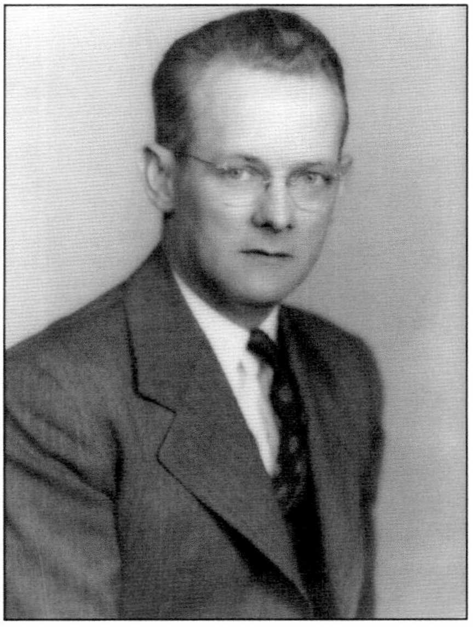

Albert Swift was the youngest mayor in Ohio when he first held office in 1938 and 1939; he also served from 1942 to 1944. He helped to form the Hamilton County Police Association and a river cleanup system. (Courtesy Daniel D. McDonald.)

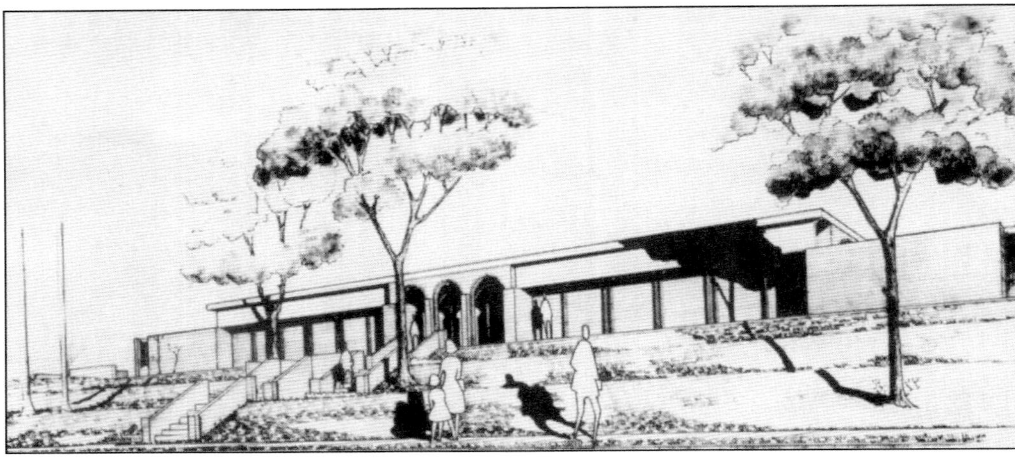

When the branch library inside the Madeira Municipal Building proved inadequate for patrons, the Hamilton County Library Board considered two new locations: one at Shawnee Run and Miami Avenue in Columbia Township and one at Miami and Euclid Avenues. City council and the Madeira School Board wanted the library within walking distance of the majority of Madeira students. The Madeira council offered the library board $30,000 over a 10-year period if the branch was located in the city. After much debate, the Miami and Euclid Avenues location was picked. Pictured below at the July 1964 ground-breaking, from left to right, are city manager John Griffin, contractor William Lichtenberg, associate architect Ray Roush, architect Carl Strauss, library business manager Howard Uible, Mayor Daniel D. McDonald, library board president Ina Warner Broeman, and librarian Ernest I. Miller. The library opened on June 14, 1965. (Both courtesy Madeira Historical Society.)

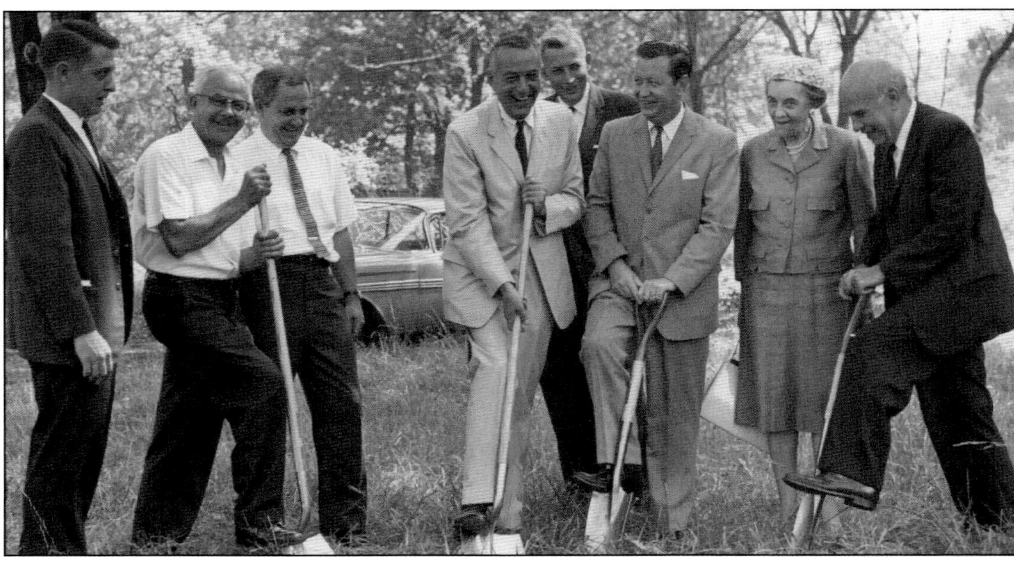

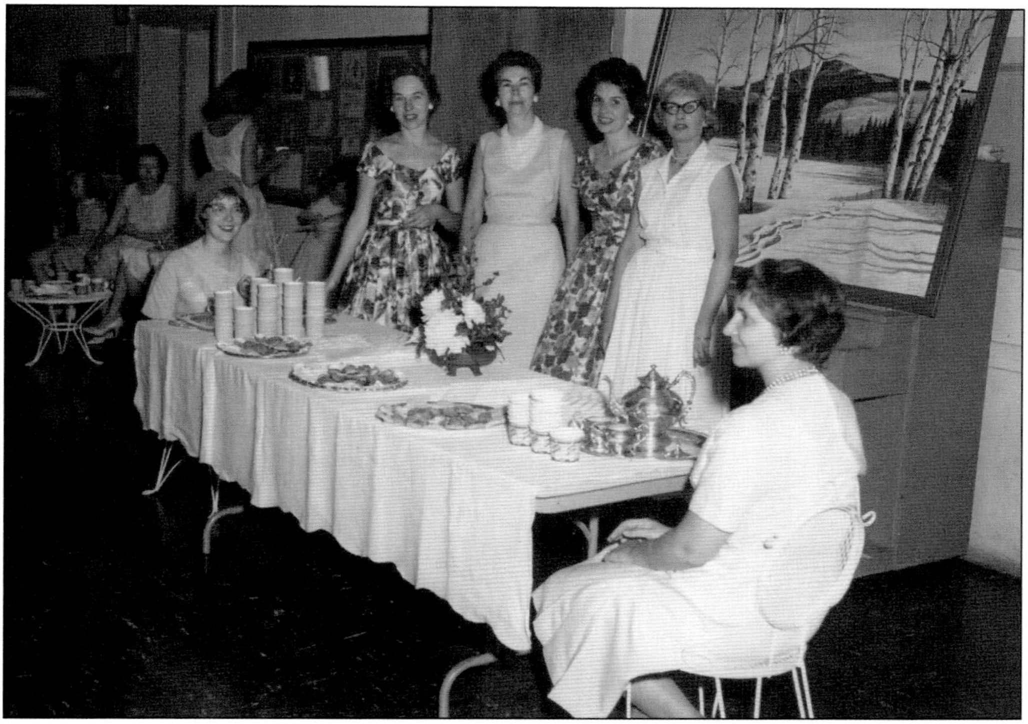

Members of the Eastern Hills Jr. Woman's Club prepare for an art show in 1962. Still active today as the Madeira Woman's Club, the group operates the Clothes Closet to generate money for charitable causes and sponsors the Madeira Art Fair each spring. From left to right are Myra Griffin, Betty Gerber, Mary Jane Cullen, Hattie Lou Schneider, Jean Bachman, and Marilyn Glasgow. (Courtesy of the Madeira Woman's Club.)

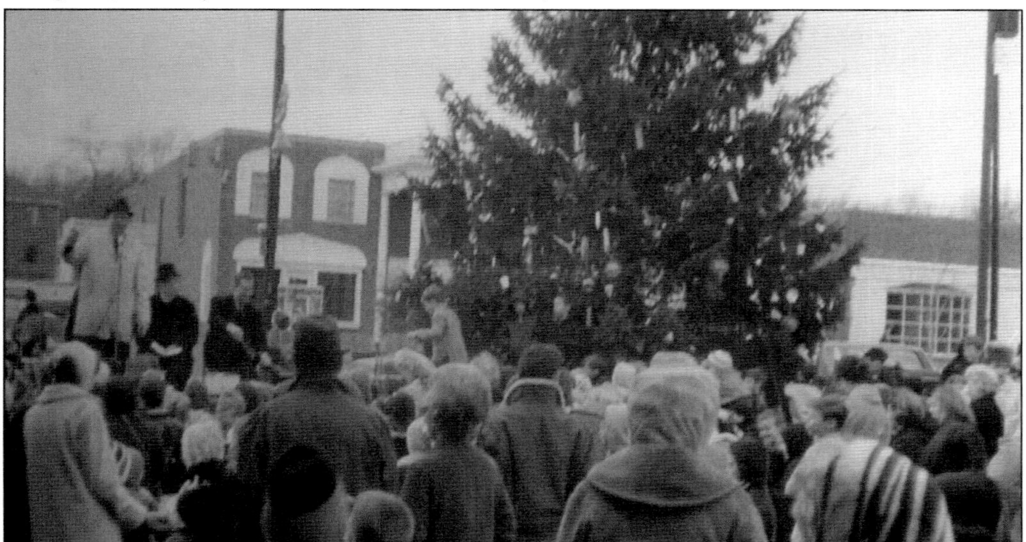

Residents gather for the community Christmas tree–lighting ceremony in 1966. The Madeira Recreation Association coordinated the annual event with various civic groups. Santa's visit was always a highlight. (Courtesy Madeira Historical Society.)

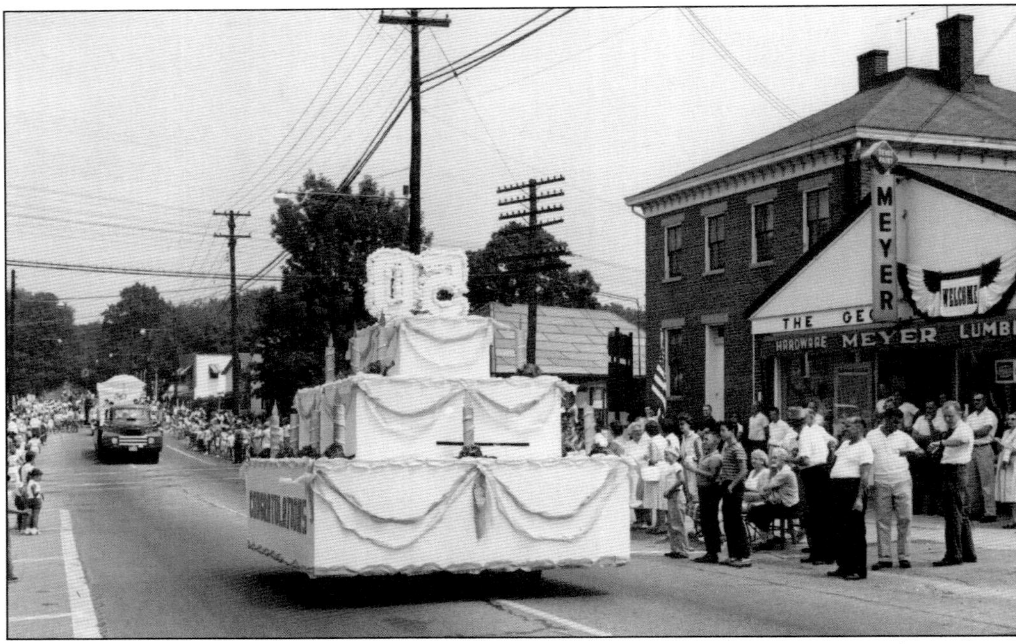

Fifty years of change are reflected in this scene during the Golden Anniversary Parade on Miami Avenue, as the birthday cake float glides by the George Meyer Hardware and Lumber Store on August 13, 1960. The Meyer company started out as a coal, feed, and building-supplies store. (Courtesy Madeira Historical Society.)

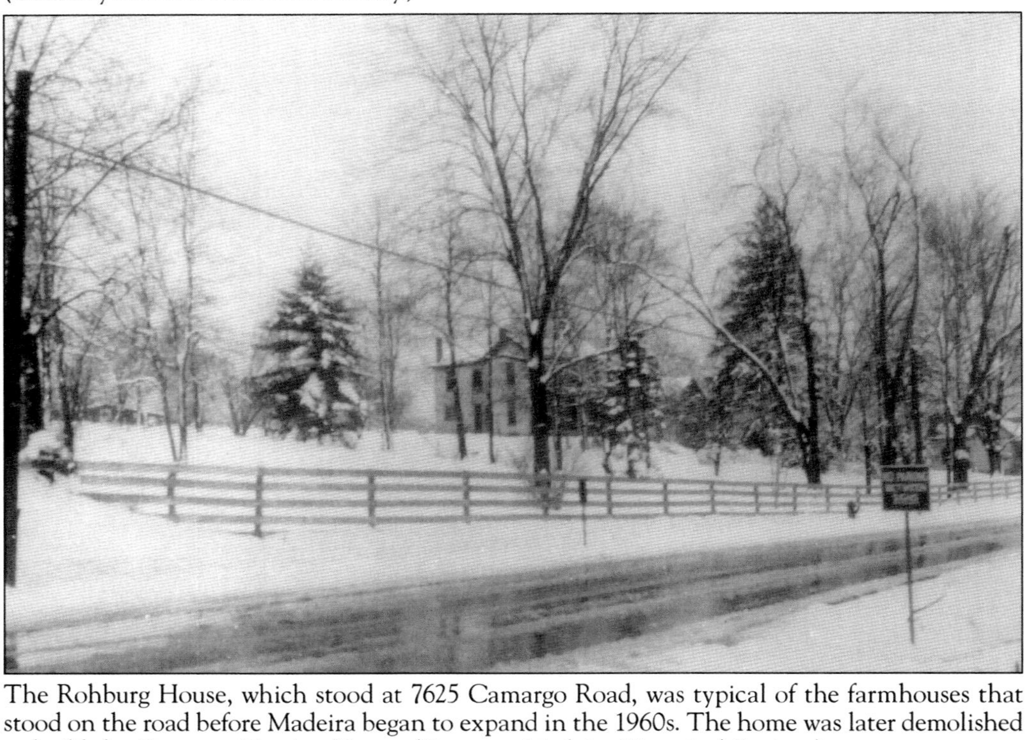

The Rohburg House, which stood at 7625 Camargo Road, was typical of the farmhouses that stood on the road before Madeira began to expand in the 1960s. The home was later demolished to build the Camargo Nursing Home. (Courtesy Madeira Historical Society.)

Mayor Daniel D. McDonald presides over a city council meeting in this *c.* 1962 photograph. From left to right are Harold Caldwell, Carl Schneider, Carl Thornton, solicitor Aldon Kinney, Fr. James G. Joyce, McDonald, city manager John Griffin, Lewis Krehnbrink, Allen Reed, and James B. Long; clerk-treasurer Ed Hillman is seated in front of the mayor's desk. (Courtesy Daniel D. McDonald.)

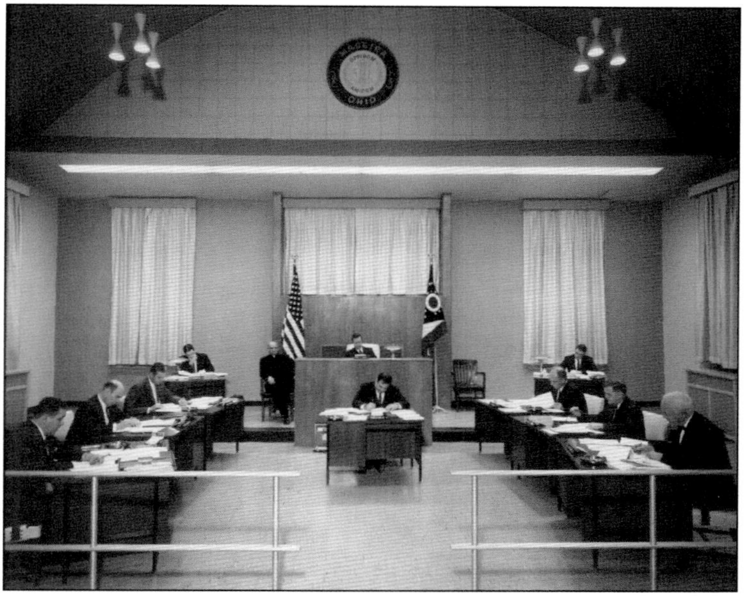

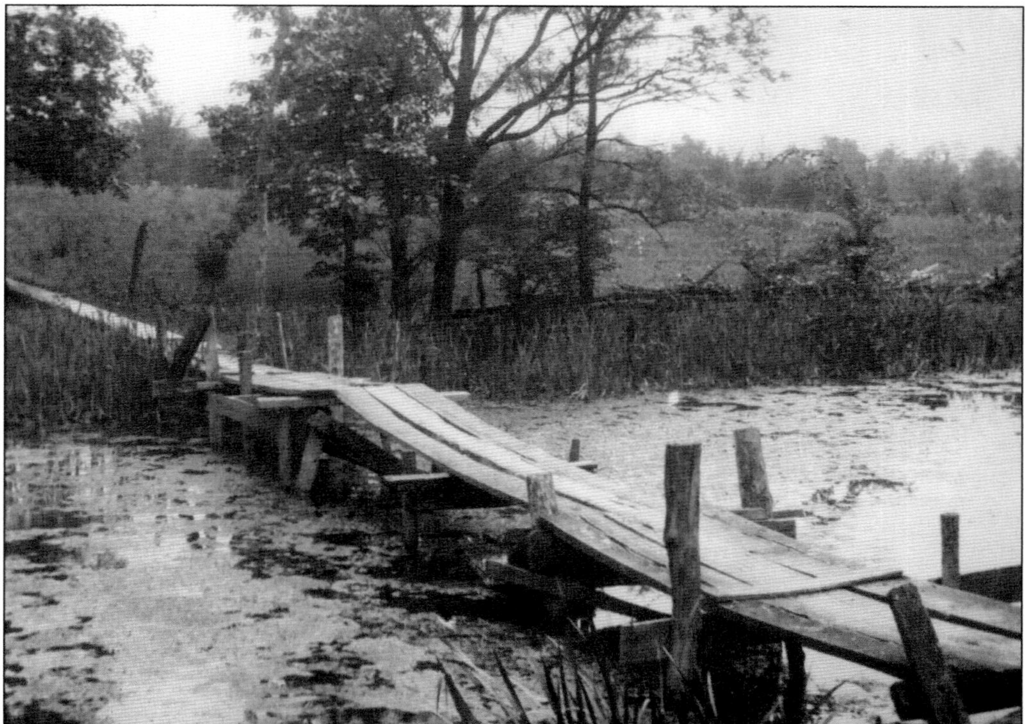

From Homer Hosbrook's backyard, now a subdivision, "a path led all the way to Miami Avenue through the Hosbrook Woods. It passed between two ponds, the larger one to the south, crossing on a plank bridge," wrote Naomi Bain Henn in her reminiscences. The larger pond was a popular spot for ice-skating. Sled riding down Laurel Hill was another favorite winter pastime. (Courtesy Madeira Historical Society.)

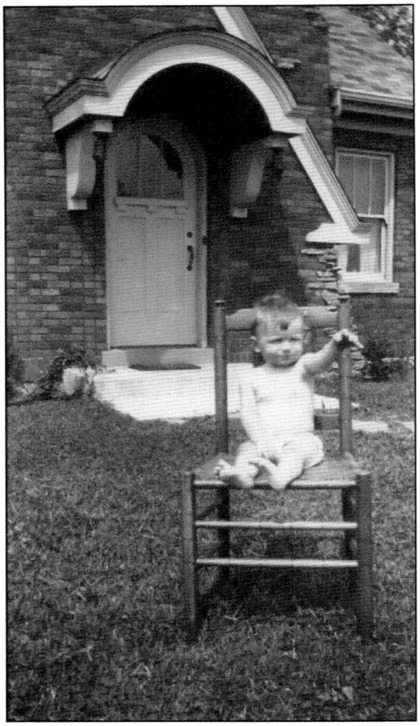

Young Norbert L. Henke sits in front of his home at 6462 Shawnee Run Road in 1929. His home was five houses down from his grandfather, William Henke's, farmhouse. Norbert would later attend school in a two-room schoolhouse in Madisonville. One room was for grades one through four; the second was for grades five through eight. (Courtesy Doris and Norbert Henke.)

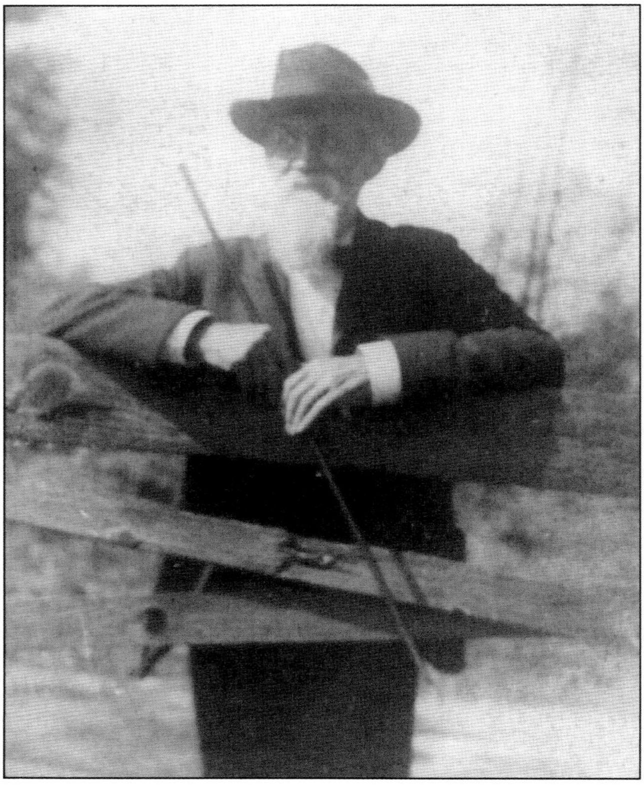

Samuel K. Druce became Madeira's first mayor after the village of 500 incorporated in 1910. He served from August 10, 1910, to December 31, 1913. The mayor was the great-grandson of William Druce, an early Madeira settler. Druce was born on what is today Miami Hills Drive; he married Sarah Dones in 1869. Her parents were among the first Madeira settlers. (Courtesy Madeira Historical Society.)

Ten

"Anudder Leedle Queez"

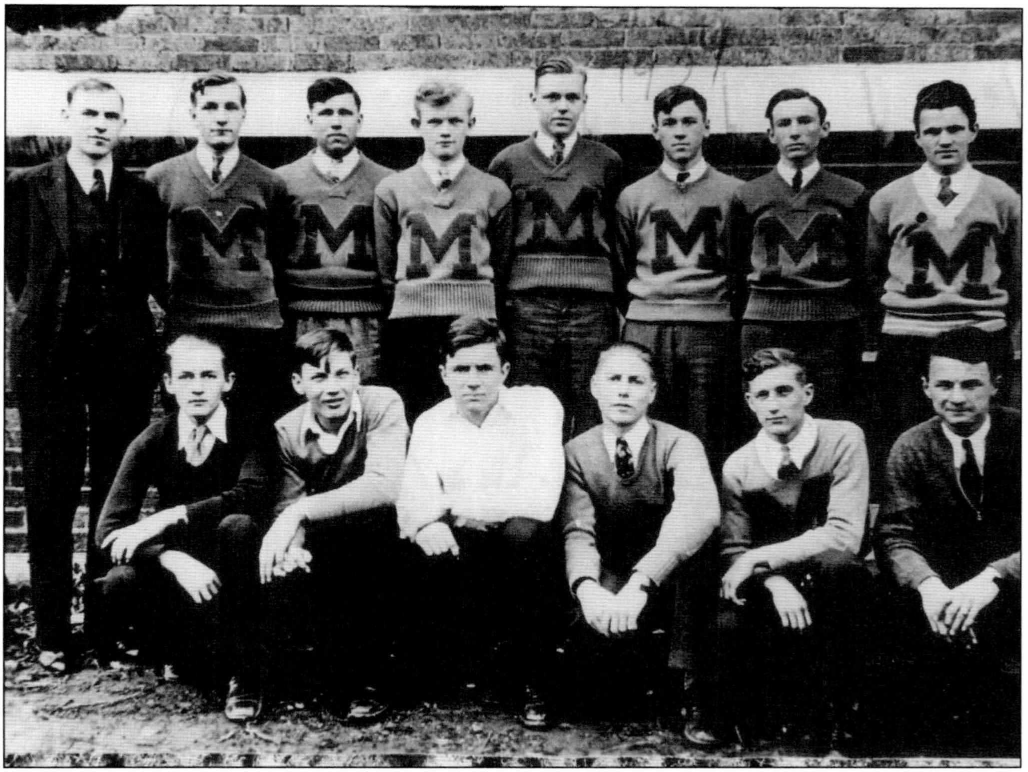

Young men in Madeira High School's HI-Y Club of 1934 pledged to adhere to a code of clean speech, clean sports, clean scholarship, and clean living. From left to right are (first row) Jack Tietz, Ted Browning, Charles (Bill) Emery, Paul Ballman, Elmer Rohman, Barney Scull; (second row) advisor W. Marshall Sellman, Ralph Borger, Warren Judd, Malcolm Bain, Don Dittler, Martin Strifler, Clifford J. Behrmann, and George Aery. (Courtesy Madeira Historical Society.)

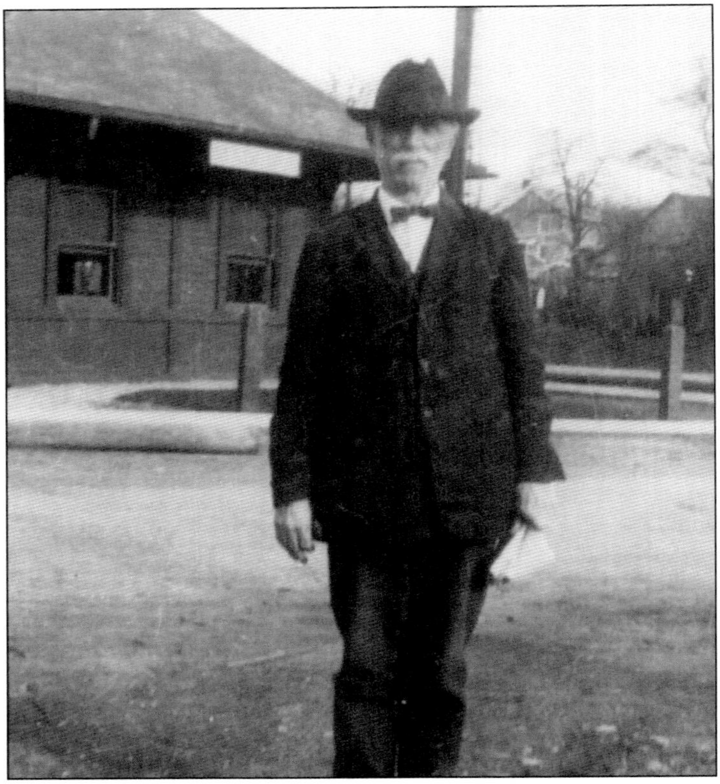

Zachary Taylor DeMar (1848–1946) taught in two other local schools before coming to Madeira schools in 1885. He was a teacher and principal in the Madeira public schools for 37 years and is acknowledged as the driving force in making Madeira schools effective in those decades. (Courtesy Madeira Historical Society.)

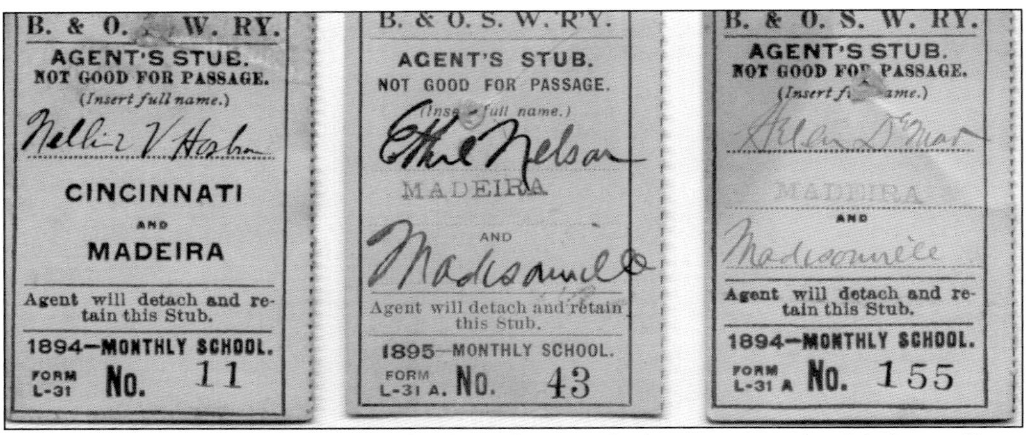

Before Madeira had its own high school, students took the train to either Madisonville or Cincinnati to pursue their diplomas. Here are the monthly train passes for pupils Nell Hosbrook, Ethel Nelson, and Helen DeMar. (Courtesy Madeira Historical Society.)

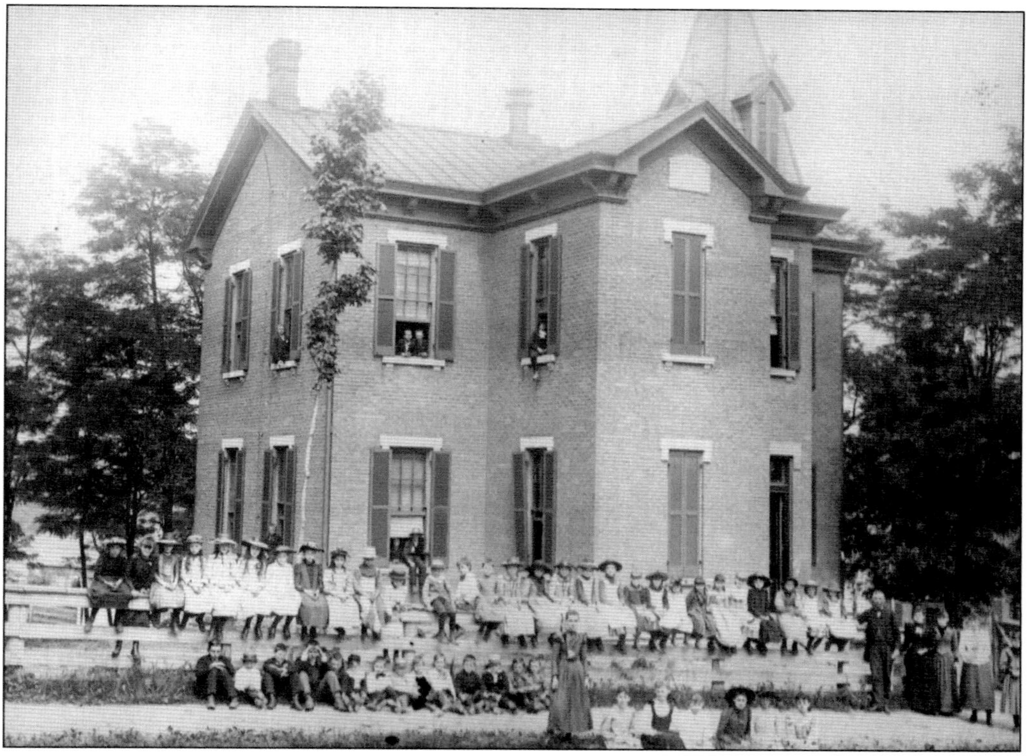

The Madeira student body is shown at Madeira District No. 6, popularly known as Camargo School, around 1910. The school was built at the southwest corner of Miami Avenue and Camargo Road in 1875 on land once owned by pioneer David Black that was later used as a brickyard. The school was razed in 1914 to make way for a new building. (Courtesy Roger Ward.)

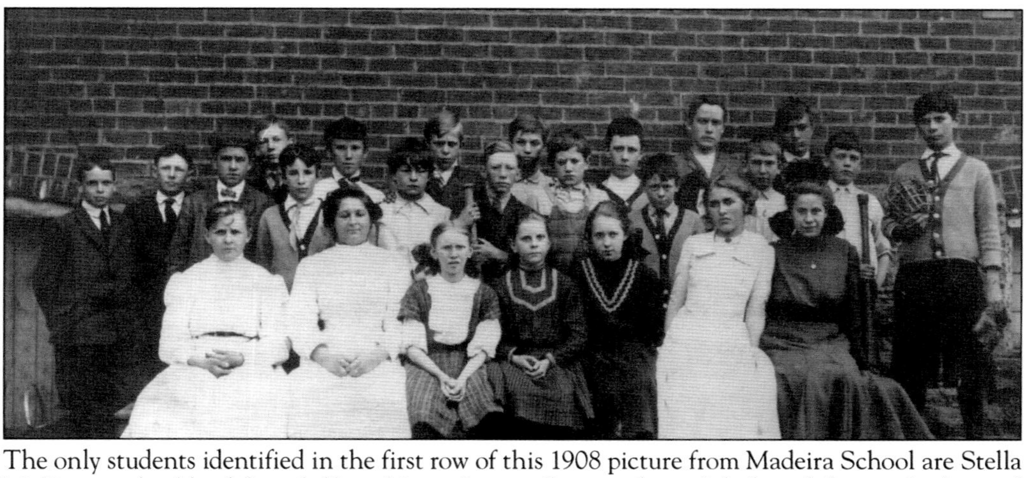

The only students identified in the first row of this 1908 picture from Madeira School are Stella McConnaughy (third from left) and Irene Logan (last on the right); from left to right (second row) are Harry Knight, Russ Atkins, Ray Sampson, Ralph Sorn, Howard DeMar, Al Stoll, Carl Flack, Floyd Hoes, Ben McConnaughy, Ray Crofts, Peter Dodson, Ira Nelson, Ed Burns, Herman Decatur, Eugene Sorin, Robert Brown, Walter Burman, and Delbert DeMar. (Courtesy Madeira Historical Society.)

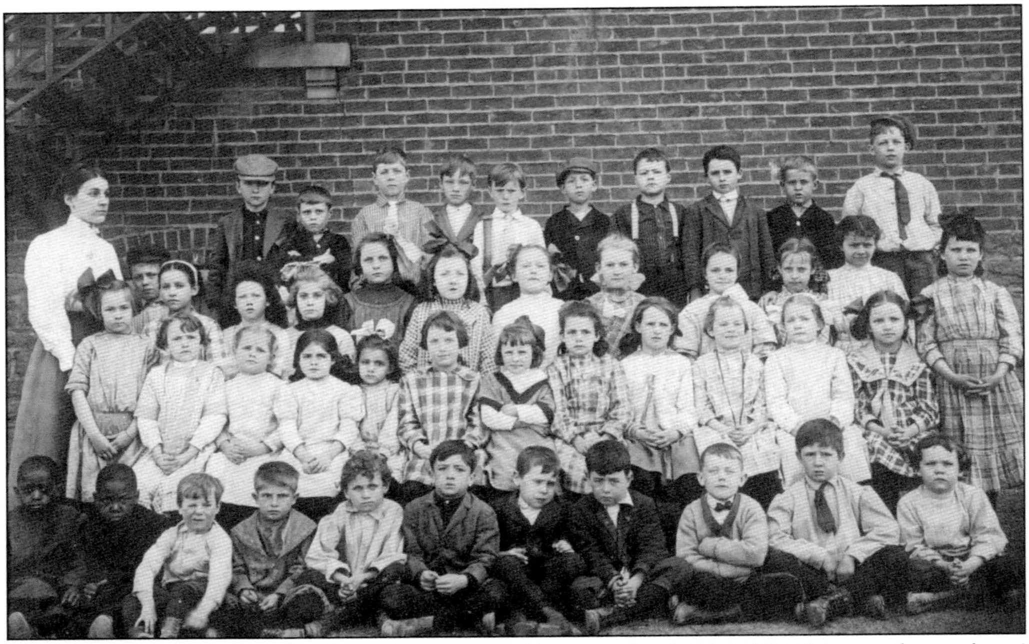

Students from Madeira School are photographed here on April 25, 1912. This was the students' last year in this building at Miami Avenue and Camargo Road. The condition of the old school and an increase in students led to the passage in November 1912 of a $25,000 bond issue for a new building. (Courtesy Madeira Historical Society.)

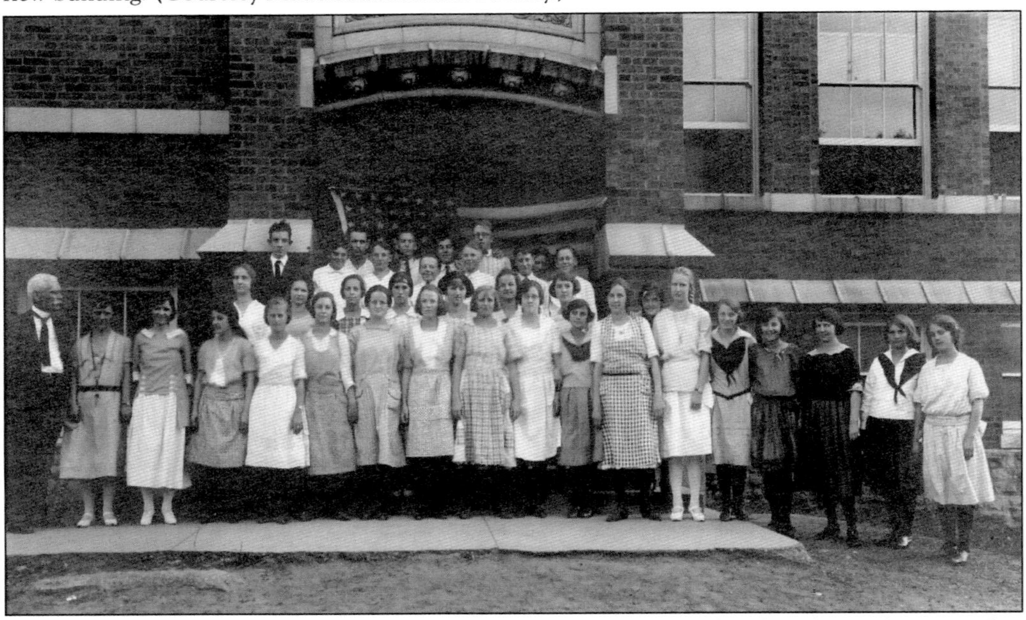

Madeira High School opened in September 1922. Before that most local students who wanted to graduate attended Withrow High School in Cincinnati on a tuition basis. Members of the first Madeira High School graduation class were Harold DeMar, Julian Nelson, Alma Slagle, Bernice Surran, and Lloyd Nelson. Madeira Presbyterian Church hosted the graduation ceremony in June 1923. (Courtesy Madeira Historical Society.)

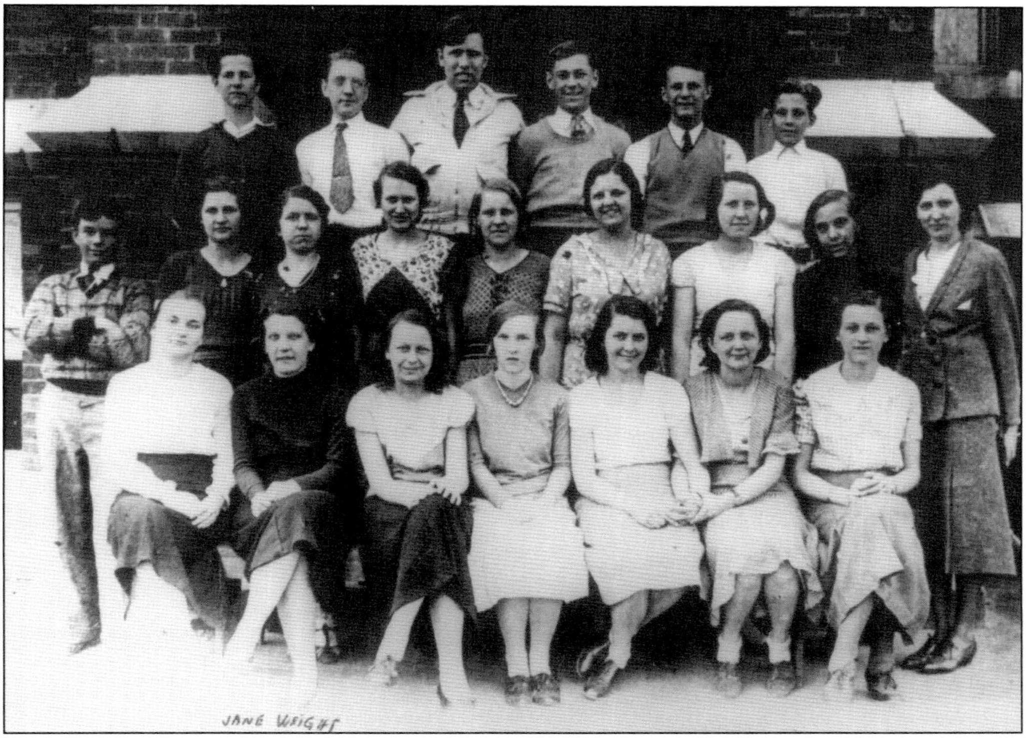

Members of the 1933 senior class included, in no particular order, Russell Brown, Melvin Ballman, Wesley Kramer, Frank Hartman, William Doer, Dorothy VanFossen, Mary Tidd, Wilma Parker, Loie Nelson, Dorothy Morgan, Betsy Myers, Ruth McDonald, Florence Gruber, Alvin Grassmar, Kathleen Gould, William Fredricks, and Virginia Richmond. A new high school on Miami Avenue was completed in 1937, financed by a bond issue and the Federal Public Works program. (Courtesy Madeira Historical Society.)

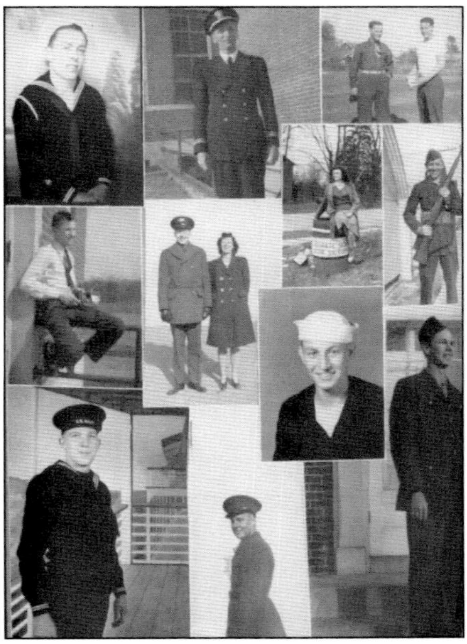

This collage in the 1944 Madeira High School yearbook was dedicated to "the boys in the service of our country." Various branches of the armed services, as well as home-front activities including scrap drives, are represented here. While students just a few years earlier pondered dances and the senior party at Coney Island, graduates were now consumed with war news. (Courtesy Madeira Board of Education.)

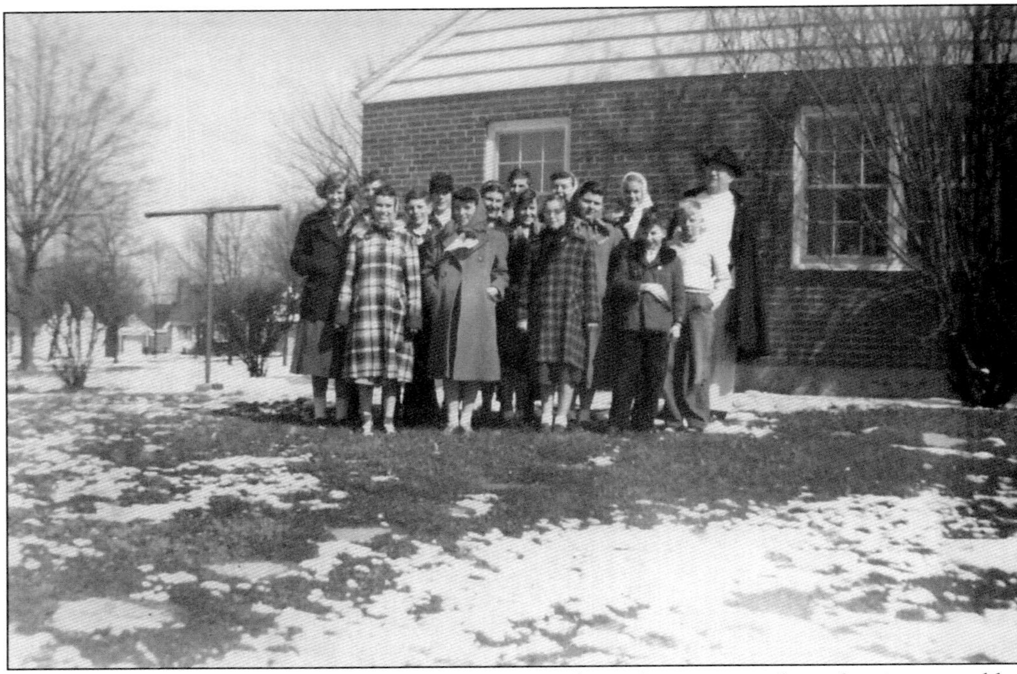

Eighth graders at St. Gertrude School pose in 1950. Three classrooms and a cafeteria were added to the original building that year. Other additions were made in 1949, 1955, and 1958, expanding space from 3 classrooms to 18. (Courtesy St. Gertrude Church.)

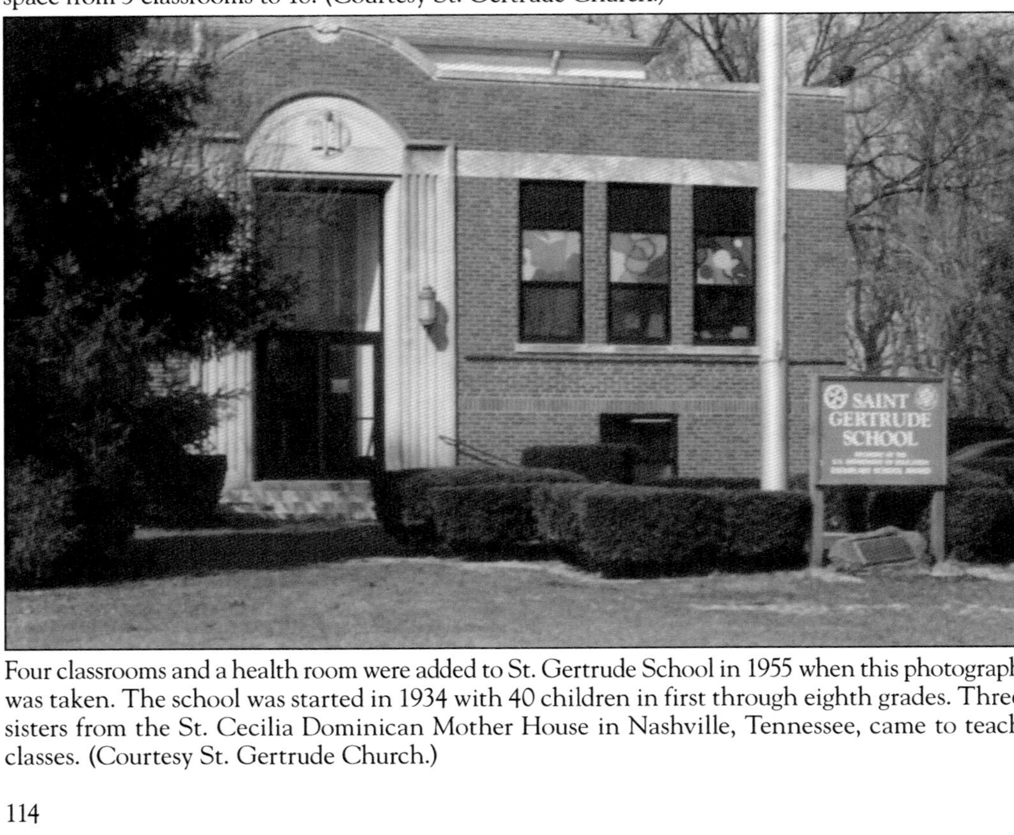

Four classrooms and a health room were added to St. Gertrude School in 1955 when this photograph was taken. The school was started in 1934 with 40 children in first through eighth grades. Three sisters from the St. Cecilia Dominican Mother House in Nashville, Tennessee, came to teach classes. (Courtesy St. Gertrude Church.)

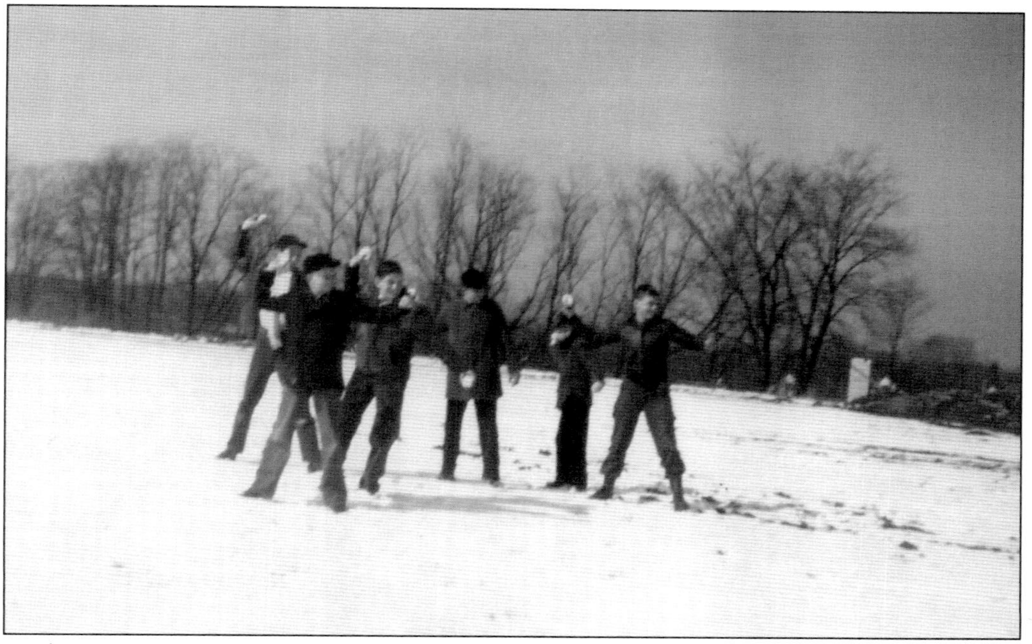

Students take a break from classes at St. Gertrude to toss snowballs in November 1950. (Courtesy St. Gertrude Church.)

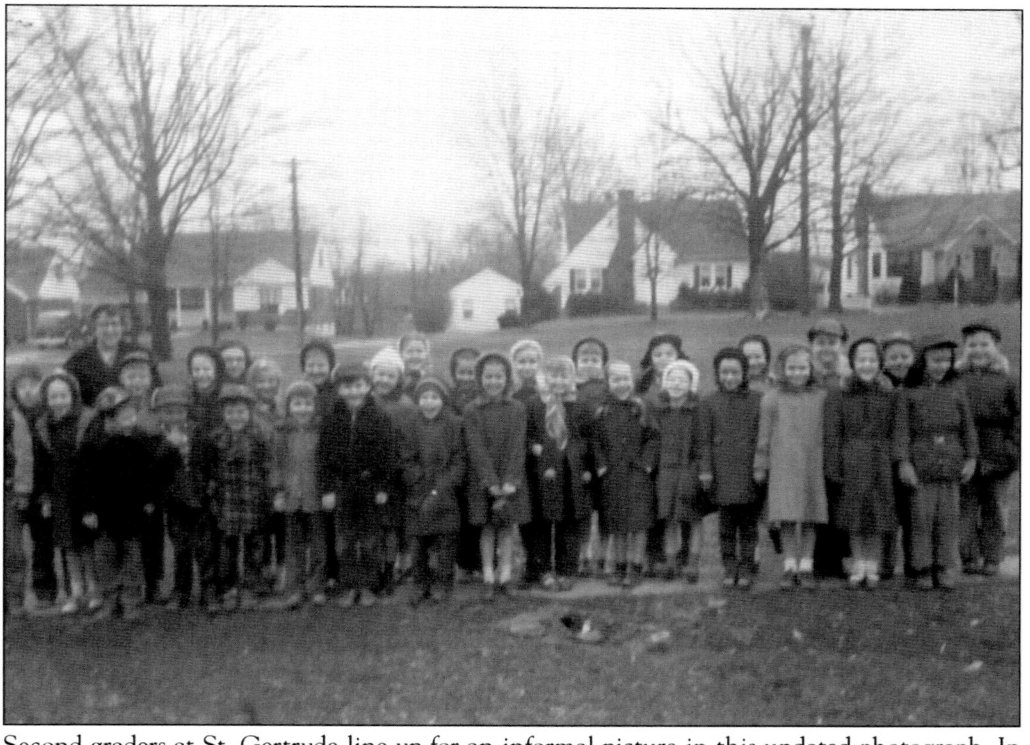

Second graders at St. Gertrude line up for an informal picture in this undated photograph. In 1963, the school had 710 students and expanded facilities for physical education, music, and the library. (Courtesy St. Gertrude Church.)

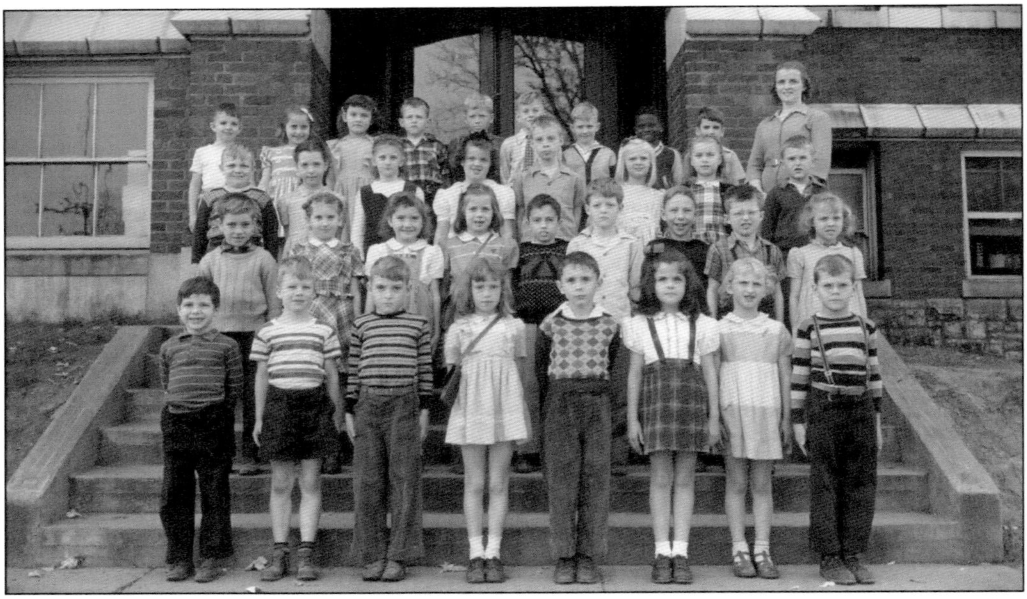

Mrs. Shirley's second graders stand outside Madeira School in 1946. Mrs. Steeb taught another second-grade class where a little girl named Patti Patten was enrolled. Patten was one of many students who began building fond memories of her Madeira school days as she matured. Her father, Russell Patten, served as mayor in 1958 and 1959, and the whole family was involved in the community. (Courtesy Madeira Historical Society.)

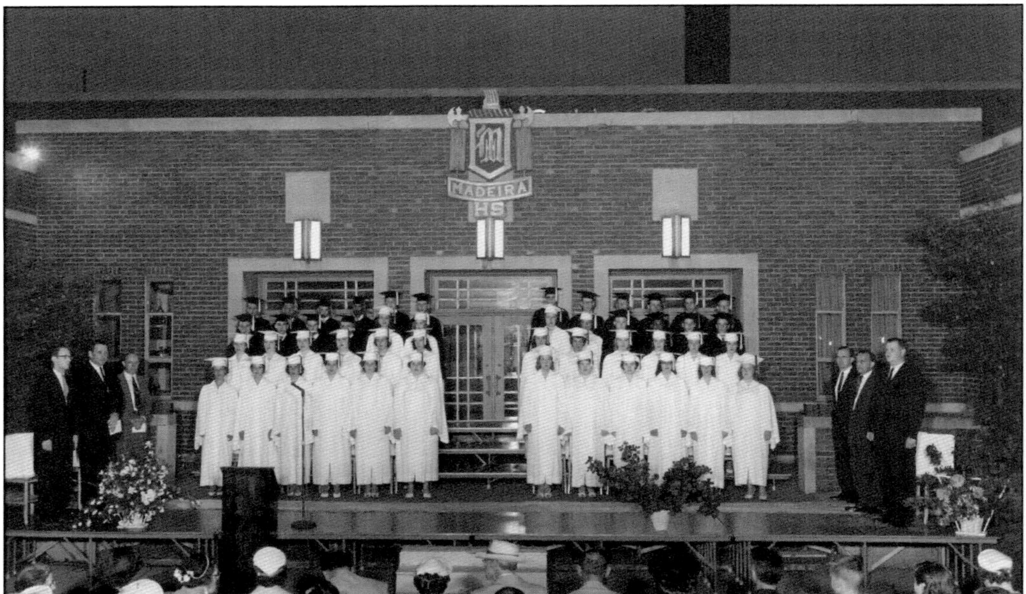

The Madeira class of 1956 (some of whom are shown above as second graders) graduates at the high school at 6612 Miami Avenue. Graduate Patti Patten dreamed of being a teacher and coming back to the elementary school to work with respected principal John F. Dumont. While she evaluated her college options for a year, she worked as a secretary at the school. (Courtesy Madeira Historical Society.)

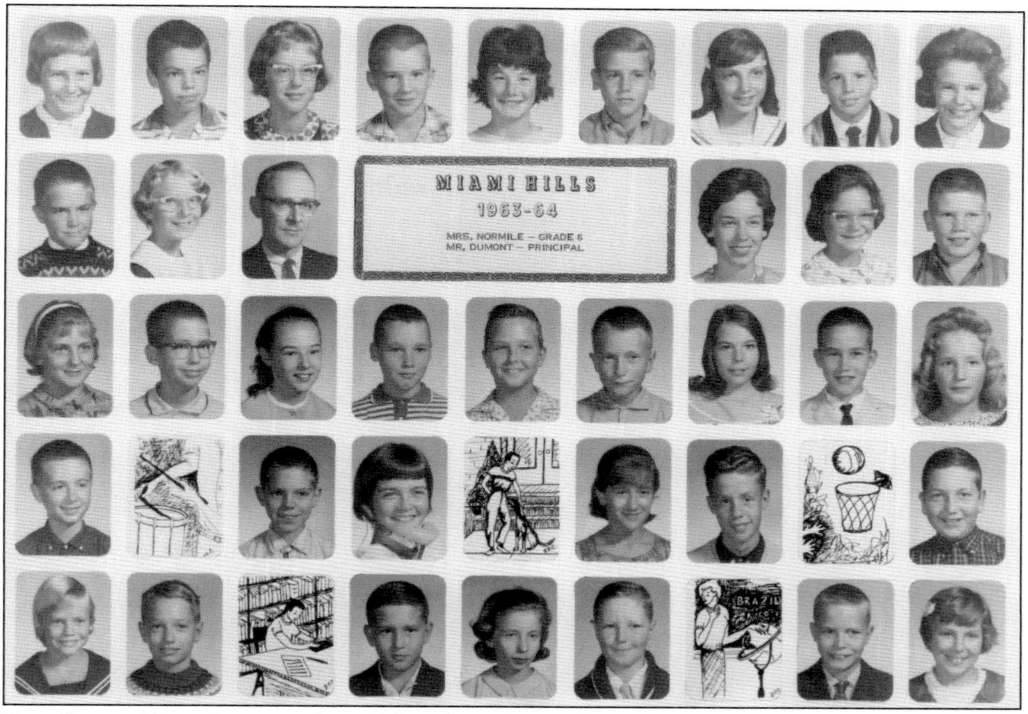

Patti Patten Normile, a member of the class of 1956 shown on the opposite page, was a sixth-grade teacher at Miami Hills during the 1963–1964 school year. Although she only taught full time for a few years before starting a family, Patten was the kind of teacher who students lovingly remember. Today she writes books about spirituality and pastoral care, and she still remembers her former students. (Courtesy Stephan Johnson.)

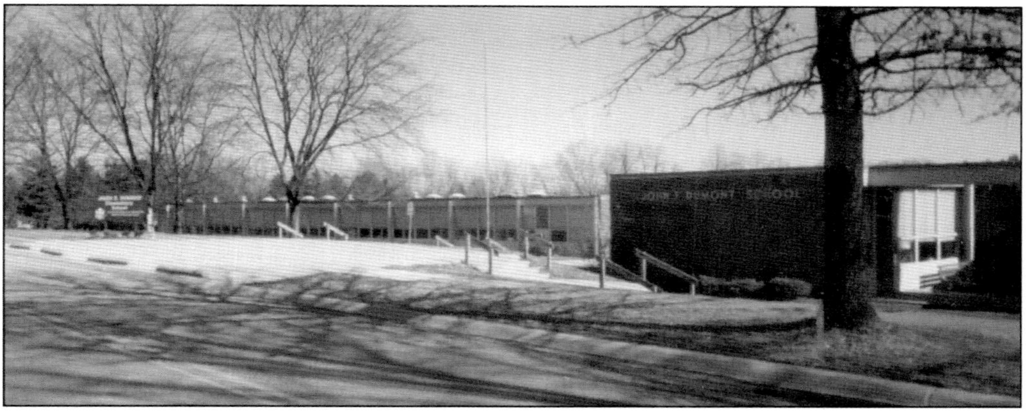

Built in 1954 as Miami Hills Elementary, this school was renamed for long-time principal John F. Dumont, "a lovely man," recalls former teacher Patti Patten Normile. This photograph of the school on Thomas Drive was taken sometime after 1965. (Courtesy Madeira Board of Education.)

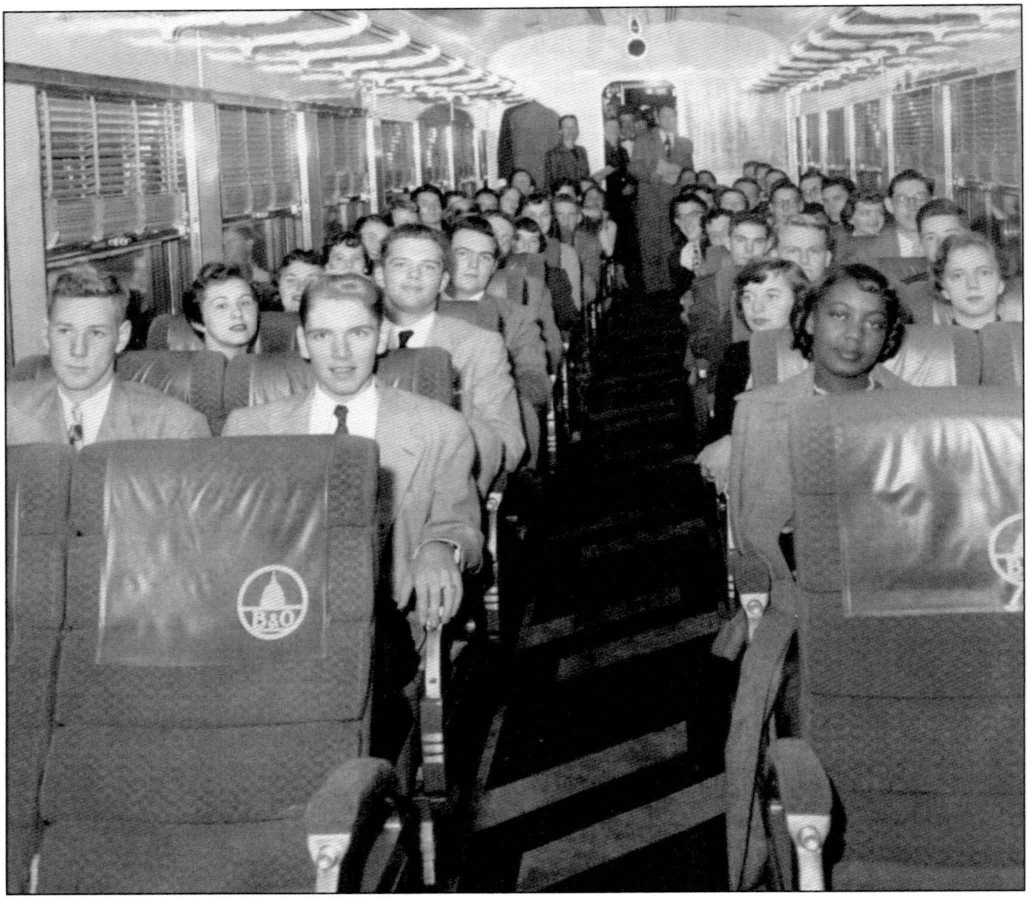

Members of the Madeira class of 1952 ride the train to Washington, D.C., for their senior class trip. (Courtesy Madeira Board of Education.)

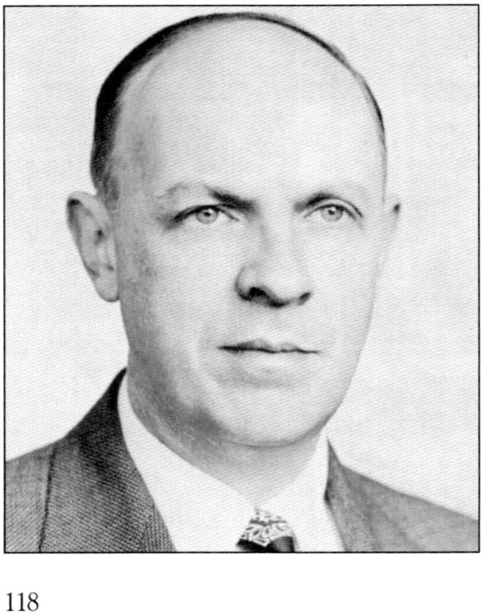

W. Marshall Sellman came to Madeira as a teacher in 1932, became high school principal in 1938, and superintendent in 1948—holding that position until he retired in 1966. During his tenure, a new elementary building and high school were constructed, and student achievement and effective teaching were continually emphasized. Camargo Elementary was renamed for him, and today the middle school bears his name. (Madeira Historical Society.)

Herbert L. Dericks became a teacher at Madeira in 1946. He was high school principal from 1948 to 1966 before succeeding Sellman as superintendent. Dericks is credited with maintaining and improving high academic standards in the district. Many additions and improvements to buildings were completed during his tenure. He retired in 1975. (Courtesy Madeira Board of Education.)

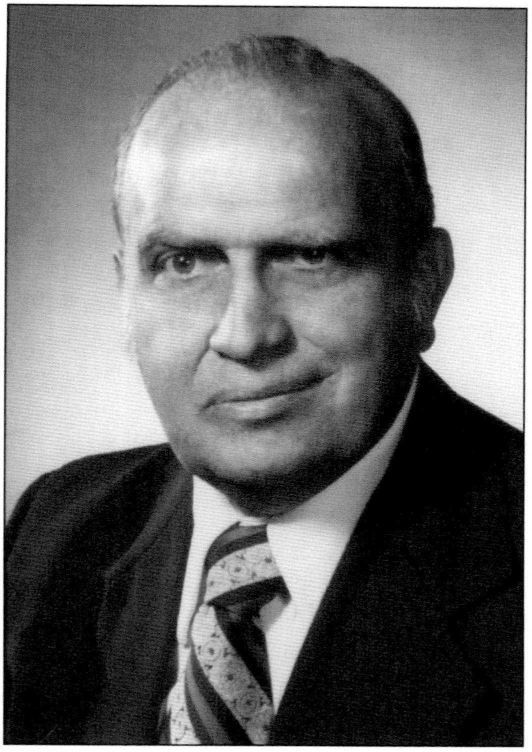

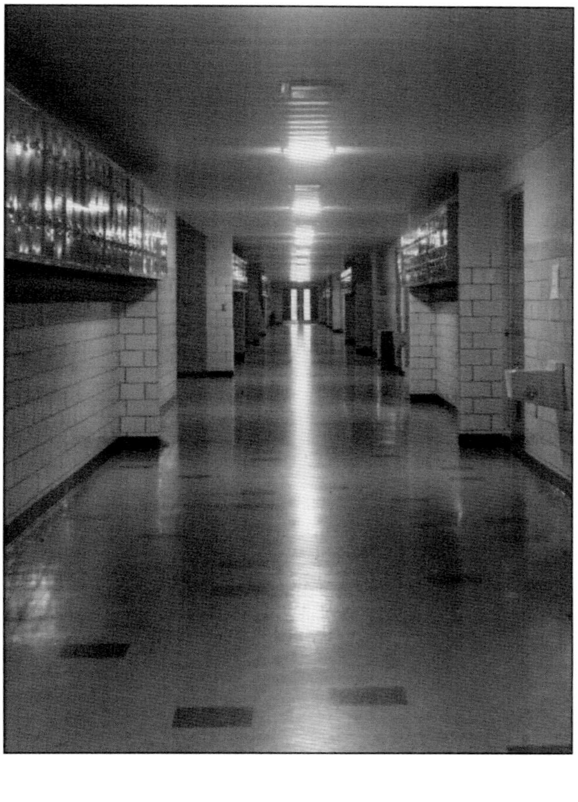

Gleaming new hallways and lockers await students in the Madeira High School addition on Loannes Drive in 1964. The district had grown to 2,175 students by then. The campus-style high school was built in 1958 for $1.3 million. (Courtesy Madeira Board of Education.)

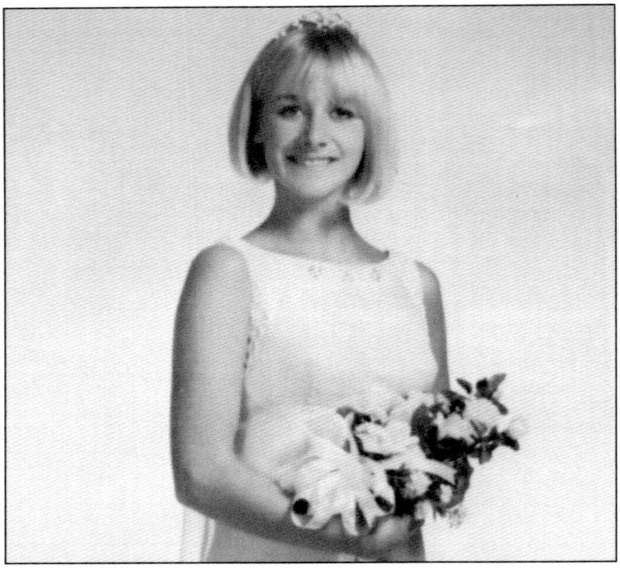

Susanna K. Honsinger, a junior, became homecoming queen in October 1967. She captained the cheerleaders in her sophomore and senior years, worked on the school paper, participated in the variety show for four years, and performed with the chorus and glee club. (Courtesy Madeira Board of Education.)

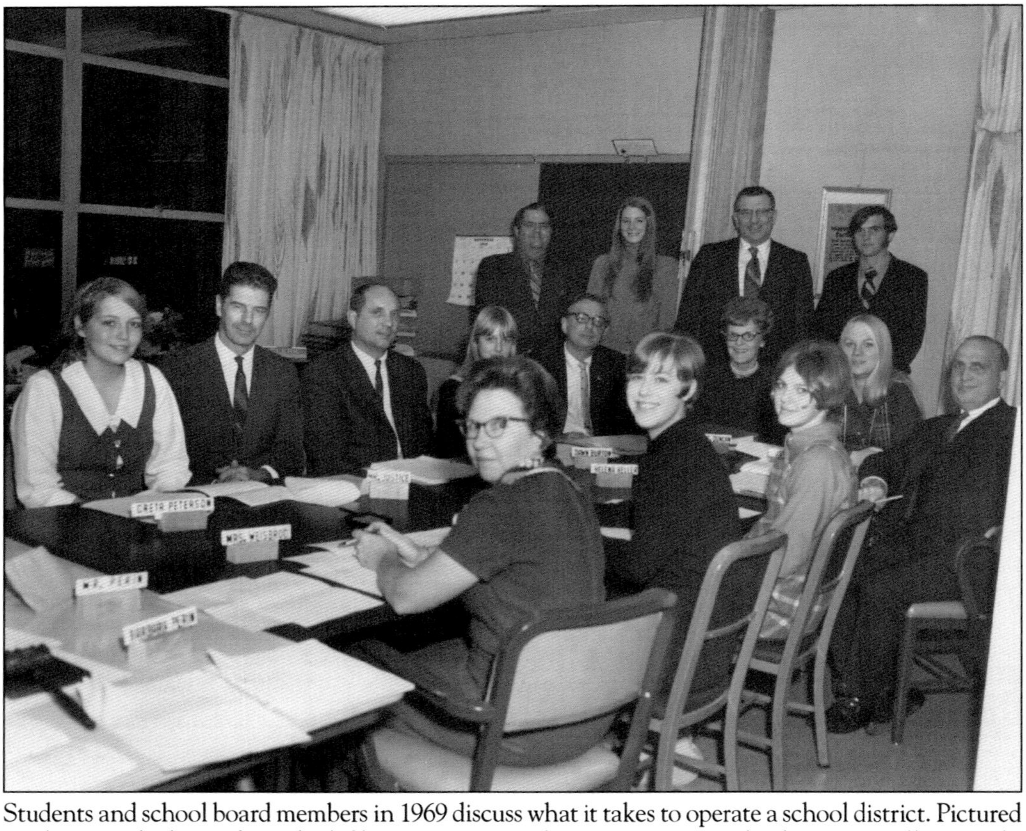

Students and school board members in 1969 discuss what it takes to operate a school district. Pictured are (sitting, clockwise from the left) Greta Peterson, business manager Lloyd Justice, William Toth, Dawn Burton, Ray Siefert, treasurer Verna Duncan, Susan West, Supt. Herbert Dericks, Helena Keller, Laurie Frank, and Phila Weisbrod; (standing, from left to right) Frank Garrett, Barbara Perin, James C. Perin, and William Crump. (Courtesy Madeira Board of Education.)

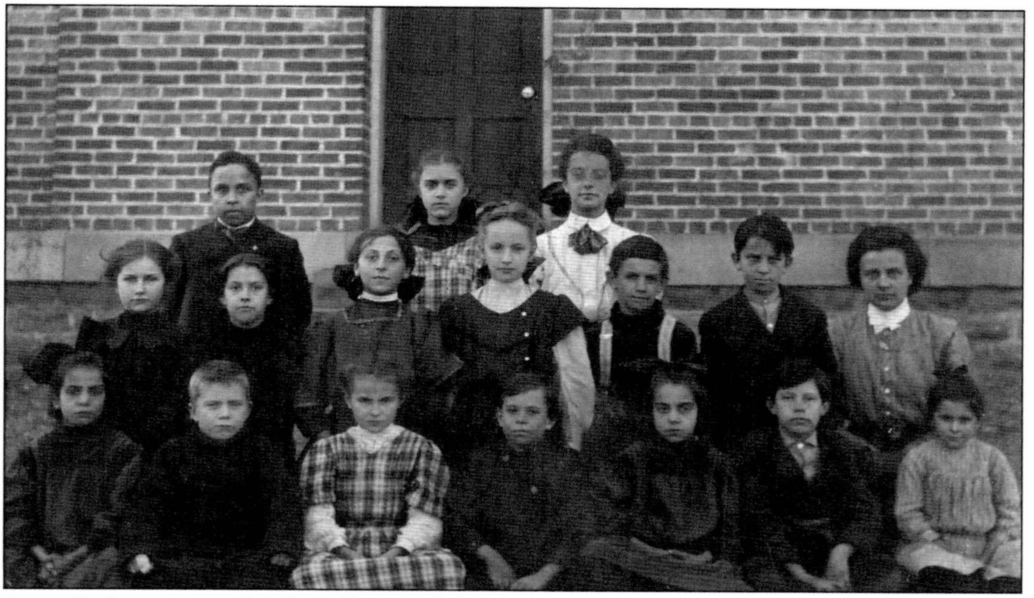

A small class poses at Madeira District School No. 6 in this undated photograph. From left to right are (first row) Carrie Beard, Carl Grob, Ruth Lodwick, John Grob, Florence Beard, George Brown, and Ester Lodwick (Ruth's twin); (second row) Dorothy Dennientz, Ida Grob, Edna Lodwick, Bertha "Birdie" Beekley, Orland Fishback, Harry Lodwick, and teacher Gertrude Schlertzenbader; (third row) Robert Taliofero, Margaret Brown, and Clara Lodwick. (Courtesy Roger Ward.)

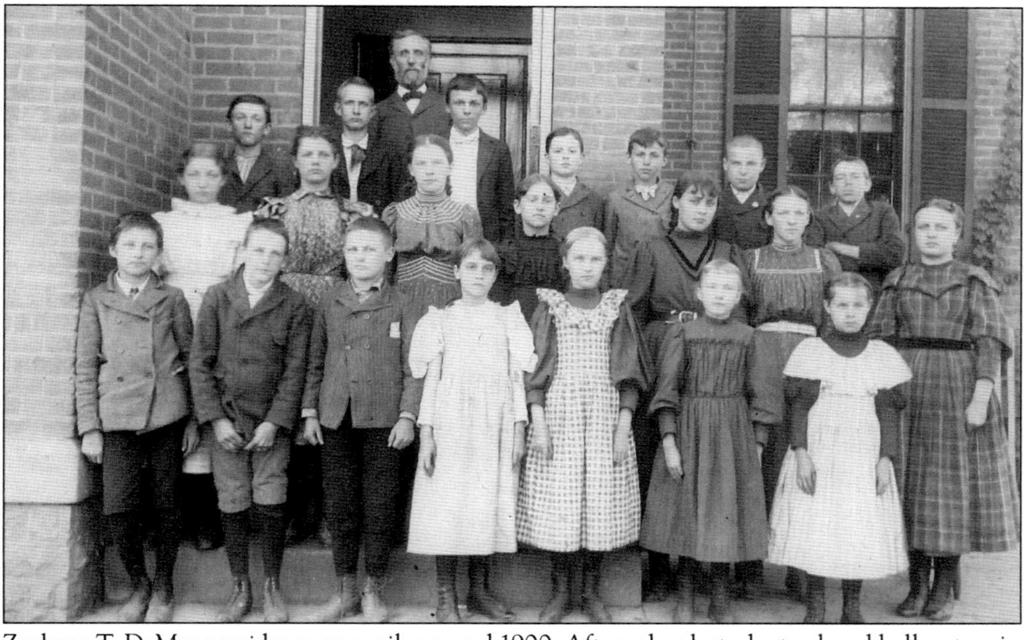

Zachary T. DeMar presides over pupils around 1900. After school, students played ball or tag; in the winter, they staged snowball battles and coasted down across Camargo Road and past the railroad tracks. Student Will Crist had a memorable ride one day. He dug his toes into the snow to stop, but the ground was so slick that he kept moving. He coasted—safely—underneath a train. (Courtesy Roger Ward.)

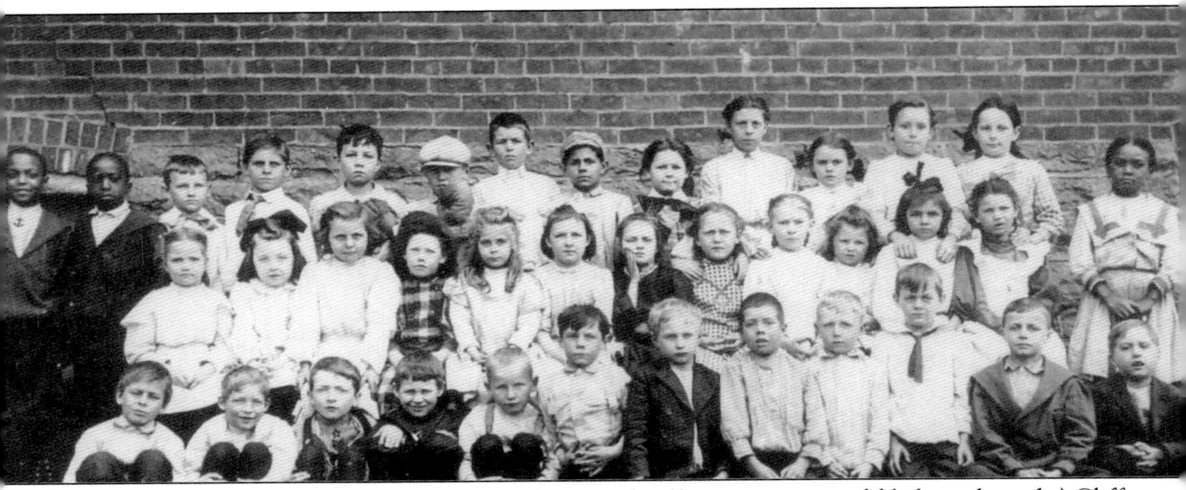

Madeira students in 1910 included, from left to right, (first row, starting fifth from the right) Cliff DeMar, Guy ?, ? Meyer, unidentified, and George Luckey; (second row) Rachel Clark, Margaret Heabron, Amelia Kramer, Catherine Aikin, Olivia Kaiser, Ruth Sampson, Ruth Croft, Maria Galvin, Cleo Hosbrook, ? Wilson, Ruth Berger, May Currie, and Anita Dean; (third row) Lorenzo Dean, Walter Spaulding, Horace Clark, George Kramer, Vehons Durragh, Charles Dodson, Joseph (?) Nelson, Frank Berger, Nancy Wilson, Alice Doer, Mary Burns, Mary Gier, and Mary Groves. Students studied reading, grammar, writing, and arithmetic. Although clothing, curriculum, and teaching styles have changed over the years, a few student concerns are timeless: homework, quirky teachers, and the groans that accompany the news that "it's time for anudder leedle queez" delivered in an Alabaman twang by Madeira High School math teacher Ernest Combs to hundreds of students in the 1960s and 1970s. (Courtesy Madeira Historical Society.)

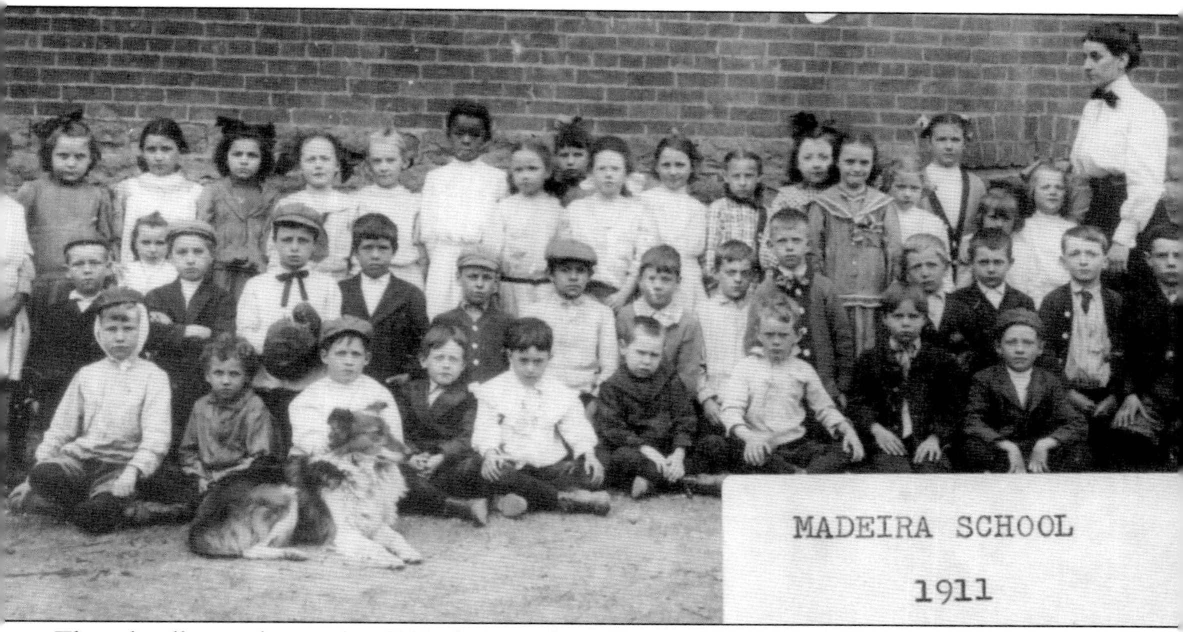

The schoolhouse dog in this 1911 photograph is not named but must have been a welcome distraction during recess at Madeira School. The students are, from left to right, (first row) Howard Dodson, Russell Currie, Telford Sullivan, Frank Galom, Julian Nelson, Charles Laffery, Spider McConnaughy, unidentified, and Wesley Betzer; (second row, starting fifth from the right) Don Pierret, Harold DeMar, Fred Laffey, John Hudson, and Frank Doer; (third row) Anita Dean, Amelia Kramer, Junior Brown, Ruth Berger, Mary Galom, Cleo Hosbrook, unidentified, Rachel Clark, May Currie, Catherine Aikin, unidentified, Alma Slagle, Margaret Heabron, Ruth Croft, Helen Stauffer, Ruth Sampson, Irma Dodson, and Mae Fischer; Miss ? Watkins (far right) was the teacher. (Courtesy Madeira Historical Society.)

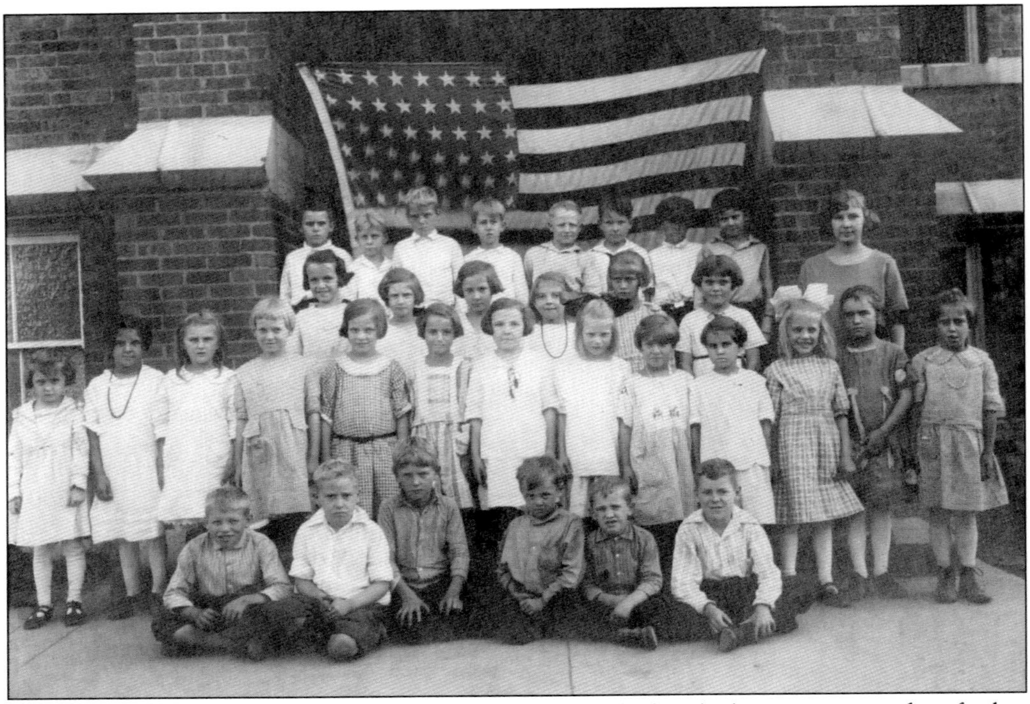

Students at Madeira School in this *c.* 1925 photograph studied in the largest, most modern facility that the school system had ever built. Coal-fired furnaces warmed four classrooms on the first floor as well as two classrooms and an auditorium on the second floor. Perhaps most importantly, after 1925, students and faculty enjoyed indoor plumbing. (Courtesy Madeira Historical Society.)

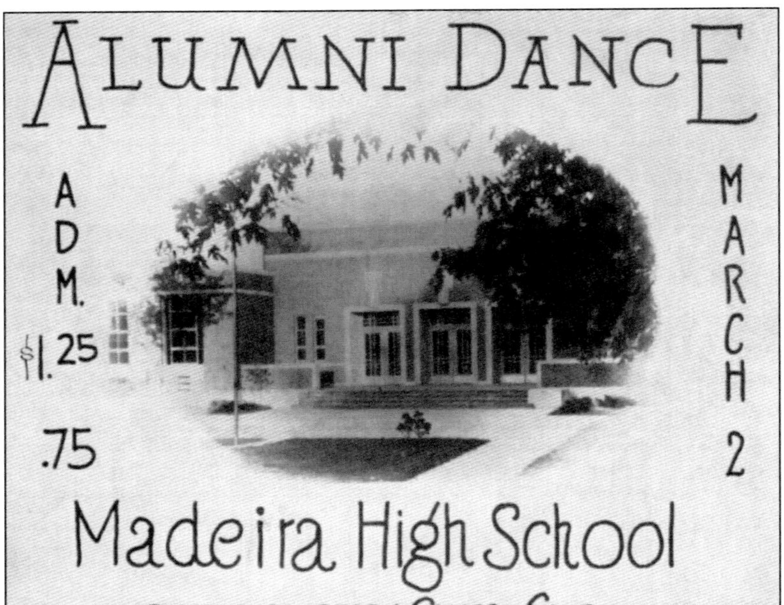

The newly formed Madeira Alumni Association held a moonlight boat ride (without the moonlight, noted president Elmer Rohman) in 1941. The group is still active today, periodically publishing an alumni directory and organizing reunions. (Courtesy Madeira Board of Education.)

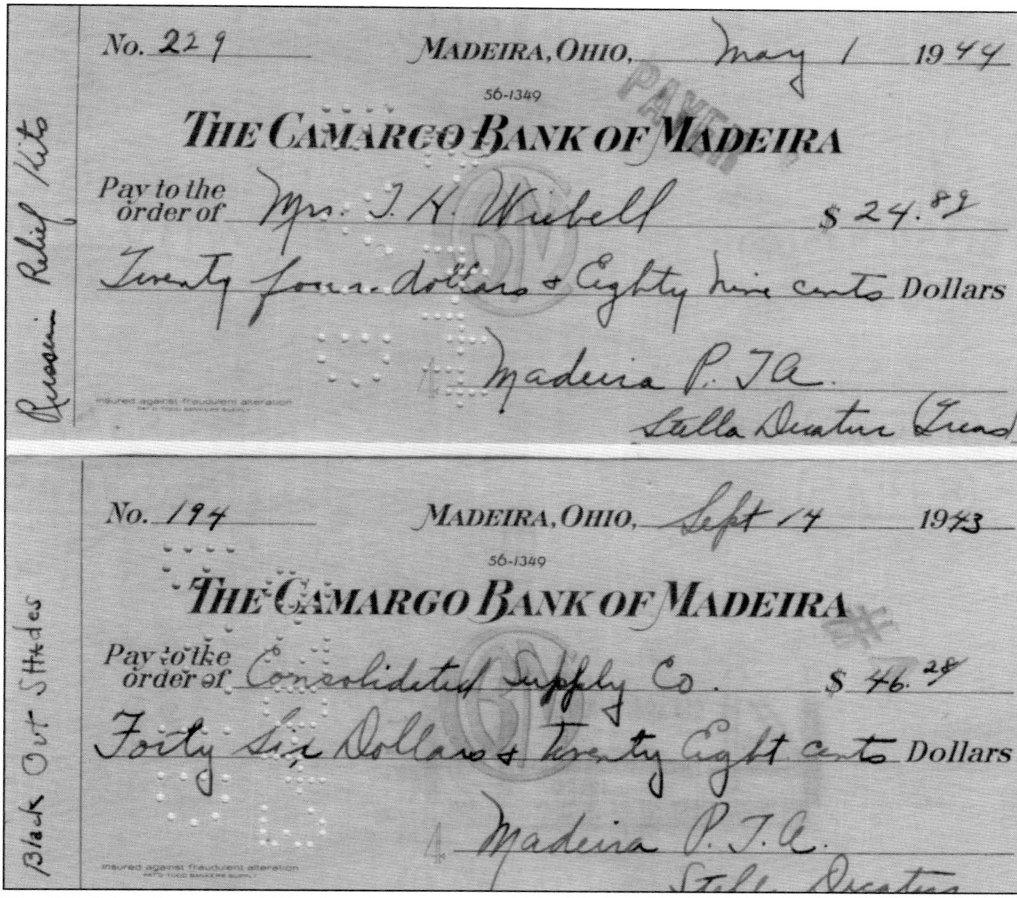

The Madeira Parent and Teacher Association aided relief efforts during World War II by donating funds for blackout shades and for relief kits to be sent to Russia. The group first organized in 1901 as the Madeira's Mothers' Club before involving fathers by joining the state and national Organizations of Parents and Teachers in 1924. (Courtesy Madeira Historical Society.)

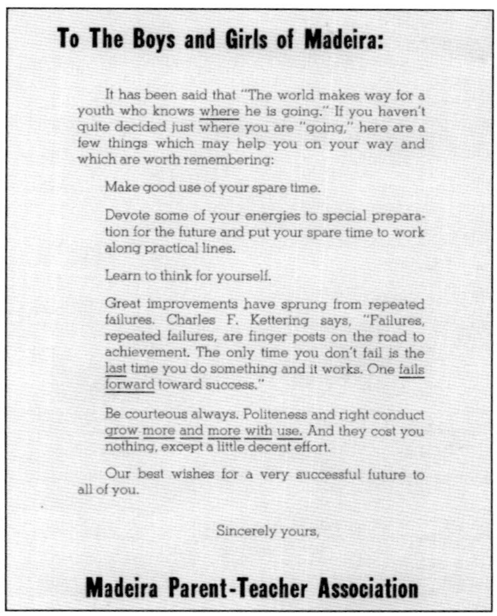

To The Boys and Girls of Madeira:

It has been said that "The world makes way for a youth who knows where he is going." If you haven't quite decided just where you are "going," here are a few things which may help you on your way and which are worth remembering:

Make good use of your spare time.

Devote some of your energies to special preparation for the future and put your spare time to work along practical lines.

Learn to think for yourself.

Great improvements have sprung from repeated failures. Charles F. Kettering says, "Failures, repeated failures, are finger posts on the road to achievement. The only time you don't fail is the last time you do something and it works. One fails forward toward success."

Be courteous always. Politeness and right conduct grow more and more with use. And they cost you nothing, except a little decent effort.

Our best wishes for a very successful future to all of you.

Sincerely yours,

Madeira Parent-Teacher Association

Wholesome sentiments of courtesy, stewardship of time, perseverance, and independent thinking are expressed in the PTA's message to seniors around 1950. (Courtesy Madeira Board of Education.)

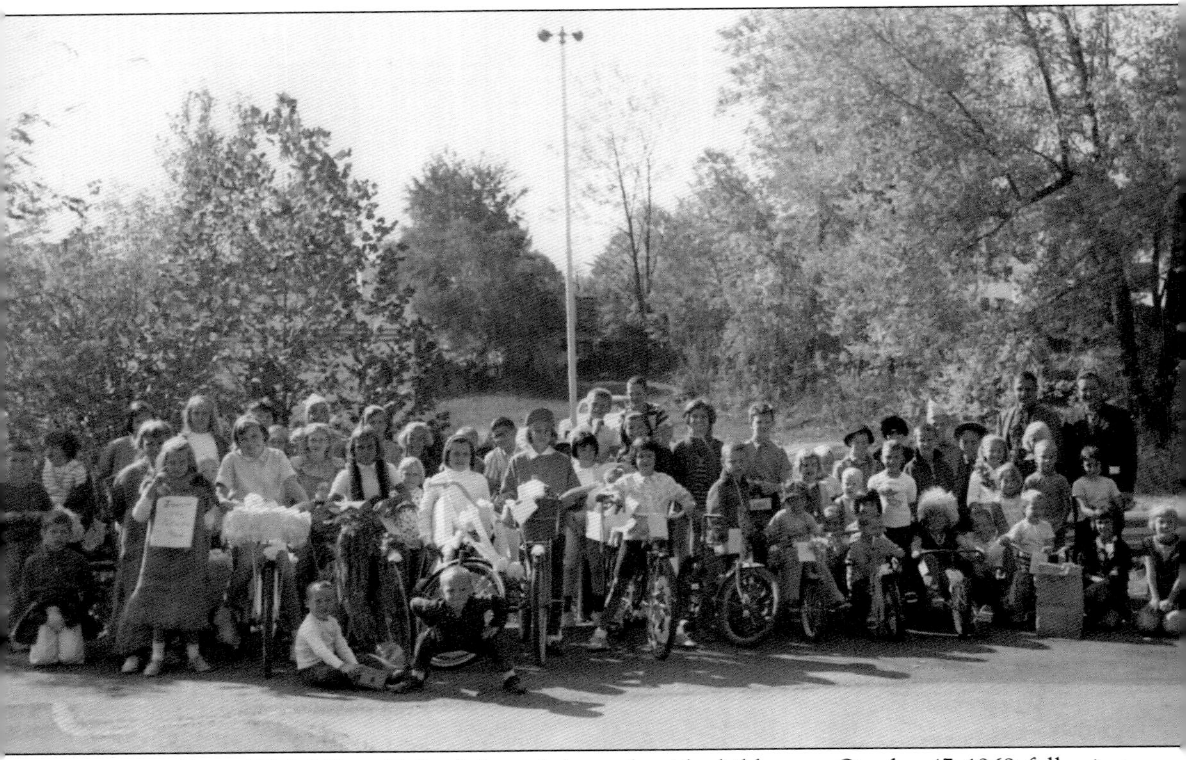

Mayor Daniel D. McDonald (back far right) stands with children on October 17, 1969, following a bicycle parade. McDonald was born in a Laurel Avenue home in 1924 and has lived in Madeira most of his life. McDonald Commons Park was named for him in recognition of a lifetime of public service. As mayor from 1960 to 1977, McDonald helped to plan and implement many policies and projects that have enabled Madeira to arrive at its 2010 centennial as a thriving community. Generations of children, filled with promise, have grown up and been educated in Madeira. From pioneer Daniel Hosbrook's c. 1808 subscription school to computer-enhanced classrooms in 2010, education and constant improvement have been community priorities. In 1985, William J. Bennett, U.S. Secretary of Education, commended Madeira High School as one of the country's model schools. In 2009, Madeira seniors had the 10th-highest achievement ratings in Ohio. (Courtesy Daniel D. McDonald.)

INDEX